Rebellious Histories

Rebellious Histories

The *Amistad* Slave Revolt and the Cultures of Late Twentieth-Century Black Transnationalism

MATTHEW J. CHRISTENSEN

SUNY PRESS

Published by State University of New York Press, Albany

Printed in the United States of America

For information, contact State University of New York Press, Albany, NY
www.sunypress.edu

Production by Eileen Meehan
Marketing by Anne M. Valentine

Library of Congress Cataloging-in-Publication Data

Christensen, Matthew J.
Rebellious histories : the Amistad slave revolt and the cultures of late twentieth-century black transnationalism / Matthew J. Christensen.
p. cm.
Includes bibliographical references and index.
ISBN 978-1-4384-3969-3 (hbk : alk. paper) 978-1-4384-3970-9 (pbk. alk. paper)
1. Slave insurrections—United States. 2. Amistad (Schooner). 3. Influence (Literary, artistic, etc.)—History—20th century. 4. Antislavery movements—United States. 5. Sierra Leonean literature. 6. Sierra Leone—History. I. Title.

E447.C48 2011
326'.80973—dc22 2011008544

10 9 8 7 6 5 4 3 2 1

For Shirley

Contents

Illustrations

Acknowledgments

Rebellious Histories explores the problem of late-twentieth-century popular cultural deployments of the 1839 *Amistad* slave rebellion—and the trans-Atlantic slave trade against which it was directed—as a historical and allegorical antecedent to contemporary forms of resistance to global capitalism. My curiosity about the scope of the Sierra Leonean and American resurrection of the *Amistad* slave rebellion in this period and about the critical contours of the body of texts that emerged was sparked while I was a Kalamazoo College undergraduate on a study abroad program at Fourah Bay College in Sierra Leone from 1990 through 1991. It was there, in a course taught by Joseph Opala, that I first learned about the rebellion, and it was there that I first saw *Amistad Kata-Kata*, Charlie Haffner's dramatic rendition of the shipboard revolt. I was initially drawn to the historical narrative for personal reasons. As a twenty year old trying to make sense of my subject position as a white man with U.S. citizenship in a deeply impoverished country such as Sierra Leone, I found that the *Amistad* rebellion historicized the problems of privilege, power, and global capitalist violence that I was grappling with. I did not think much about the rebellion again until the late 1990s after an education in postcolonial studies and transnational cultural studies gave me a critical framework to recognize the unique and richly multivalent perspectives on the intertwined effects of the slave trade, colonialism, and contemporary global capital flows that writers such as Haffner in Sierra Leone and Clifford Mason and Barbara Chase-Riboud in the United States were exploring with their historical fictions. While this book is rooted in my personal quest to understand my place in the world, it is ultimately a testament to their aesthetic and political endeavors.

With such a long gestation, *Rebellious Histories* and its author owe many individual and institutional debts. I am particularly grateful for the early support and critical engagement of Richard Yarborough, Donald Cosentino, Shu-mei Shih, and the late Teshome Gabriel. My most enthusiastic champion, my most dedicated reader, and my most insistent voice of ethical consciousness remains Shirley Jennifer Lim. She never let me forget that I was writing this book for people whose struggles deserve a broader audience.

Joseph Opala deserves a hearty thank you for being the first to teaching me the history of the *Amistad* revolt, as he has for many others in Sierra Leone and elsewhere. Joe also introduced me to many of the Sierra Leonean writers and artists discussed in this book. Without their acquaintance, *Rebellious Histories* would not have come into being. For similar reasons I thank Iyunolu Folayan Osagie for her work recovering forgotten *Amistad* revolt histories in Sierra Leone and the United States and for generously sharing a copy of *The Broken Handcuff*, Raymond DeSouza-George's unpublished play about the rebellion.

Without generous financial and institutional support *Rebellious Histories* would be little more than an idea. The following institutions and organizations provided support at crucial moments: the West African Research Association; Princeton University's Center for African American Studies; Columbia University's Center for the Study of Ethnicity and Race; Australia National University's Humanities Research Centre; the James S. Coleman African Studies Center at UCLA; the University of California Office of the President; SUNY Stony Brook's History Department; and the University of Texas-Pan American's Faculty Research Council, Faculty Development Leave Program, Department of English, and College of Arts and Humanities. In particular, I would like to thank Valerie Smith, Ed Keller, Jennifer Yanco, Gary Okihiro, Debjani Ganguly, my department chairs Steven Schneider and Pamela Anderson-Mejias, and deans Rudolfo Rocha and Dahlia Guerra for providing me an intellectual home in these institutions. Special recognition goes to Liza Porras, Nora Duran, Elena Reyna, Alma de la Rosa, Kerry Allen, Leena Messina, the WARA staff in Dakar, and all of the other overworked office managers and administrative assistants who went out of their way to take care of paperwork and other bureaucratic procedures during the long periods I was away from various campuses. My abiding appreciation also goes to the various archivists and staff members at the British Library Newspaper Library, the Gilder Lehrman Library, the Schomberg Center for Research in Black Culture, the Institute for Sierra Leonean Cultural Studies at Fourah Bay College, the Sierra Leone National Library, the Freedom Archives in San Francisco, and Bolerium Books, also in San Francisco. I am also deeply grateful to

Charlie Haffner and Raymond DeSouza-George for sharing their time and personal papers.

This is a better book with images by Tim Waites and Konrad Tuchscherer. I want to thank them and the New Haven Museum for permission to include their photographs of *Amistad*-related artwork. I also want to thank the Sierra Leone Adult Education Association for permission to reprint Waites' photographs, which originally appeared in Joseph Opala's book *"Ecstatic Renovation!" Street Art Celebrating Sierra Leone's 1992 Revolution*. I am equally grateful to Indiana University Press Journals for permission to reprint an earlier version of chapter 2, "Cannibals in the Postcolony: Sierra Leone's Intersecting Hegemonies in Charlie Haffner's Slave Revolt Drama *Amistad Kata-Kata*," *Research in African Literatures* 36, no. 1 (February 2005): 1–19, and chapter 4, "Enslaving Globalization: Slavery, Civil War, and Modernity in Sierra Leone," *The Global South* 2, no. 2 (Fall 2008): 54–74.

I have benefited intellectually, professionally, and emotionally from friends and colleagues. I do not know how to express my appreciation for their interlocutions, incitements, cajoling, conversation, companionship, dinner parties, happy hours, procrastinations, and lessons about the world without sounding saccharine, so in no particular order, I thank Simon Gikandi, Jennifer Wenzel, Lloys Frates, Victoria Sams, Jim Wallace, Eileen Julian, Eustace Palmer, Abioseh Porter, Patrick Muana, Chris Corcoran, Gail Griffin, Laura Murphy, Rachel Gabara, Daphne Brooks, Danika Brown, Rebecca Mitchell, Sandhya Shukla, Cynthia Schmidt, Katherine Sugg, Ira Livingston, Cynthia Tolentino, Manthia Diawara, Mbye Cham, Abu-Hassan Koroma, Kathleen Wilson, Nick Mirzoeff, Ned Alpers, Ali Behdad, Susette Min, David Eng, Abubakar Kalokoh, Arrow Bokarie, Mary Dillard, Gibril Cole, Jasamin Rostam-Kolayi, Tamara Ho, Katherine King, Sondra Hale, Susanna Wing, Mike Miller, Mercedes Ibarra, Mark Quigley, Sanda Lwin, Farhad Karim, Sue Englander, John Durham, Gisele Fong, Arleen DeVera, Dennis Laumann, Cymone Fourshey, Linda Murray, Marilyn Manners, Gary Marker, Mike Mahoney, and Russell Schuh. I would also like to thank my current and former colleagues at University of Texas-Pan American, especially Debbie Cole, David Anshen, Jose Skinner, Gary Schneider, Dora Ramirez-Dhoore, Caroline Miles, Rebekah Hamilton, Lynda Nuss, Ed Cameron, Linda Belau, Angela Vergara, Barbara Vielma, Marilu Salazar, and the late Lee Davinroy for their intellectual engagement and support.

To my family, I owe an enormous debt. I am grateful for my parents' insistence that I get the best education I could when the circumstances of my birth had made it impossible for them to do the same. My intellectual engagements are almost unthinkable without my mother, whose foreshortened life was not fair but instilled in me an unequivocal commitment to justice.

Last, I thank Larin McLaughlin for her faith in my project, my anonymous readers for their insightful critiques, and Andrew Kenyon and the rest of the staff at State University of New York Press for their exacting labors.

Introduction

Rebellious Histories

One-hundred-fifty-three years after the *Amistad* shipboard slave rebellion, young Sierra Leonean men celebrated the country's April 29, 1992, military coup by parading a twenty-foot-long papier-mâché replica of the *Amistad* schooner through their capital city's streets.[1] With a measure of success as improbable as the 1839 slave uprising, the twenty-seven-year-old army captain Valentine Strasser and a cadre of fellow junior military officers had just toppled the seemingly omnipotent governing regime whose twenty-four-year reign of profiteering had driven the country to civil war. Self-described revolutionaries, the new military rulers promised a quick end to the war and to political vice. For the country's young male celebrants, the *Amistad* slave rebellion captured all the symbolism of the coup: resistance to dehumanizing economic exploitation, self-rule over illegitimate governance, and youthful idealism over aged corruption. The *Amistad* history also offered the young men a direct lineage to the nineteenth-century slave rebels with whom they shared a common history. Like the coup's young supporters, Sengbe Pieh and his fellow rebels hailed from communities inside the modern boundary lines of the Sierra Leonean nation-state and could be claimed as fellow Sierra Leoneans. In a nation whose capital, Freetown, was established by successive waves of Africans liberated from American plantations and from slave vessels captured by the British navy after the diplomatically negotiated end of the trans-Atlantic slave trade in 1807, the *Amistad* mutineers' narrative of escape from enslavement in the Americas and return to Africa as free men and women resonated all the more powerfully. As one young man exclaimed, "Sengbe Pieh and Captain Strasser are the same person—both revolutionaries" (Opala 10). For nearly a year after the coup, Sierra Leone's young, mostly urban, often undereducated and underemployed young men used the *Amistad* revolt to shape the popular interpretation of their government with plays about the slave rebellion and a public art campaign that covered city walls throughout the country with portraits of *Amistad* leader Sengbe Pieh, Valentine Strasser, and a panoply of supporting heroes.

For the young Sierra Leonean men who reclaimed the history of the *Amistad* rebellion in this moment of political upheaval, the 1839 slave revolt resonated both politically and culturally. But it did so far more deeply, however, than as a simple political warning sign to corrupt politicians or as a cultural marker of an "imagined community" constructing a heroic past for itself (Anderson, *Imagined Communities*). The exuberant rhetoric of revolution broadcasted by the young participants overshadowed a more carefully considered examination of the libratory narratives of postcolonial nationalism in light of the reterritorializing imperatives of global capitalism. Discussing his reasons for featuring *Amistad* leader Sengbe Pieh among the public portraits he painted in Freetown in the months following the 1992 coup, visual artist and secondary school history teacher Josee Lahai explained:

> You go to school, come to the United States, because the United States is like really the heaven where you come, educate yourself, and go back to Sierra Leone, get a good job, you know have your family, live well. So, now when we thought about Sengbe Pieh . . . we thought other Sierra Leoneans have come to the United States and have survived and succeeded . . . So we youngsters thought . . . one day Sierra Leoneans would have easy access to the United States like the United States people have easy access to Sierra Leone. (Lahai interview)

For Lahai, Sengbe Pieh's refusal to submit to an earlier manifestation of global economic exploitation symbolizes the possibility of harnessing U.S. political and economic hegemony. With this argument, Lahai simultaneously frames the modern condition of postcolonial national citizenship in Sierra Leone as one in which physical presence within the geographical boundaries of the nation-state is replaced by a citizenship of extended transnational migration. Implicit in Lahai's declaration that young Sierra Leoneans see their best chances for individual betterment in an economic sojourn to the United States is a sense that the long-term success of the Sierra Leonean nation itself requires the migration of its most able bodied. Given the general patriotic fervor of the arts movement as a whole, Lahai's *Amistad*-informed redefinition of citizenship reveals a complicated understanding of the nation and global capital and of the way that the history of the trans-Atlantic slave trade is apprehended. More than a simple heroic narrative for the young manufacturers of a new national imaginary, the history of the *Amistad* slave rebellion functions allegorically to help frame a critique of the postcolonial nation under global capitalism.

By no means are the young Sierra Leoneans alone in recognizing the resonance of the *Amistad* rebellion in the workings of contemporary transnational culture. Twenty-two years prior to the celebratory march through Freetown and several thousand miles to the west in California, San Quentin Prison–inmate Ruchell Magee began signing his name Ruchell "Cinque" Magee to articles published in *The Black Panther Paper* and *The Berkeley Barb*, adopting *Amistad*-rebellion leader Sengbe Pieh's Hispanicized moniker, *Joseph Cinque*, as his own. In the U.S. context, the *Amistad*'s story of armed liberation from illegitimate servitude offers a potent retelling of the American foundational myth of revolutionary struggle, and does so in a way that incorporates—rather than excludes—acts of rebellion by people of color. What is particularly striking for Magee is that the *Amistad* also functions in much the same way as it does for Lahai to comprehend the racialized effects of global capital. Incarcerated almost continually since he was fifteen, the thirty-year-old Magee chose Cinque's name at the moment he faced his most serious criminal charges and his political critique of the racist and capitalist structure of the American penal system gained a public audience. Led by Jonathon Jackson, brother of famed prison revolutionary George Jackson, Magee and two other African American inmates took over the San Rafael courthouse in California's Marin County in August 1970. Proclaimed by the Black Panthers and other radicals on the American Left to be the first shot in the imminent revolution ("We Are the Revolution" 2), the armed action in San Rafael ended abruptly in a hail of bullets that left one hostage and all three of Magee's accomplices dead and Angela Davis famously charged with conspiracy. For Magee, the relative fame stemming from the Marin events gave new impetus to his efforts to historicize incarceration—which he argued was a component of U.S. imperialism in Southeast Asia and elsewhere—as a direct outgrowth of plantation slavery and the trans-Atlantic capitalism that perpetuated it. Imprisonment, then, was nothing less than a modern-day form of slavery within a global capitalist system. And, as Cinque, Magee cast himself as a twentieth-century slave rebel at the helm of an incipient worldwide revolution to end enslavement once and for all.

While slave rebellions often live on for generations in the cultural memory of the communities with the most at stake in the outcome of the uprising, the memory often slips to the back of the collective consciousness only to resurface and take on new life in moments of danger when the circumstances and utopian aspirations of the earlier slave rebellion resonate particularly strongly, as the *Amistad* did in Sierra Leone during the year following the 1992 military coup or as it did for Ruchell Magee in 1970. Retaining such images "of the past which unexpectedly [appear] to man singled out a moment of danger," Walter Benjamin asserts, protects both "the tradition and its receivers . . . from becoming tools of the ruling classes" (Benjamin 255). For Benjamin, isolating that moment when the image of the past appears, comprehending its content, and analyzing the historical condition of its recipients safeguards a counterhistory resistant to capitalism's totalizing narratives. As especially adept vehicles for conceptualizing "the telos of black struggles" (Adéẹ̀kọ 1), armed uprisings against enslavement remain among the most potent expressions of the will to freedom from the subjugating forces of individual slave owners, the legal and economic structures in which those slave owners operate, and the philosophical discourses governing state-sanctioned global slave economies. C. L. R. James, for whom the memory of the Haitian Revolution was singled out during the global tumult of the 1930s, asserts this point forcefully in *The Black Jacobins* when he proclaims that "the transformation of slaves, trembling in the hundreds before a single white man, into a people able to organize themselves and defeat the most powerful European nations of their day, is one of the great epics of revolutionary struggle" (ix), and as such must serve as a powerful example to colonized Africans and trembling Europeans alike.[2] For as easy as it is to celebrate slave revolts, James is careful to note, however, that if the black Jacobins of San Domingo "could seize opportunity they could not create it" (25). In other words, the slave rebel's unequivocal claim to his or her liberty obliges subsequent historians, cultural producers, and activists alike to consider also the problems of agency and resistance within the dominant epistemologies underwriting chattel slavery, colonialism, and neoliberal capitalism. In moments of heightened danger, slave rebellions crystallize the historical conditions of possibility, enabling and limiting alike.

During Jim Crow, the Great Depression, and the militant black nationalism of the late 1960s, slave rebellion texts proliferated as writers and artists grappled with the unrealized promises of the freedom imagined by enslaved Africans in centuries past.[3] Given that slave rebellions so powerfully evoke utopian longings and the problems of agency, resistance, race, nation, and historical practice, even interrupted uprisings such as those associated with Nat Turner, Gabriel Prosser, Denmark Vessey, and the Stono plantation served as forceful symbols of the will to freedom in bleak times. In fact, their "failure" provided the added opportunity to reflect on the economic and social structural obstacles to effecting societal transformation. For Arna Bontemps, for example, who wrote novels during the 1930s about both the Haitian Revolution and Gabriel Prosser's 1800 aborted uprising in Virginia, organized slave rebellion on the scale that the two men envisioned offered a model of revolution for a radicalized global proletariat. But, in Bontemps' estimation, Prosser's failure to account for the African cosmologies that still shaped the slaves' worldview was equally instructive for leaders of the 1930s who would need to work as much with the cultural consciousness of the proletariat as to radicalize it.[4] For Aimé Césaire, too, developing a political consciousness attentive to possibilities and limits of slave rebellion was key to achieving freedom from racism and colonialism. In his epic poem "Cahier d'un retour au pays natal," begun in 1939, Haiti is where "negritude got up on its feet for the first time and said it believed in its humanity" (Césaire 67), and Toussaint Louverture "is the medium through which Césaire acquires self-knowledge and envisions the consciousness necessary for liberation within the context of colonization" (Hurley 111).[5]

As my opening examples about Josee Lahai and Ruchell "Cinque" Magee attest, the *Amistad* slave rebellion gives artists a multivalent Atlanticwide counterhistory to capitalism's totalizing narratives during moments of acute danger just like the Haitian revolution and Gabriel Prosser's uprising did for Césaire and Bontemps. In the same way that the crises in Europe and its colonies, mass poverty at home, and the radicalization of American intellectuals and workers catalyzed counterhegemonic historical narratives in the 1930s, a civil war fought in Sierra Leone over the spoils of the global diamond trade and the disproportionately racialized violence of the American carceral system, itself symptomatic of globalizing capitalist forces, triggered explorations of the historical and allegorical meanings of enslavement and resistance during the final decades of the twentieth century. Between 1970 and the late 1990s, Lahai and Magee were joined in revisiting the *Amistad* rebellion by a wide cast of actors with divergent, and sometimes competing, claims to the emergent order of late capitalism: the Sierra Leonean playwrights Charlie Haffner, Raymond DeSouza-George, and Yulisa Amadu Maddy; the Sierra Leonean artists Alusine Bangura, Amadu Tarawalie, Mustapha Lawal Turay, and Chernoh Bah; the Sierra Leonean government; the United States Information Service in Sierra Leone; the African American novelists Barbara Chase-Riboud and Clifford Mason; Hollywood filmmaker Steven Spielberg; and even the cultish Symbionese Liberation Army. The three-decade span also generated an opera libretto, a comic book, two collections of essays on African American culture and politics, numerous popular histories, sculptures on both sides of the Atlantic, and an art gallery and publishing imprint named after the shipboard rebellion.[6] In an era defined by the global reterritorializations of late capitalism, the collapse of the narratives of decolonization, and the rhetoric liberal multiculturalism, the specter of the *Amistad* rebellion flashed up again and again in novels, on stage and screen, in murals, and in political writing in what may be the two most geopolitically distinct locations at this time—Sierra Leone and the United States—to lay bare the racialized, regional stratifications undergirding the seemingly triumphant advance of the capitalist world order.

That the *Amistad* rebellion would capture popular attention at this time, like the Haitian Revolution did in the 1930s, is not surprising because few individual uprisings illuminate the material history of Atlantic capitalism and its symbolic imaginary more than the revolt that took place in the early morning hours of July 1, 1839, when fifty-three Africans broke their chains, took up a cache of cane knives, and escaped a ship's hold to kill the captain and cook, force two ship hands overboard, and shackle the two Spaniards who had recently purchased them at auction. Once liberated, the Mende and Temne men and women attempted to sail the schooner from Cuba back to their home in West Africa. While the mutiny ultimately resulted in the successful completion of the return trip, the initial freedom that it secured was short-lived. Unschooled in navigation, Sengbe Pieh, Grabeau, Burnah, and the other mutineers found themselves at the mercy of the Spaniards, Pedro Montes and José Ruiz, to sail the ship. With radically opposing interests to their African masters, the Spaniards sailed east by day and west by night, ensuring that the *Amistad* never strayed far from North America. On August 25, after slowly zigzagging northward for nearly two months, during which time eight of the Africans died, the *Amistad* dropped anchor near Montauk, New York, where the rebels hoped to find fresh water and a skilled captain who would be willing to trade his services for possession of the schooner. While a delegation of the rebels sought out resources on shore, the *Amistad* was sighted, approached, and boarded by the crew of the U.S. naval ship *Washington*, who hoped to make a salvage claim for the ship as well as for its flesh-and-blood occupants. Hurriedly rowing back out to the *Amistad*, the shore party arrived too late to avoid capture and were seized anew and transported to New London, Connecticut, where they were jailed on piracy charges and made the curious objects of a legal battle over the regulation of international commerce, national sovereignty, and, of course, the natural right to liberty. By its conclusion a year and a half later in the U.S. Supreme Court, the drama involved no less than the queen of Spain and U.S. presidents Martin Van Buren and John Quincy Adams.[7]

In a nation riddled with the tense contradictions of enslavement and still shaken by the Nat Turner rebellion of 1831, the Africans aboard the *Amistad* sparked a firestorm of media attention, but none more than the vocal and charismatic Sengbe Pieh. Identified later by the other mutineers as the leader of the revolt, Sengbe gained added fame for imploring his fellows to one last stand against the U.S. navel officers even as they were being reshackled, a fiery speech that though indecipherable by the Americans present was widely reported in the press. Declared a savage pirate by the proslavery papers and a "lover of liberty" in the tradition of "Webster," "Washington and the heroes of the revolution" by the antislavery press, Sengbe Pieh was singled out as either a dangerous threat to the fabric of American society or a noble embodiment of the core values of the American revolutionary spirit (Sale 101, 108). For the abolitionists in particular, Sengbe Pieh's ascension from a modest farmer to a captive of roving slave merchants and, ultimately, to a leader of a rebellion against tyranny fueled their cause by powerfully legitimating the natural rights claims with which so many of them justified their demand for the end of slavery.

The public contest over the *Amistad* rebellion's symbolic significance unfolded against the backdrop of a courtroom battle in which claims over the Africans' right to resist slavery and, in fact, their very status as human beings competed with, and were often overshadowed by, legal wrangling over the regulation of international commerce. In many ways, the case served as a much more important juridical test for nineteenth-century global capitalism than for the constitutionality of slavery. Ruiz and Montes, the *U.S.S. Washington*'s captain, and the white men the Africans encountered near Montauk all filed salvage claims for the ship and its human cargo. Quickly, both the queen of Spain and prominent U.S. abolitionists entered the fray. Wanting neither to give up its sovereignty rights nor to cede economic power over Caribbean trade, the Spanish monarch invoked a treaty that would force the United States to give up the mutineers and the ship (Jones, *Mutiny on the Amistad* 52). The abolitionists sensed an opportunity in the plight of the mutineers to generate a nationwide emotional and moral debate over the problem of slavery. Hence, they submitted writs of habeas corpus, which, if acted upon by the judge, would force the courts to concede that the Africans were human and, therefore, not property on which salvage claims could be made (63). Moreover, once James Covey, a Mende interpreter, was found, and the Africans told their version of events, revealing that they had been born in the Mende region of West Africa and not Cuba as the Spaniards claimed, the abolitionist supporters fashioned a much more advantageous second line of legal defense predicated on a series of international treaties that had banned all transatlantic slave trading. In the end, attorney Roger Baldwin's unflagging efforts to prove that the Africans had been transported in violation of the treaties banning the transatlantic slave trade and former president John Quincy Adams' argument that President Van Buren had exceeded executive power in his attempts to sway the outcome of the case culminated in legal victory. The abolitionists prevailed, and the *Amistad* mutineers, against overwhelming odds, were set free.[8]

Theirs was not, nor would ever be, a completely unqualified triumph. For the next half year, Sengbe Pieh and his comrades traveled throughout New England to raise funds for the return trip by speaking and performing in front of church congregations and antislavery societies, where they recited the prayers and hymns that their Christian abolitionist allies compelled them to memorize, performed acrobatics, sang songs in their native Mende language, and otherwise subjected themselves to involuntary self-display and the performative racial spectacle typical of the nineteeth century (Sale 96).[9] Their return, too, underscores what an ambivalent success the revolt was, for it highlights how deeply the trans-Atlantic slave trade decimated the African political and economic landscape and how drastically the continent was about to be radically transformed by colonialism. Upon his long-awaited return to his village, Sengbe Pieh found his wife, children, parents, siblings, aunts, uncles, neighbors, and his entire village, in fact, vanished, all swallowed by the voracious appetite of the slave trade. Their disappearance derogated the victories that he won in his quest to attain the anticipated pleasure and relief of homecoming. Moreover, neither he nor the other mutineers, nor any other inhabitant of Mendeland for that matter, would ever be able to escape fully the patronizing and paternalistic oversight by white Westerners, for the Christian mission set up by the white Americans accompanying the *Amistad* mutineers would eventually blossom and later be turned over to the British-based United Brethren of Christ Church (UBC), which, in turn, paved the path for British colonization of what was to become Sierra Leone (Osagie, *The Amistad Revolt* 64, 67).[10] Even though Sengbe Pieh quickly abandoned the mission, he never really escaped its shadow. His unwillingness to aid the missionaries led them to brand him a heathen and a slave trader in their reports; and while never substantiated, the rumors highlight the hypocritical racial paternalism embedded in the rhetoric of civilization and conversion that the British colonial invaders were beginning to deploy in justifying their scramble for Africa.[11]

When this image of the past flashed up one-hundred-fifty years later, its primary recipients were writers, visual artists, activists, and other organic intellectuals on the streets of cities like Freetown, behind bars in U.S. prisons, or otherwise severed from global intellectual communities. With the exception of Hollywood director Steven Spielberg and, perhaps, novelist Barbara Chase-Riboud, they were also among the most vulnerable to the violence of emergent forms of economic production and accumulation. As a historical antecedent to contemporary racialized capitalist exploitation and as an allegory for how individuals adapt, appropriate, and deflate those global economic forces to their own lives, the *Amistad* slave rebellion, I argue here in *Rebellious Histories*, provides these writers and artists a crucial locally resonant formulation to analyze the social conditions of late capitalism. As a revolt that took place on the open waters of the Atlantic by Africans yet to see a plantation, and as a revolt that led its protagonists into the heart of a legal battle over questions of national sovereignty and the legalities of international trade, the *Amistad* rebellion focuses attention, in ways that, say, Nat Turner's rebellion or Denmark Vesey's cannot, on how both continental and diasporic Africans engage and are engaged by the global flows of bodies, cultural practices, nationalist ideologies, and capital. Carried out on a slave ship—that vessel that Paul Gilroy describes as the defining chronotope of Atlantic capitalism and the forms of dissent organized against it (17)—by men and women who only recently had been captured and redefined as chattel, the *Amistad* rebellion powerfully symbolizes contemporary patterns of racialized, global inequality as well as the complex dynamics of black transnational subject formation within the global networks of capitalist production, past and present.[12] For all the triumph the young Sierra Leonean men saw in the *Amistad* victory, the narrative also signals the fraught dynamics of resistance. After all, the *Amistad* mutineers' efforts to claim their freedom placed them in complicated position to the white American abolitionists, including former U.S. president John Quincy Adams, on whom they were dependent to navigate the U.S. legal system. To contemporary African communities subject to NGOs, foreign aid packages, visa application officers, and IMF programs, the *Amistad* mutineers' situation rings strikingly familiar.[13]

In the way that Toussaint L'Ouverture's assertion of a radical vision of Enlightenment freedom in San Domingo repeatedly sparks efforts to work through the Enlightenment's problematic racial and colonial legacies, the *Amistad* rebellion potently indexes a range of material and epistemological tensions at the heart of contemporary global capital's reconfiguration of culture and subjectivity.[14] As the frisson of Josee Lahai's patriotic nation-state nationalism and simultaneous faith in the redemptive promise of transnational migration reveals, the *Amistad* narrative speaks directly to the persistent incommensurability of liberal national citizenship and black transnationalism. Despite the disciplinary efforts of modern nationalism to produce "compliant national citizens" (Appadurai 190), subjectivity for Africans and African Americans alike continues to operate along different sets of borders than national citizenship, overlapping in significant ways, but nevertheless exceeding and transgressing the boundary markers laid out by the interpellating powers of the state. Subjectivity in this regard is transnational: rooted in the nation-state and simultaneously routed across its borders, mirroring the transatlantic, transnational circuits taken by the *Amistad* mutineers and their supporters. As a result, postcolonial Africans such as Lahai and their counterparts in the diaspora continue to negotiate the conflicting forces of national citizenship and transnational subjectivity. In the United States, the intersection of Enlightenment claims that blackness is incompatible with the modernity of national citizenship with the state-sponsored violence of chattel slavery and segregation have left "the African diaspora's consciousness of itself . . . defined in and against constricting national boundaries," thereby "making Afro-diasporic people's relation to the nation-state 'contingent and partial' " (Hanchard 248). As scholarship on citizenship and political subjectivity in Africa shows, colonial policy and pedagogy, postcolonial patrimonial politics, and the transnationalization of primary production have generated similar disjunctures.[15] However, the enduring hegemony of nation-state nationalisms reproduces the binaries insider/outsider, citizen/foreigner, nation/race that make critical analysis of political and subject formations that cross borders and resist binary categorization so challenging. Moreover, postcolonial nationalism's persistent grip on the practices of epistemological decolonization—that is, to define "a discursive space outside of the Western way of knowing" (George 75–76)—still delimits efforts to imagine transformation outside the rubric of the nation-state.[16] In its elaboration of the dynamics of black transnationalism as it is produced at the intersection of local and global hegemonies, the *Amistad* narrative offers its contemporary interpreters rich critical valences for exploring contemporary modes of knowing and interpreting in the wake of the unrealized and, likely, unrealizable promise of nationalist decolonization.

In the process of forging locally specific, historically informed analytical frameworks for theorizing place, nation, and globalization, the American and Sierra Leonean authors who turn their attention to the *Amistad* history face the challenge of developing a historical practice attentive to the material legacy of slave-trade-era capitalism in the present, without, however, emptying the signifier *enslavement* of its historical and political specificity. Some, such as African American prison writer and antiprison activist Ruchell "Cinque" Magee, unapologetically assert that labor conditions in the contemporary global economy continue undifferentiated from plantation slavery. Others, such as African American detective novelist Clifford Mason whose protagonist, Joe Cinquez, uses his sleuthing skills to halt the economic exploitation of African and African diaspora communities, do not go so far as Magee but do suggest that neoliberal capitalism's production of contemporary black communities and black subjectivities shares clear affinities with the slave-trade economies of the past. In Sierra Leone, where the capital city was founded by liberated slaves from the Americas and where those liberated slaves were almost immediately placed under colonial control by their British benefactors even while the trans-Atlantic slave trade raged on unabated just outside of the city's environs, playwrights such as Charlie Haffner and Raymond DeSouza-George do not so much disentangle the historical forces of enslavement, colonial governmentality, and neoliberal late capitalism as they use the *Amistad* narrative to highlight their ongoing mutual constitution. As cultural texts mining and shaping the material of the cultural imaginary, neither the North American nor African *Amistad* works shy away from making historical claims about global capitalism's history in the trans-Atlantic slave trade or about colonialism's entanglement in this genealogy. Thus, they are no less valuable for the ethical demands they place on historians or for intervening in debates about colonialism's place in the longer history of global capitalism or over the "value of postcolonial studies in our globalizing world" (Loomba et al. 2). Moreover, by contrasting the utopian ideals of the *Amistad* mutineers with contemporary conditions of poverty, inequality, and "failed" nationalisms in places like Sierra Leone, their texts reveal how incomplete the projects for liberation remain and demonstrate, too, the persistence of specific structural inequalities inherent to the trans-Atlantic slave trade in the practices of contemporary global capitalist production, accumulation, and consumption.

The one other scholarly work that compares contemporary Sierra Leonean and American *Amistad* revolt narratives, Iyunolu Folayan Osagie's *The Amistad Revolt: Memory, Slavery, and the Politics of Identity in the United States and Sierra Leone* (2000) provides a valuable emplotment of the multiple avenues by which the revolt history has reentered collective memory. Osagie's analysis does not, however, interrogate its assumption that all humanity strives toward stable, coherent national identity. Arguing that the revolt's "reappearance as a collective act of memory is influencing and revitalizing nation-building and cultural identity" (xiv), Osagie proposes that we read these texts as critical interventions seeking to resolve the racial crises confronting the United States and the impoverishing effects of postcolonial tyranny in Sierra Leone, without, however, investigating the ways in which the works might critique the very foundations on which the nation-state rests as a political construct. Therefore, Osagie's otherwise compelling thesis that the work of collective memory involved in recovering the *Amistad* history represents an important development in the production of African American and Sierra Leonean national identities leaves the nation-state itself unproblematized and the cultural effects of globalization obscured. For me, the *Amistad* texts demand our critical attention precisely because they challenge the very national categories and transnational effects that Osagie takes for granted.[17]

By assessing the material and epistemological tensions produced where global capitalism exacerbates contradictions of subjectivity and citizenship as they are explored in this body of texts, I trace in *Rebellious Histories* the contours of a popular cultural critique of modernity and its history as a part of the global capital networks of the Atlantic world. The writers, visual artists, and activists for whom the *Amistad* rebellion resonates most are not those whose voices are typically heard in debates over the meanings of globalization and modernity. Some, like Sierra Leonean street art painter Josee Lahai and African American detective novelist Clifford Mason, have been overlooked by scholars altogether. Others, like Steven Spielberg and Barbara Chase-Riboud, are well known but not commonly recognized as participants in a discourse on transnationalism. By looking at the writings, actions, and visual art by such culture producers, *Rebellious Histories* explores the way that Atlantic capitalism, modernity, and their histories are understood by individuals and groups outside the structures of authority that shape hegemonic discourse—by this I mean both political and economic authorities as well as transnational theorists working in the academy. *Rebellious Histories* is also attentive to the publics for which their *Amistad* texts were, and, in some cases, continue to be produced.[18] With the exception of Steven Spielberg's film *Amistad* and, perhaps, Barbara Chase-Riboud's novel *Echo of Lions*, the texts I examine target highly localized audiences and, thus, facilitate the formation of local public spheres—Lahai's paintings, for example, were seen by few outside of the rough-and-tumble area around Freetown's dockyards (made famous in the global north by Graham Greene's novel *The Heart of the Matter*) where they generated discussion and debate about the slave-trading past and the natural resource- and arms-trading present.

Rebellious Histories reads the body of *Amistad* texts as a counterdiscourse to hegemonic intellectual formulations of globalization's modernity and its history, in other words, as rebellious histories. But, like any discourse, it is only legible and its governing structures only apparent when the individual texts are read in tandem. Of the dozen texts I examine, only Sierra Leonean playwright Raymond DeSouza-George's play *The Broken Handcuff*, Clifford Mason's novels *The Case of the Ashanti Gold* and *Jamaica Run*, and Ruchell "Cinque" Magee's antiprison writings explicitly reference contemporary modes of capitalist accumulation or practices of black transnationalism. Yet even texts that do not overtly signal the context of their production, like Spielberg's film *Amistad,* reveal their ideological investment in debates over U.S. national sovereignty and black transnationalism when read within the larger body of works. Focused as I am on the confluences of the *Amistad* materials, I am no less alert to the fissures, disjunctures, and gaps between and among individual texts, especially across the Atlantic divide where historical, economic, and political disparities radically differentiate lived experience. In fact, while connected historically via the rebellion they recall and via the liberated African American slaves who returned to Africa to settle Freetown in the eighteenth century, the Americans and Sierra Leoneans produced their works on the *Amistad* slave revolt largely in isolation from each other. It was not, in fact, until the mid-1990s when Steven Spielberg hired the Sierra Leonean author of a United States Information Service pamphlet on the rebellion as a consultant for his film *Amistad* that Americans and Sierra Leoneans actively collaborated across the Atlantic, and only then because of Hollywood's disproportionate global influence and capital. The absence of direct dialogue is itself symptomatic of the stark economic inequalities that hinder African access to global publishing and distribution markets and obstruct all but the most mainstream Hollywood products from circulating in places like Sierra Leone. To read the trans-Atlantic discourse generated by the *Amistad* texts with recognition of the disjunctures and gaps is to articulate, as Brent Hayes Edwards does in *The Practice of Diaspora*, a discourse "of cultural and political linkage only through and across difference in full view of the risks of that endeavor" (13).

Like literary critic and theorist Simon Gikandi, I argue that globalization and modernity are often defined and understood outside the centers of economic, political, and intellectual authority quite differently than from inside. While some of the texts gesture toward an instrumental, delocalized understanding of national identity in line with popular academic arguments about flexible citizenship and alternative modernities, they might simultaneously express a deep faith in the redemptive possibilities of the nation-state quite at odds with hegemonic intellectual discourse. Moreover, while the texts are keen to draw attention to the newness of the new imaginaries generated by the shifting global flows of capital, ideologies, culture, and human bodies, their focus on the nineteenth-century *Amistad* rebellion suggests that these new figurations of self and diaspora are not so different from those of the past. For these reasons, I share Gikandi's claim that new global cultures cannot be understood without recognition of their "genesis in modernity" (Gikandi 642). However, given the way that many of the *Amistad* texts themselves locate that genesis in the trans-Atlantic slave trade, I challenge Gikandi's contention that modernity "cannot be conceived outside colonial governmentality" (642).

Despite *Rebellious Histories*' genealogical debts to Paul Gilroy's *The Black Atlantic*, I shy away from the term *black Atlantic*, preferring instead variations on the term *transnationalism*. Without a doubt, Gilroy's theorization of the Atlantic as a single unit of analysis offers a compelling analytical framework for conceiving a politically transformative racialized subject formation that takes shape through the process of "intercultural positionality" (6) and of "the fractal patterns of cultural and political exchange" (15) across the overlapping spaces of racial, cultural, intellectual, and political borders. However, as I detail in chapter 4, Gilroy's formulation of modernity makes no room for theorizing the modernity of those Africans who remained on the African continent during and after the Atlantic slave trade. Moreover 'black Atlantic' obscures the broader Indian and Pacific Ocean networks alongside which the Atlantic slave trade operated and the Enlightenment took shape. With the encompassing word 'transnationalism' I hope to preserve a sense of the larger economic and cultural forces at work, even if the focus of my study is, in fact, very much an African and African diasporic Atlantic world. Moreover, while 'transnationalism' signals a more generic framework than 'black Atlantic,' it simultaneously specifies a very particular condition of modern subjectivity. Defining transnationalism as a mediator "between nationalism and globalization," Emily Apter posits that transnationalism is "a way to designate the claims of minoritarian languages and cultures and of diasporic communities" (Apter 70). This understanding of transnationalism as a contradictory space of mediation recognizes that the clash of global capital and the nation-state produces the conditions for the articulation of altogether original forms of identification and resistance just as readily as it engenders new and aggravated practices of domination. Dislocated from the home nation-state (or simply from nation-state citizen-subjectivity) by force, desire, or imagination, the individuals situated at the interstices of global capital and cultural flows give shape to distinct, if fluidly provisional, transnational cultural practices—what Arjun Appadurai terms "diasporic public spheres" (21)—to negotiate their feelings of displacement and belonging as transnationals. These territorially contingent transnational cultural practices defy the logic of coherence and stability that underwrite hegemonic conceptions of nation-state and racial identity; therefore, they constitute transgressive and destabilizing alternatives to the modernities of the Enlightenment and the nation-state.

Taken together, the *Amistad* texts form a unique body of cultural work that interlinks the histories of colonialism, trans-Atlantic slavery, postcolonial independence, civil rights and black power struggles, and global capitalism. In order to capture the complex critical questions that necessarily arise out of this constellation, *Rebellious Histories* brings the theories of postcolonialism, diaspora, and globalization into a productive encounter to explore a more complex understanding of modernity and of the relationship between Africa and the United States. Individually, these theoretical frameworks refashion hegemonic definitions of modernity, which still too often pose Africans and African Americans as Euro-America's inescapably premodern others. Yet, diaspora studies too often holds the moment of terrifying rupture of the Middle Passage as the constitutive element of slavery's modernity, which effectively renders those who remained on the African continent spatially outside of and temporally prior to that modernity. Similarly, despite Achille Mbembe's declaration that "the [slave] trade was *the* event through which Africa was born to modernity" (Mbembe 13), trans-Atlantic slavery rarely features in African discourses of modernity. Rather, postcolonial African studies routinely subsume the transformative effects of Atlantic slavery to colonization as the determinate factor in the formation of African modernities. *Rebellious Histories* charts a more expansive cartography of the Atlantic world with its ever-morphing circuits of exchange—of which colonialism represents but one spatiotemporal element—to bring a new focus to the residual traces of the trans-Atlantic slave trade's remaking of village social structures, practices of violence, and definitions of personhood in Africa. With this focus on the modernity of the slave trade in Africa, *Rebellious Histories* opens up diaspora and postcolonial African studies more fully to each other and to a more nuanced understanding of modernity in the Atlantic world. Moreover, I argue that with closer attention to colonialism's global capitalist slave-trading past, postcolonial critiques of globalization can be more effectively mobilized to historicize global capitalism and to theorize its reconfiguration of culture and subjectivity.

For all the trans-Atlantic correspondences linking the Sierra Leonean and American *Amistad* texts, differences in history, political economy, and relative geopolitical power produce distinct, if overlapping, transnational effects in the two locations and, thus, produce different stakes for claiming the *Amistad* history. For these reasons I begin the book with two comparative chapters. The first reads African American and Sierra Leonean acts of claiming the revolt leader's name as a discursive process of naming the material conditions and racialized effects of global capitalism. In the chapter, I examine African American texts by antiprison activist Ruchell "Cinque" Magee and detective novelist Clifford Mason in which the author or his fictional character inhabits the name and persona of *Amistad* slave revolt leader Joseph Cinque. Alongside these American texts, I decode a Sierra Leonean visual arts movement that aimed to reclaim Cinque's birth name, *Sengbe Pieh*. Renaming practices like these are, of course, part of a long history of shedding "slave" names, forging Pan-African or diasporic identities, and preserving histories of resistance. These dynamics are at work in the act of taking Cinque's name and in asserting his birth name, but I argue that such acts also discursively locate the self or selves historically in new economic and political conditions. Reclaiming the name 'Cinque/Sengbe,' I argue, charts the recognition of how the neoliberal denationalization of "legitimate" capital and the expansion of "phantom" global economies trading clandestinely in diamonds, drugs, and arms have disproportionately impacted material security and practices of self-representation. However, by juxtaposing Magee's writings with Mason's novels, and by counterposing their U.S.-based works with the Sierra Leonean paintings, I assess the productive possibilities and the limits of formulating a transnational black subjectivity vis-à-vis the differential privileges afforded Africans and African Americans under global capital.

Through an examination of publications by the Sierra Leonean president's office, the United States Information Service, and Sierra Leonean playwright Charlie Haffner, chapter 2 traces how the narrative of the *Amistad* revolt emerged in the late 1980s as a key modality through which meanings of Sierra Leonean nationalism and claims to state power were contested in a global frame. I argue that through its dialogic engagement with the two governmental texts, Charlie Haffner's play *Amistad Kata-Kata* transforms the fear of cannibalism that sparked the rebellion into a politically charged trope whereby it couples cannibalism as a name for the excesses carried out by local authorities with cannibalism as a description of the dehumanizing consumption of African bodies within the Atlantic slave system. The trope thus forms a key for translating the slave revolt into a discrediting, disrupting critique of the complex interrelations between global capitalism and excessive elite consumption in the postcolony.

In my effort to most effectively attend to the differential demands placed on the rebellion history by the Sierra Leoneans and Americans, chapters 3 and 4 focus individually—rather than comparatively—on U.S. and Sierra Leonean texts, thereby permitting me to better contextualize works coming from the two locations. In chapter 3, I read Steven Spielberg's film *Amistad* (1997) and Barbara Chase-Riboud's novel *Echo of Lions* (1989) as mass culture artifacts produced in the wake of black nationalism and in the context of intensified anxiety about the United

States' place in an increasingly globalized world. In each text, I argue, the *Amistad* leader's presence inside U.S. nation-state borders threatens the hegemonic narratives of U.S. nationalism. As a figure that refuses incorporation into the body politic and that simultaneously offers African Americans a transnational mode of affiliation, Sengbe/Cinque reinvigorates the specter of black nationalism, but in a fashion that has as much to do with early 1970s' militancy as it does with the new diasporas forming in the 1980s and '90s. Where Spielberg's *Amistad* contains this threat to the white, patriarchally defined nation by characterizing Cinque as the quintessential neoliberal individual and by denying him a transnational affiliation with America's black population, I show how Chase-Riboud foregrounds how black subject formation has historically taken shape transnationally in the shadow of the global capitalist slave trade and thereby highlights how such formations destabilize the monologic nationalism and neoliberal individualism the film's gendered constructs reproduce.

During the first years of Sierra Leone's civil war (1991–2002), at least two playwrights and dozens of visual artists depicted the *Amistad* revolt or its leader Sengbe Pieh as part of what I contend was an effort to develop a new explanatory framework for historicizing the corruption, exploitation, and violence of political life in the country. The war was fought largely over control of the country's diamond mines and, consequently, over access to global markets. Where earlier Sierra Leonean and American *Amistad* texts call attention to the intersections of local and global hegemonies at work in the nation-state and to the racialized configurations of national citizenship, they do not fundamentally question the centrality of the state itself to modern subjectivity. Impending state collapse and mass population displacement across national borders, however, focused attention sharply on the genealogical birth of the nation-state in the modernity of Atlantic slave-trade capitalism and on the tenability of transnational citizenship under late capitalism. My analysis in the final chapter turns to texts produced during the civil war that make a more explicit critique of the categories of the nation-state and citizenship. In chapter 4, I assess Sierra Leonean writer Raymond DeSouza-George's 1994 play *The Broken Handcuff* and his compatriot Josee Lahai's commentary about his 1993 public portrait of Sengbe Pieh given retrospectively in December 2000 from a West African diaspora community just outside Atlanta, Georgia. Their texts, I assert, deploy the rebellion to develop a historically informed postcolonial critique of globalization to account for its history in the trans-Atlantic slave trade. Lahai, I contend, filters his understanding of citizenship and temporality for the contemporary transnational Sierra Leonean through the history of the *Amistad* slave rebellion. DeSouza-George, similarly, brings a new focus to the residual traces of the trans-Atlantic slave trade's remaking of village social structures, practices of violence, and definitions of personhood to historicize the violence and fragility of the nation-state.

In the subsequent pages, I deploy the terms *Amistad history* and *Amistad narrative* to identify the collection of events and experiences beginning with the *Amistad* rebels' initial capture in and around their homes and ending with their return and the establishment of the Christian mission by their American benefactors. As a necessary shorthand, the term simplifies a complex history of motivations, desires, tactics, and effects. It also risks obscuring the chronologies that the writers and artists privileged. Ruchell "Cinque" Magee, for instance, showed no interest in the narrative beyond the point of the Supreme Court decision, whereas Raymond DeSouza-George makes the tragic denouement of Sengbe Pieh's return to the destruction of his family and village a fundamental element of his thematic. I do my best to specify the author's usage and my own. Where I do not, I trust that the context will. For similar reasons but with opposite effect, I identify the rebellion leader by the names *Joseph Cinque, Joseph Cinqué, Joseph Cinquez*, and *Sengbe Pieh* to reflect how each author or artist chooses to name him and when they choose to name him by which name. At times, this mixing of names and spellings can get unwieldy. In chapter 3, for example, I use the spelling *Cinqué* to describe the character who appears in Steven Spielberg's film *Amistad* and *Cinque* and *Sengbe Pieh* in accordance with Barbara Chase-Riboud's novel where the name shift signals a period when he verges on succumbing psychologically to enslavement. When making general comments or when describing the historical figure, I typically use *Sengbe Pieh*, attempting as best possible to respect the man so fiercely dedicated to preserving his liberty.

1

Cinque/Sengbe

Naming the Transnational Subject

With an agenda to destroy all institutions of incarceration, dismantle the nation-state, and form a new transnational race, the Symbionese Liberation Army was nothing less than the United States' radical Left's most spectacular failure, bringing both unparalleled media focus and public derision for its idealistic and bizarrely contradictory revolutionary agenda. Introducing itself to the San Francisco Bay area in November 1973 with a bold gesture that can only be taken as emblematic of its contradictory politics, the SLA assassinated the Oakland Schools superintendent, Dr. Marcus Foster, who was the only African American in the country at the time to occupy the helm of a major urban school district. Widely condemned as irresponsible and adventurist by the likes of Angela Davis and Huey Newton, Foster's assassination would prove to be only a tame precursor to the SLA's most spectacular action.[1] In the spring of 1974 the SLA jolted to life middle America's nightmarish fantasies about revolution, black power, and the moral decay of white suburban youth when it kidnapped media heiress Patty Hearst, ransomed several million dollars in food donations from the Hearst family for California's poor, magically transformed Patty into a revolutionary, and, only four months later, died a real-time televised death in a massive firefight with the Los Angeles Police Department. Only Hearst and two other core members escaped the shootout. Said to be "more whoopticians than theorists" by one leftist would-be sympathizer (Hinckle 12), the SLA repeatedly demonstrated a penchant for carrying out its revolution as a "guerrilla theater" that was equal parts militant and absurd but wholly televisable.[2] In a manner sure to draw widespread attention, its actions were often carried out by white revolutionaries in blackface and under the threat of death by cyanide-tipped bullets. As an almost exclusively white terrorist cell led by a black male exconvict that mixed its quasi-Marxist antiprison rhetoric with messianic mysticism, the SLA became a caricature of the revolutionary Left and magnified the movement's problems of masculine privilege and charismatic leadership to epic proportions. For the group and its observers, the name *Cinque Mtume*, taken by SLA leader Donald David DeFreeze and modeled on *Amistad* leader Joseph Cinque, became a focal point around which many of these challenges were debated.

By way of an extended introduction to this chapter on the use of the *Amistad* rebellion on both sides of the Atlantic to name the material conditions and racialized effects of global capitalism, I sketch out in these opening paragraphs how DeFreeze's choice of Cinque Mtume as his *nom de guerre* opened a space for outside observers and members of the SLA alike to contend with the group's, and its leader's, problematic political identity. For social commentators, the uneasiness over and oftentimes grudging recognition of the SLA's revolutionary leadership were repeatedly expressed through attempts to explicate DeFreeze's choice of 'Cinque' as a name. These observers sought clues in the history of the *Amistad* revolt that might reveal something about the SLA's political goals and agenda but that could also be used to contest its revolutionary credentials. For the SLA, explicating the symbolism of the name offered yet one more opportunity to display the outlandish and fundamentally patriarchal revolutionary sensibility that undermined its own inchoate agenda. Where it advocated an egalitarian, nonhierarchical revolution, it managed also to identify a messianic meaning in the name 'Cinque,' thereby turning its bearer, DeFreeze, into the Fifth Prophet, a modern-day messiah and heroic patriarch quite at odds with the group's vision of a communitarian utopia.

That Donald David DeFreeze's *nom de guerre*, 'Cinque Mtume,' would become an important signifier in the contest over the SLA's meaning to American culture and politics should come as little surprise considering that for each SLA novice, the revolution began with personal rebirth, a process that saw initiates renounce their prior identities and names. Members Emily Harris and Joe Remiro emerged as "Yolanda" and "Bo," for example, and Patty Hearst as "Tania." These new names were intended to capture the revolutionary spirit of past anti-imperialist militants. Patty-as-Tania would write, "I have been given the name Tania after a comrade who fought alongside Che in Bolivia for the people of Bolivia. I embrace the name with the determination to continue fighting in her spirit" ("SLA Communiqué, April 3, 1970" qtd. in Avery and McLellan 301). It appears that Cinque Mtume brought the renaming practice to the SLA from California's Vacaville prison, where, as a member of the Black Cultural Association (BCA), he shed his "slave" name *Donald David DeFreeze* (Avery and McLellan 20). Founded in 1968, the BCA aimed to help black prisoners take control of their own rehabilitation through education in literacy, math, African culture, and radical politics (Cheevers 1, 5). Members of the BCA were encouraged to shed the names that they had inherited from the white men and women who had enslaved their ancestors. Implicit in the choice to rename themselves was the recognition that one of the most powerful acts carried out by slave masters was to deny an enslaved African's identity by giving him or her a new name, a violent practice of erasure that, according to Orlando Patterson, functioned as one of the constitutive elements of enslavement (Patterson 55). To reject one's "slave" name and adopt a new self-fashioned name, as innumerable African Americans did during the 1960s and 1970s, was thus far more than a means of expressing one's individuality. By adopting a new name, one's moniker was made a contested signifier in the fiercely fought battles over race and power and signaled in no uncertain terms one's political opposition to hegemonic power. Consequently, Donald David DeFreeze, the chronically underemployed petty criminal and repeat inmate, was reinvented as an embodiment of Joseph Cinque's proud resistant spirit and the Swahili word for "disciple" or "apostle."

Names played a central part in the SLA's agenda, and because they did, observers seeking to comprehend the SLA's extravagant political performativity focused on them. To say that the popular media had a field day with Hearst's transformation into the bank-robbing, machine-gun-toting Tania would be an understatement; but in a more restrained manner, the press also sought to construct an explanatory narrative for the SLA's revolution by unpacking the historical meanings embedded in DeFreeze's revolutionary name. Voicing ambivalence about the SLA's contribution to racial politics and about the contradictions in its revolutionary agenda, at least two publications would latch onto the persistent, though now discredited, claim that *Amistad* leader Joseph Cinque became a slave trader upon his return to West Africa.[3] *Dawn Magazine*, the national periodical supplement included with such venerable middle-class African American newspapers as the *Amsterdam News* and the *Baltimore Afro-American*, signaled its anxiety about how to characterize Cinque Mtume's legacy as an African American leader by running an article shortly after the May

1974 shootout with the LAPD that simultaneously eulogized the slain black SLA field marshal and recollected Joseph Cinque's legacy as an ironic hero who had bravely challenged the institution of slavery while personally benefiting from it (Henegan, "There Was Another Cinque" 15). Without linking the slave-trading legacy to DeFreeze directly, the article nevertheless associates the original Cinque's taint with the slain SLA leader's character.[4] Likewise, in an effort to make sense of the SLA's rampant contradictions of leftist theory and its routine political *faux pas*, Warren Hinkle repeats the slave-trading rumor in a 1974 *San Francisco Phoenix* article. Hinckle queries:

> Donald DeFreeze adopts the name Cinque, an African chief who took control of a slave ship but lost his abolitionist brownie points when he became a slave trader himself . . . What obtains with these names? Is the SLA perverse? Or uninstructed? Such questions bait the theory recently propounded by conspiracy theorists on the left that the SLA is a creature of the CIA. The Ivy League delinquents in the Agency's dirty tricks department are known to do their communist homework and it is unlikely that even the lads who brought us the Bay of Pigs would make a boo-boo such as giving so obviously less than 24-karat left wing handles. As to whether the SLA is being perverse or dumb, the smart money is with the former. The leftist double entendre in the names Cinque and Tania[5] served to further provoke the left, already near to spitting teeth over the lumpen brazenness of the SLA. I believe or half believe that the SLA gets its kicks out of jerking off the left. (1)

For Hinckle, then, DeFreeze's choice of the name 'Cinque' reveals less a series of contradictions rooted in ignorance than a calculated pattern of manipulating expectations. Hinckle takes a bemused pleasure in the SLA's thumb nosing but nevertheless remains apprehensive about the group's politics. For each of these journalists, DeFreeze's revolutionary sobriquet opens a space to both explain and contest the SLA's revolutionary program.

In turn, the SLA made its own exegesis of the name the source of one of its most troublingly problematic contradictions. Against the backdrop of its egalitarian rhetoric, the SLA produced a document in which Cinque Mtume is cast as a patriarchal messiah come to deliver the oppressed masses from exploitation. As one might expect from a group whose leader took his name as part of a cultural nationalist organization, the SLA initially associates Cinque Mtume with the symbolism of rebellion against tyranny so clearly identified with the *Amistad* revolt. The SLA communiqué dated April 4, 1974, proclaims, "Cinque Mtume is the name that was bestowed upon him by his imprisoned sisters and brothers. It is the name of an ancient African chief who led the fight of his people for freedom" ("SLA Communiqué, April 4, 1974," qtd. in Avery and McLellan 521). But what begins as a move to refashion the *Amistad* revolt narrative for the contemporary struggle quickly turns into a nightmare of gender, race, and class fetishism. While Cinque Mtume is shown initially to embody the original Cinque's freedom-loving resistant spirit, he comes to represent less a man of the people than the new patriarchal messiah: "The name means Fifth Prophet, and Cin was many years ago given this name because of his keen instinct and sense, his spiritual consciousness, and his deep love of all the people and children of this earth" (521). Congnizant of the Left's widespread distrust of messianic rhetoric, the statement clumsily backtracks to assure that Cinque was in no way inflicted with an "ego problem" (521). Ultimately, however, it reaffirms his God-like status: "He has ONE WORD to the children of the oppressed and the children of the oppressor: COME" (523). Cinque Mtume, then, is revealed to his people as the patriarch who gathers up his children to lead them to salvation. The black male excon becomes the new messiah and the only true leader of the people.

Clearly, a whole host of factors contributed to DeFreeze's cultish veneration, not least of which is the misapprehension of how the original Cinque received his name. Apparently unaware that 'Cinque' was a slave name imposed on Sengbe Pieh by a Spanish plantation owner, the SLA interprets the name as the Spanish number 5, turning DeFreeze into the Fifth Prophet. Already encumbered with a penchant for mystical interpretation, the SLA emphasizes this quasinumerological exegesis rather than link its revolution against incarceration and imperialism to the *Amistad* revolt and Sengbe Pieh's own battle to protect and preserve his African identity. The history of the *Amistad* revolt could easily have given the SLA a more materialist narrative for explaining the structural bases of domination and resistance and for articulating a theory of transnational oppositional identity. The SLA's critique of incarceration, after all, often included the language of enslavement, and the group was adamant about the culpability of multinational corporations for race, gender, and class oppression (Pearsall et. al., "Communiqué addressed to the *San Francisco*

Phoenix April 4, 1974;" "Communiqué #3, February 4, 1974"). However, belying Hinckle's faith in the SLA's historical acumen, the group eschews the materialist historical narrative for the cultish, mystical, and messianic. By deifying its sole black male member, by turning DeFreeze into the prophetic father figure of the oppressed masses, the SLA repudiates its own rhetoric of gender equality and nonhierarchical social organization. The shortsighted interpretation of what the name 'Cinque' could signify and the hagiographic romanticization of DeFreeze that resulted quite clearly emblematize the SLA's inchoate revolutionary agenda.

Its celebrity status notwithstanding, the SLA ultimately not only ensured its own downfall, but, in the analysis of at least one later observer, contributed significantly to the dissolution of the revolutionary Left as a whole.[6] Yet even in this apparent failure, we see a glimmer of how critical the *Amistad* revolt history could be to the United States' radical leftist movements of the 1970s and to subsequent critiques of global capitalism in the 1980s and '90s. Despite the SLA's troubling hermeneutics, Joseph Cinque's armed revolt against enslavement offered precisely the narrative structure that the revolutionary left of the 1970s required. At a moment when the state was ascribed little legitimacy and incarceration was defined as nothing more than a new brand of enslavement, the *Amistad* revolt's imagery of bold, bloody, and legally legitimated violence symbolized the direction toward militancy in which the revolutionary Left believed it ought to move. As we shall see, another self-fashioned Cinque—Ruchell "Cinque" Magee—in fact, had already used the *Amistad* revolt four years earlier to redefine the hegemonic definitions of tyranny and enslavement in much this way, and, as it would turn out, Cinque's name would remain a compelling—and deeply contested—signifier in the United States even after militant black power gave way to an era of racialized neoliberal Reaganomics, as it would also in Sierra Leone where the failures of post-colonial political independence fueled trenchant poverty, civil war, and large-scale migration. On both sides of the Atlantic, the names 'Cinque(z)' and 'Sengbe' would tell powerful stories about the place of continental and diasporic Africans in the larger structures of global capitalist geopolitics, and they would locate people of African descent in a longer history of global trade, exploitation, and violence.

Because self-given names reveal so much about an individual's conception of his or her place in society, and because the names 'Cinque' and 'Sengbe' contain such rich historical significations, I focus this chapter on African American and Sierra Leonean acts of claiming revolt leader

Cinque/Sengbe's name as a discursive process of naming the material conditions and racialized effects of global capitalism. The following analysis examines African American texts by Ruchell "Cinque" Magee and Clifford Mason in which the author or his fictional character inhabits the name and persona of *Amistad* slave revolt leader Joseph Cinque(z). Alongside these American texts, I explicate a Sierra Leonean visual arts movement that aimed to reclaim Cinque's birth name, 'Sengbe Pieh.' Certainly, the cultural logic of shedding slave names is at work in the act of taking Cinque's name and in asserting his birth name, but I argue that such acts also discursively locate the self or selves historically in specific material conditions. Reclaiming the name 'Cinque/Sengbe,' I argue, charts the recognition of how the neoliberal denationalization of "legitimate" capital and the expansion of "phantom" global economies trading clandestinely in diamonds, drugs, and arms have disproportionately impacted material security and practices of self-representation. However, I show that juxtaposing Magee's writings with Mason's novels, and their U.S.-based works with the Sierra Leonean paintings, reveals both the productive *possibilities* and the *limits* of formulating a transnational black subjectivity vis-à-vis the differential privileges afforded Africans and African Americans under global capitalism.

In the first part of this chapter, I look to the *Amistad*-informed rhetoric of California inmate activist Ruchell Magee, who adopted the name 'Cinque' in 1970, to consider how the original rebel leader's name and the historical narrative of his 1839 slave revolt were deployed to designate the ontological status of incarcerated people of color under the regime of U.S. imperialism and the attendant rise of multinational capitalism. An improbable hero and inmate intellectual in an era of best-selling prison manifestos and larger-than-life celebrity revolutionaries, the seventh-grade-educated, Louisiana-born, folksy jailhouse lawyer Ruchell Magee scored his radical credentials with antiprison leftists and his fifteen minutes in the national limelight almost by accident. On August 7, 1970, four years before Patty Hearst's kidnapping by the SLA, a firestorm of bullets rained down on the occupants of a getaway van in the parking lot of the Frank Lloyd Wright–designed Civic Center in San Francisco's wealthy white suburban Marin County, leaving four dead, two wounded, and three, including Magee, miraculously uninjured. Minutes earlier, while testifying on behalf of a fellow San Quentin inmate that day in the Marin County Courthouse, Ruchell Magee took the gun and the opportunity for freedom offered to him by the seventeen-year-old Jonathon Jackson, and joined two other San Quentin inmates in the courtroom in taking Judge Harold Haley, the district attorney, and three jurors hostage. In an apparent attempt to move the captives to a nearby radio station where Jackson likely intended to demand that his brother, the famed prison radical George Jackson, be released from San Quentin, they came under a barrage of fire from prison guards and police in the parking lot. As the only survivor among the would-be revolutionaries, Magee was charged with kidnapping and murder, and soon after he would see a conspiracy charge added in conjunction with Angela Davis's arrest. Davis was implicated because the guns used were registered in her name and because of her rumored romantic attachment to Jonathon's brother. As much as the events in Marin County themselves catapulted Magee into the public's eye, Davis' high-profile defense campaign lent him a broader audience for his analyses of race and incarceration.[7] Largely forgotten today by the canonizing activist machine that deifies figures such as George Jackson and Mumia Abu Jamal, Magee remains incarcerated on the Marin conviction in California's Corcoran State Corrections Facility, extending a life behind bars that began in 1955 at the age of fifteen when he was charged with the attempted rape of a white woman in his Louisiana hometown and sent to the infamous Angola State Prison. Magee would be free only a few months of his adult life between his release from Angola and an arrest in 1963 in Los Angeles on a marijuana-related kidnapping charge (Thiel, chapter 3, 6).[8]

Because Jonathon Jackson's goals for the courtroom takeover were erased with the bullets that took his life, both the Left, which lauded the Marin County action, and the Nixon-Reagan Right, which stepped up its law-and-order rhetoric as a consequence, ascribed dense layers of meaning to the events of August 7. At the same time that President Nixon made a special television appearance after Davis's arrest to thank J. Edgar Hoover and the FBI for protecting the moral fabric of the nation, the Black Panthers held a revolutionary funeral for the slain martyrs, about whom an editorial writer for the *Berkeley Tribe* exuberantly proclaimed, "They strode beyond the world as we know it, Huey [Newton] says beyond the experience of Watts, of Detroit, beyond even the most romantic fantasies of young whites. In death they redefined life. Where they fell we begin" ("We Are the Revolution" 2).[9] Capitalizing on the spirited rhetoric bandied around by both the Left and the Right, Ruchell Magee tapped the politically charged atmosphere to declare himself a slave in the government's possession and his participation in the takeover as nothing less than a slave rebellion. In the process of fashioning himself as a revolutionary slave rebel, Magee added the *Amistad* revolt leader's name, 'Cinque,' to his own.[10] Like so many other African Americans influenced by black power and cultural nationalism, Magee considered his given name to be a "slave name" and Cinque to be his "African name" ("Interview with Dave Stevens").[11]

Magee's politicization took place in the context of increasing frustration with the pace of social and political change that turned activists involved in the U.S. civil rights and antiwar movements toward the militant rhetoric of black power and racial nationalism. Angered, one on hand, by the belligerent resistance to civil rights legislation, by the disproportionate numbers of African Americans killed in Vietnam, and by the racial disparities of the early 1970s' economic recession, and inspired, on the other, by Marxist anti-imperialist movements in other parts of the world, many black activists began to argue that full racial integration into American society was an untenable goal. Racial stratification was considered to be so ingrained in American national culture and economic organization that, without completely dismantling the nation-state or dividing the United States into separate racially defined nations, black economic and political power could never be reached. Similarly, the example of militant freedom fighters in Southeast Asia and southern Africa rendered violence a viable option for securing change. In moving away from a nation-state-bounded conception of race-based domination, activists among the increasingly militant black Left also began to contextualize their struggle for freedom as part and parcel of the concurrent battles against imperialism in Africa and Southeast Asia. Accordingly, African Americans were argued to be a colonized nation, exploited economically as modern-day slaves to benefit a white capitalist elite whose multinational corporations were responsible for colonialism the world over (Allen 12). Resistance, in the thinking of black power militants, had to be choreographed and targeted correspondingly.

Several political shifts within this milieu ensured that U.S. prisons took the spotlight in leftist politics. The most significant was Richard Nixon's successful 1968 "law and order" presidential campaign, which engineered a moral panic over President Johnson's inability to contain the social disorder caused by the country's proliferating political movements.

After Nixon's election, FBI and police repression of groups such as the Black Panthers escalated, leading to arrests, imprisonment, and killings of activists by police and undercover FBI agents (Gilmore, "Globalization and U.S. Prison Growth"). It was not just the Panthers who were entering prison in increased numbers, at least not in California, where the inmate population increased 15 percent between 1970 and 1973, with African Americans comprising almost 30 percent of the overall numbers, compared with their 7 percent representation in the state as a whole (Avery and McLellan 47–48; Cummins 65).[12] With prominent Panthers in prison, the Left began to apply its analysis of the racist, capitalist, and imperialist underpinnings of America's aggression in Vietnam to domestic social relations and came to the conclusion that penitentiaries were nothing less than American concentration camps designed to exploit and exterminate people of color. A similar analysis had begun much earlier inside the prison walls led by Elijah Muhammad's Black Muslims and, later, by the Black Panthers, who encouraged prisoners of color to redefine themselves as political prisoners incarcerated for economic crimes that they committed only because of the institutional racism practiced by the state (Berkman 2; B. Aptheker 58).[13] Additionally, outspoken activists pointed out how prisons functioned as revenue-generating factories and were disproportionately populated by blacks and Chicanos, thus intimating they were also slave-labor plantations (Kasirika and Muntu 220).[14] In the analysis that emerged from the Left, the modern judicial and penitentiary systems, then, functioned as a prison-industrial complex coterminous with the imperialist military-industrial complex to exploit the labor and quash the dissent of nonwhite people worldwide.

Twenty-one years after the Marin courtroom takeover, Ruchell "Cinque" Magee would recollect the circumstances under which he adopted his slave rebel moniker and what it symbolized to him:

> Cinque was added to my name upon my 1971 court appearance, after learning the Supreme Court decision in regards to the 1841 trial of Joseph Cinque and the other captives aboard the slave ship Amistad.
>
> The film version of the slave ship Amistad event by Steven Spielberg's missed my ordeal by a mile. Perhaps, because many journalists do not see the big picture of the courts-system becoming the modern day slave-ship. Poor people (blacks in particular) are railroaded into prison the past 30-years, and

> declared having no rights. Had Cinque and others not took over the ship Amistad, they may had never lived to prove slavery. Slaves was sold as criminals with no rights.
>
> Just before the Marin County Courtroom was taking over August 7, 1970 by one Jonathan Jackson and James D. McClain, I was on the witness-stand testifying against the Los Angeles Police frame-up of 1963/65 that got me in prison (isolated in a dungeon cell).
>
> Appellate judges had denied me access to court almost 7 years than. Upon told of my chances to expose the L.A. police frame-up by T.V. news, obviously, I went along with the rebellion.
>
> Caught up in unlawful imprisonment based on racism, I didn't choose the rebellion, the rebellion choosed me. (Personal correspondence, March 9, 2002)

By no means an African American Gramsci in his writing style or output, the seventh-grade-educated Magee nevertheless reads the *Amistad* revolt—and all the racial, national, and legal contestations to which it alludes—as both allegory and historical antecedent for his own place in the American carceral system. For Magee, the courtroom is like the slave ship insofar as it conveys free individuals to indentured servitude, stripping their rights in the process. But, by invoking the favorable Supreme Court decision that released the *Amistad* mutineers from state incarceration, Magee suggests that contemporary enslavement is no more legally legitimated than its antebellum equivalent and that violent rebellion is just as sanctioned now as then. Thus, in comparing himself to Cinque, Magee casts himself as a heroic slave rebel. Like the *Amistad* Africans who were taken illegally as slaves across the Atlantic in violation of numerous international treaties and had their mutiny legally upheld in American courts and morally supported by many American communities, Magee justifies his actions in the Marin County courtroom as a rebellion against unjust tyranny.

Magee's analyses of the prison-industrial complex and his use of Cinque's name as a marker of his subject status in a particular historical moment of racialized global capitalism is given fuller treatment in a series of short essays and a creative text that he published in radical newspapers around northern California's Bay Area during the period following the Marin rebellion. The most suggestive piece is a two-page play titled "Miscarriage of Justice." Written in a solitary confinement cell at San Quentin, "Miscarriage of Justice" tells the story of Cinque and Kitabu, two political activists framed for crimes ranging from robbery to drug possession. The majority of the action takes place in a courtroom presided over by Judge Black-Get-Back, a caricature of a self-righteous proponent of Nixon's law-and-order society. The play ends in a public park where Cinque initiates a worldwide revolution against global capitalism and its attendant forms of racism. The character Cinque, whose full name is Ruchell Cinque Magee and who shares an autobiography almost identical to Magee's, is clearly intended as a representation of its author. Cinque's most identifiable trait is his ability to speak authoritatively about structural inequality. Cinque speaks when he is expected to be silent and aggressively antagonizes white men in positions of power when he is expected to display unquestioning deference. Yet, in several key respects, the two are very different, suggesting that in Cinque, Magee fantasized a revolutionary alter ego for himself. Where Magee's verbal interventions in court once led to a judge's order to shackle and muzzle him ("Ruchell vs. Reagan" 8), Cinque's orations secure his liberation. And where Magee's pronouncements about race, incarceration, and enslavement were overshadowed by those of his codefendant, Angela Davis, and by radicals such as George Jackson, Cinque's inspire a multiracial coalition to rise up in revolution.

In a scant two pages, the play refracts a picture of the courts' systematic psychological subjugation of its victims, who are rendered voiceless and therefore without agency to resist their conditions of servitude. "Miscarriage of Justice" imagines slave rebellion, accordingly, as a multistage process beginning with the reclamation of the prisoners' independent and authoritative voice, ending with revolution against global capitalism under a multiracial, transnational banner. Among Cinque's primary obstacles to initiating revolution is Judge Black-Get-Back's effort to belittle and humiliate him into speechlessness. By naming the principal antagonist Judge Black-Get-Back, Magee concocts a racist judge whose personal mission is to push uppity blacks back into their place of subservience to whites. Judge Black-Get-Back is particularly adept at humiliating his defendants into silence. At one point, for instance, he attempts to shame Cinque and Kitabu by smugly asserting, "Personally I don't think Black is beautiful because the only beautiful people are those who work for a living and do not go around robbing people. In fact, you all look awful silly wearing those Black is Beautiful buttons in my courtroom." Cinque rejoins, “Yes, Mr. Frivolous Racist Dog, you would think that working people are beautiful since you enjoy the richness of their labor. And here is a Habeas Corpus and we have a civil suit in the federal court against you. Now Mr. Motherfucker, sentence that” (9). In the act of speech, in the refusal to be silenced, Cinque declines to be subjugated to the judge’s domineering will. By speaking in a race- and class-coded vernacular, he fiercely protects his independent, human subjectivity. And by drawing attention to the ways in which the judge benefits personally from class stratification, Cinque exposes the hypocrisy underlying Judge Black-Get-Back’s self-satisfied pronouncement about the value of labor. Moreover, by refusing to acquiesce to the judge’s racist paternalism, Cinque fends off a ruling long enough to address the public one more time. The time his verbal acumen proves sufficient to set the armed revolution in motion.

With no explicit references to the *Amistad* slave rebellion or to modern forms of enslavement, the name ‘Cinque’ nonetheless signals a genealogy of incarceration and resistance as a manifestation of chattel slavery and the forms of opposition organized against it. Over and over again in his writings, Magee draws connections between the antebellum plantation and the twentieth-century prison. Against the backdrop of the *Amistad* revolt, Magee characterizes all prisoners as being enslaved by a system of global capitalist economic production. In no way does Magee view enslavement strictly as a metaphor for incarceration, for he understands the judicial and penal system to operate according to a strict economics of slave-based production in the most literal sense of the term. In a newspaper article that appeared in *The Black Panther*, Magee critiques the two-cent-per-hour wage given to inmates as a direct form of plantation economics (“Ruchell Magee’s Struggle” 13). Moreover, Magee deciphered a pattern of conspiracy by the white judges and lawyers to protect a lucrative system of race-based economic production. According to Magee, lawyers and judges, whom he liked to describe as “klan-pig oppressors” (Magee and West, “The Right to Kill” 12), worked in collusion with each other and with the police and prison authorities to arrest and try sufficient numbers of individuals to preserve their high salaries (paid by tax dollars extorted from the poor):

> The materials necessary for [legal professionals’] employment is the steady supply of slaves readily found in the poverty areas. On the streets these slaves represent only a person to be counted at census time. But as slaves in numerous prison

> slave camps, they represent the lubrication necessary for the continuous advance of the oppressive capitalist machine, which if not soon brought to an abrupt halt, will consume us all. (Magee and West, "Ruchell Speaks Out, Continued" 8)[15]

That people of color and the poor were arrested for legitimate crimes and provided due process looked like nothing other than an elaborate farce to hide the truth that legal professionals reaped lucrative wages for feeding captive laborers to penitentiaries. Magee was convinced that the judges and lawyers manipulated laws concerning the right to self-representation and the right to a court-appointed attorney to ensure that the ill-equipped incriminated themselves, and the legally literate were kept silent (Magee and West, "Ruchell Magee Speaks Out" 8). For Magee, the legal apparatus's sole function was to render the poor useful to the capitalist plantation economy of the penitentiary.[16]

Magee's heavy-handed reliance on the exuberant radical rhetoric of his day, his frequent recourse to offensively sexist language, and his disdain for the rigorous historical and economic analysis found more consistently in the writings of contemporaries such as George Jackson can mask the force—and insight—of his claims. Recent studies of the political economy of the prison industrial complex bear out many of Magee's underlying arguments. Dylan Rodriguez, for example, argues that what makes imprisonment a distinct regime of power is the nature of its bodily objectification. Rodriguez explains, "[T]o the extent that the prisoner or 'inmate' is conceived as the fungible property of the state . . . the captive is both the state's abstracted legal property/obligation and intimate bodily possession" (41). Thus the line between slave and inmate blurs almost beyond recognition, especially in the context that prisons, not unlike plantations, as Rodriguez contends, "construct a nexus for the production and sustenance of varieties of racialized domestic warfare, the articulation of the neoliberal states, and massive containment of surplused and racialized populations" (112). In this reasoning, the state's economic survival is predicated on racialized incarceration just as the antebellum economy was predicated on chattel slavery. Ruth Wilson Gilmore extends this argument by making the case that deindustrialization, the growth of finance capital, the post-1965 influx of documented and undocumented immigrants, tax revolts, and the dismantling of the welfare state—in other words, the localized effects of economic globalization—have all produced racialized labor surpluses that the U.S. economy has been unable to absorb (*Golden*

Gulag 88). In other words, high unemployment pushes larger numbers of individuals into various forms of illegal economic competition, such as drug dealing, which contributes further to the sense of moral panic and social crisis fostered by Richard Nixon and Ronald Reagan. Despite the neoliberal mandate to contract government, the expansion of the prison system, according to Gilmore, offered a solution to the problem of increasing labor surpluses and to the potential political unrest such surpluses might produce if politicized. Thus, political and economic stability under globalized late capitalism is as dependent on the "prison fix" as the plantation-based agricultural economy was on enslavement. Inmate labor is not as essential in Gilmore's conception of the prison industrial complex as Magee maintains nor as is it was on the plantation, but as she so convincingly argues, incarcerated bodies nevertheless remain crucial for the reproduction of capital in an era of intensifying globalization.

Magee's incarceration renders him, paradoxically, distinctly transnational. Unlike the more militant nationalists or Pan-Africanists, and despite his own revolutionary rhetoric, Magee never completely abandons his faith in constitutional law or in the ideals of individual liberty promised by the Constitution itself. In the routine habeas corpus petitions he has filed over the past four decades, Magee reveals his faith that the legal system will eventually act responsibly and recognize the injustice of his incarceration as it did the *Amistad* mutineers in 1840. With this faith, Magee acknowledges his political constitution by the state as it is enacted through the prison regime and its economic imperatives. So too the original Cinque's rebellious, racialized political subjectivity only materialized once he was subjected to the Atlantic slave economy and interpellated by the U.S. judiciary and the Christian abolitionists who took up his cause. Yet, like the *Amistad* rebellion leader whose refusal to be enslaved in the Spanish empire and subsequent subjugation by the U.S. judiciary courts propelled him into a transnational space impacted by the competing claims of multiple nations but never fully incorporated by any one of them, Magee stakes a claim to a black transnational political subjectivity shaped by the U.S. nation-state, but not entirely constituted and controlled by it. As a modern Cinque taking up the legacy of antislavery resistance, Magee imagines a self produced by the United States' prison regime and its structural racism yet stakes a claim outside in a quasiliberated extranational space. In this simultaneous national disidentification and transnational affiliation, Magee performatively enacts a transnational black subjectivity capable of destablizing nation-state-based capitalist logics and their carceral foundations.

Magee's critique of the capitalist state ultimately remains underdeveloped, as does his utopian vision. But his theorization of how modern day enslavement operates places him in the long tradition of diasporic theorist-practitioners who have sought to "contend that Negro expression is both constitutive of the American 'cultural store' and excessive to it" (Edwards 47). Magee, obviously, would replace the word "expression" with labor, but the sense of exceeding the space allotted to African Americans by the U.S. nation-state and embracing the diasporic and transnational excess that Edwards highlights, resonates deeply in Magee's own transnational identification, no matter how immobilized his incarceration renders him. Moreover, his richly evocative effort to recast himself as a modern day Joseph Cinque illuminates the productive means by which transnational subjectivities can be harnessed toward anticapitalist and antistate political action. The tragedy of his life-long "enslavement" is, consequently, matched only by the way his interventions have been so thoroughly forgotten, even by the subsequent writers and artists who would lay a similar claim to Cinque's name.

The Symbionese Liberation Army's kidnapping of Patty Hearst four years after Magee's brief moment in the national spotlight effectively heralded the end of radical militancy for the American Left. Decimated by the FBI's counterintelligence program (COINTELPRO) and by disillusionment with the inability to affect significant structural change, the radical Left limped along into the 1980s when Ronald Reagan's "New Morning in America" ushered fully into public discourse the conjoined ideologies of neoliberalism and neoconservativism. Uneasy bedfellows, neoliberalism's secular individualist, yet antidemocratic, market-based political rationality would seem to grate against neoconservatism's moral, authoritarian, and regulatory rationality, but as political theorist Wendy Brown points out, "the moralism, statism, and authoritarianism of neconservatism are profoundly enabled by neoliberal rationality" because of their shared descaralization of "egalitarianism, civil liberties, fair elections, and rule of law" (701–02). The marriage of the two found fruition in the presidency of Ronald Reagan, who routinely threaded his neoliberal attacks on welfare, social services, unionized labor, and other New Deal and Great Society programs through a neoconservative moral indignation toward so-called welfare queens and teenage mothers, a not-so-subtle racialized and gendered rhetoric that channeled white resentment in support of his political goals. Both people of color and working-class whites bore the brunt of the resulting deindustrialization, weakening of labor laws, and cuts to health care services, but for communities of color, Reagan-era neoconservative neoliberalism had the effect of further eroding an already fragile social and economic security. Moreover, Reagan-era racialized discourse reanimated antiaffirmative action, anti-Asian, and anti-immigrant sentiments. In the vacuum created by shrinking labor opportunities and social supports, gangs and other entrepreneurs forged alternate globalized economies trading in drugs, arms, and other consumer goods. Nixon's law-and-order rhetoric, not surprising, found new life in this environment, as did a displaced—and certainly disavowed—Keynesian effort to stimulate a deindustrializing and globalizing economy by building out the prison system at an unprecedented scale (Gilmore, *Golden Gulag* 126). In this context, African American populations in particular found themselves in increasing confrontation with the neoliberal state's repressive apparatus.

Despite this, migrants from the Caribbean, Africa, and other parts of the world continued to seek economic security in the United States, in large part because of how neoliberal political rationalities promulgated by international aid agencies and local technocrats had helped destabilize their home countries. Most of the formerly colonized world found itself after political independence with fragile export-based economies highly dependent on imported oil and other manufactured goods. The oil shocks of the early 1970s crippled many and forced them to turn to international banks for loans to keep the state functioning at the most basic level. In return for these loans, the International Monetary Fund, World Bank, and other regional development banks imposed strict neoliberal, market-based structural adjustment conditions on the recipient governments, including the radical reduction of government employment rolls and the privatization of parastatals and other state services. Such conditions radically restricted the state's ability to manage the economy and its surplus labor, which typically included large numbers of highly educated workers with few job opportunities outside the civil service. Weakened state sovereignty and high unemployment generated further social instability. Add to the mix a self-enriching independence-era old guard unwilling to relinquish power, and countries such as Sierra Leone, Ghana, and Nigeria suffered large-scale out migration to England and the United States, the creation of sophisticated informal economies, and the proliferation of shadow-state formations. Meanwhile, an increasingly globalized economy set workers and manufacturing alike in constant motion across state borders to more advantageous locations. So, even as U.S. deindustrialization was systematically jettisoning manufacturing jobs to Asia and Latin America, workers in search of economic security continued to seek fleeting refuge in the United States. Ultimately, members of the global south came to bear the brunt of market-based neoliberal policies wherever they went.

Another result of the global neoliberal turn was to severely circumscribe the nationalist imperatives of both postcolonial African independence efforts and the civil rights and black power movements in the diaspora. Given the absolute centrality of nationalism in its various iterations to decolonization in Africa and the diaspora, neoliberalism's transformation of the national citizen into a transnational subject sent hegemonic notions of national collectivity and freedom into crisis. Nationalism could hardly any longer hold out the promise of collective development after the state's role shifted from ensuring the well-being and development of its citizens to securing the efficiency of markets, and the markets themselves began to serve privatized individual interests rather than the collective good. Not that the nationalist master narrative had yet made good its promises, especially in Sierra Leone where, by the time neoliberalism's misbegotten child, structural adjustment, was imposed, the state was already beginning to collapse. But, for communities historically betrayed, if that word can adequately describe enslavement and colonization, by capitalism's promises, neoliberalism's narrative of "human dignity and freedom" (Harvey 1) through the free market hardly proffered a welcome alternative to the narratives it supplanted.

In this context, the *Amistad* leader reemerges in both the United States and Sierra Leone to name the confrontation with neoliberal global capitalism and its assault on the nationalist dreams of decolonization. In the novels of African American detective fiction writer Clifford Mason and in a grassroots Sierra Leonean public art campaign, the slave rebel's name is made to underscore the emergent racialized geopolitical inequalities produced by the market ethos. In the Reagan-era Harlem of Mason's novels and in the civil war era of 1990s Sierra Leone, competition for market advantage took an especially brutal form in the armed conflicts over drugs, diamonds, and other resources that undermined the nationalist ideals of earlier generations. Like Ruchell Magee, Mason and the Sierra Leonean artists highlight the contemporary transnational flows of African natural resources—in the form of human bodies and precious minerals alike—and the corresponding acts of transnational resistance symbolized so effectively by the *Amistad* rebellion. Mason's novels chart this new neoliberal order especially well. But where Magee and Mason reclaim the name Cinque(z), the Sierra Leonean painters insist on the rebel leader's Mende birth name, Sengbe Pieh. With the name Sengbe Pieh, they highlight the enduring historical and geopolitical ruptures dividing Africa from the diaspora, even under the increasingly global manifestation of neoliberalism. But more compellingly still, their Sengbe Pieh functions as a catalyst to reimagine the very premises of postcolonial nationalism for a postnationalist world.

Set in a Reagan-era New York City, the African American detective novelist Clifford Mason's two Joe Cinquez mysteries, *The Case of the Ashanti Gold* (1985) and *Jamaica Run* (1987), chart the "criminal" opportunities for self-enrichment by savvy black transnationals able to exploit markets opened up by the forms of neoliberal governmentality imposed on postcolonial governments desperate for cash or credibility. In *The Case of the Ashanti Gold*, a small group of well-connected Ghanaian and Nigerian diplomats work clandestinely with a U.S.-based multinational mining company to capitalize on a Ghanaian government that is distracted by its effort to retain state control over gold exports. Simultaneously, they seek advantage from a diplomatic feud at the United Nations over economic sanctions against South Africa (a market-based solution if there ever was one) to illicitly sell Ghanaian gold to the apartheid regime in South Africa. Investigating a corollary dynamic, *Jamaica Run* maps a bloody land grab in Jamaica by speculators hoping to make a fortune on the international market for the country's marijuana harvests. While IMF structural adjustment policies were not designed to promote gold smuggling or large-scale marijuana production, the formation of a privatized commodities trade and an efficient agricultural export sector more than fulfill the neoliberal fantasy of a thoroughly market-based economy. Moreover, as Wendy Brown observes, "A permanent underclass, and even a permanent criminal class, along with a class of aliens or non-citizens are produced and accepted as an inevitable cost of such a society" (695). In Mason's novels, the black entrepreneurs of global commerce, like the African slave dealers of centuries past, are more than willing to sacrifice black bodies and the political sovereignty of postcolonial nation-states in their dealings with a predominantly white Western market. Neither novel ever explicitly references the *Amistad* rebellion, but, in them, only a reincarnated Joseph Cinquez, that hero of an earlier moment when

African bodies were in motion and under duress, can halt the worst abuses faced by diasporic Africans in the 1980s.

Of the two novels, *The Case of the Ashanti Gold* more fully reveals the racialized dynamics of neoliberalism. Its narrative conflict, in fact, arises out of the tension between the violence perpetuated on African bodies under the phantom regime of neoliberal global capitalism and the opportunities for those people of African descent willing to abandon the dreams of decolonization and Pan-Africanism to claim the spoils of neoliberal capital for themselves. At the center of the narrative is a conflict between Ghana and South Africa over Ghana's financial support of antiapartheid freedom fighters. The conflict threatens Ghanaian state stability by opening the door to sabotage by South Africa's state security forces, notorious at the time for their brutal repression of the African National Congress and other antiapartheid movements. At the same time, the seemingly isolated diplomatic row imperils the very economic infrastructure underpinning business between nearly the entire Third World and the West. As a representative of a global south coalition working to mediate the conflict tells Cinquez, "We have to do business with the West. And the more democracies, the happier the West is" (195). In other words, as long as the South African apartheid regime's covert operations threaten democracies elsewhere in the global south, market-oriented politics cannot function efficiently, nor can individual states maintain their market advantage in the competition for global political resources. A threat it remains, however, because a UN Security Council vote to censure the South Africa apartheid regime precipitates acts of espionage and political sabotage from both sides of the conflict. In an effort to secure Ghana's vote against the measure, South Africa's security forces hatch a plan to steal and ransom the Asantehene's royal stool. In turn, Ghanaian intelligence uncovers the plot and devises its own plan to stick the South Africans with a fake stool and then publicly discredit the apartheid rulers. Meanwhile, the political intrigue creates opportunities for the individual operatives to effectively privatize other markets and other forms of trade. Osei, Ghana's chief intelligence operative, uses his cover to broker a deal with an executive at an American-based multinational mining company to smuggle Ghanaian gold to the very white South Africans he is officially battling. Osei's surreptitious claim to—and unofficial privatization of—state resources generates a host of other competitors and, predictably, a trail of corpses.

Like all detectives, Cinquez struggles to identify his criminal, but where most detectives' primary challenge is his or her opponent's cleverness and wit, Cinquez confronts the problem of maintaining public order, defining legal jurisdiction, and delineating sovereignty in a global city like New York, where the global flows of finance, politics, and political/economic entrepreneurs intersect and where the extranational competitive demands of diverse neoliberal states overlap. After all, his opponents include not just Osei and his criminal syndicate, but also the Ghanaian nation-state; the agents of the apartheid regime charged with protecting South Africa's economic sovereignty; the other Africans, Americans, and Europeans trying to insinuate themselves into the smuggling operation; and the coalition of global south nation-states agitating for South Africa's economic isolation with their own financial interests in mind (195). In other words, Cinquez finds himself fully enmeshed in a milieu where the disorder of global capital "seems to exceed the capacity of the state to discipline or punish" (Comaroff and Comaroff, "Criminal Obsessions" 292). In most detective fiction, narrative infrastructure and narrative resolution are contingent on a social order produced by sovereign states and sovereign bodies. Without, however, a sovereign political subject with full rights under the law and/or a stable sovereign state structure capable of rationally applying the full force of the law, Cinquez's ability to identify criminal violations is greatly diminished, as is the state's ability—or willingness—to guarantee the protection of the law. For Cinquez, discovering whodunit consequently entails investigating a far broader terrain of global capital networks, social relations, and political histories than is demanded of the average detective. And Cinquez, ever on the verge of being overwhelmed by the complexity of the case, only ever identifies a suspect, who himself is killed before confessing his crime. Cinquez disrupts the criminal network, but justice is never served, nor does the novel deliver the narrative resolution typical of the genre.

Where the protagonist Cinquez maps the vectors of this neoliberal world, "Cinquez" ultimately names the conditions for regulating and diffusing the racialized effects of neoliberal capital. Like the original *Amistad* rebellion leader, Cinquez's transnational status gives him an advantage in checking a regime of power with global reach, even if his transnational advantage fails to help overturn the hegemonic global racial order. Insofar as Cinquez succeeds at identifying a suspect in his brother's death—the incident that initially drew him onto the case—he does so because he proves to be a skilled operator in the phantom neoliberal global economy, a skill that is born as much out of his capitalist instincts as it is his subject position as an African American in Reagan-era America. With his hardboiled individualism and barely restrained self-interest, Cinquez quickly intuits what moves his antagonists' entrepreneurial self-interest will provoke, as he does, for example, when his suspicions about the integrity of a Scandinavian advocate on the global south coalition leads him to tail her and confirm that she is a mole working with the American mining executive and his white South African partners. Simultaneously, with the double consciousness inherited by generations of African Americans and put to exhaustive use by so many other ficitional black detectives (Soitos 33–37), Cinquez efficiently navigates the world of transnational smugglers and political entrepreneurs who operate on the margins of dominant national and global communities. By tapping his experiential knowledge of having to define himself through the reflecting mirror of dominant white (and bourgeois black) society, Cinquez adeptly reads the motives of the global south coalition concerned by its perception in the West, as well as of Osei, who is the second, less favored son in the royal family; Osei's recently outed lesbian wife; and Ofuate, a young man charitably educated by the Asantehene but shut out of power. Perhaps what is most significant, Cinquez enlists his own provisional, second-class citizenship as an African American to work effectively without the assurances of a stable sovereign order typically insured by secure national citizenship. His ability to operate transnationally in the disorder that exceeds the capacity of the neoliberal state stems, in large part, from the fact that he simply cannot take sovereignty or citizenship for granted as an African American in Reagan's America.[17]

In the novel, "Cinquez" names not so much the condition of possibility of radically transforming neoliberal capital as it does managing and diffusing its racialized effects. As a reincarnation of the nineteenth-century slave rebellion leader, Joe Cinquez cripples, if only momentarily, the modes of global capital that most adversely impact people of African descent worldwide. Transnational by virtue of his racialized double consciousness, Cinquez succeeds because of his ability to operate as an effective conduit linking the diverse communities of the black Atlantic. By no means a Pan-African messiah, he is, however, a figure who can navigate, and therefore articulate, African and diaspora worlds divided as much by the economic inequalities separating Africans and African Americans as by the distinct historical forces of slavery and colonization. Mason's Cinquez exists in a parasitic relationship to capital, insofar as he inhabits a para-site, dependent on the systems and networks of capital, even as he aggravates them and acts as a check on global capitalism's power.

Mason is careful to suggest that the name 'Cinquez' expresses equally his protagonist's trans-Atlantic *alienation*. After a reverie about heroically protecting the virtue of Asante culture, he asks, "Was I prepared to lay down my life to save the soul of the Asante people from being desecrated? They'd probably look at me like I was a fool if I even tried to pretend that I was one of them." (100). Cinquez's honest assessment of his historical alienation from his ancestral homes in West or Central Africa serves as an important reminder that the name 'Joseph Cinque(z),' after all, masks the Mende name 'Sengbe Pieh' of its original bearer.[18] Therefore, it can effectively designate little more than a uniquely diasporic condition under global capitalism. As we will see in more detail in chapter 2, in his 1988 play *Amistad Kata-Kata*, Sierra Leonean playwright Charlie Haffner links the cannibal-like ontological onslaught of enslavement with the practice of giving African captives slave names. In the play, Sengbe Pieh resists enslavement in no small measure by rejecting the name Joseph Cinquez. Haffner thereby highlights how the choice of the name 'Cinque(z)' by Americans such as Magee and Mason betrays a deep misunderstanding of the very history that the African Americans want to reanimate. In contrast to Haffner's imagined slave rebel, Magee and Mason's Cinque(z)s still bear the shackle of a slave name and remain at least partially entrapped by the chattel logic that they seek to disrupt. Moreoever, the slave name 'Cinque(z)' places the rebel leader firmly in the Americas, obscuring the historical specificity of Sengbe's Mende ethnicity and regional West African background. Certainly, their historical myopia is a function of the limited historical sources available to them, especially Magee writing from prison, but it is a function too of their relative privilege as Americans to comprehend the rest of the world primarily as it reflects the United States. Haffner's challenge to African Americans such as Magee and Mason points to alternative ways that West Africans might apprehend the *Amistad* history and how "Sengbe" names a distinctly West African set of material conditions under global capital. Not surprising, Sengbe's name and his "Sierra Leoneaness" would come to dominate Sierra Leonean cultural representations of the *Amistad* history in subsequent years as visual artists, especially, explored Sierra Leone's place at the nexus of the global flows of guns, diamonds, mercenaries, and refugees.

In 1991, on the heels of Haffner's play, a guerilla faction calling itself the "Revolutionary United Front/Sierra Leone" led by cashiered corporal Foday Sankoh launched an armed campaign to overthrow the government, led still at that point by President Joseph Momoh. To the limited extent that the RUF/SL articulated a political vision for its violence, it cited the vulnerabilities of the country's youth under the Momoh kleptocracy (Richards 28–29).[19] However, due to its brutal violence toward civilians, including the very populations in whose name it waged war, and its quick focus on the spoils of the country's extensive diamond mining, the RUF/SL never gained real credibility. Since the discovery of diamonds in the early part of the twentieth century, the mining, trading, and smuggling of the stones, along with the corollary business ventures arising alongside, have marked Sierra Leone's primary point of insertion into the global economy. For most Sierra Leoneans, diamonds have only brought the worst elements of globalization: private militias, forced labor, debilitating economic inequality, and environmental degradation. When the RUF/SL made clear that it planned to take over key diamond mines (by attacking diamond fields in the Kono district in September and October 1992), it signaled just one more way in which the economics of global capitalism would take their toll on the local population. In the decade-long war that unfolded, the foot soldiers and civilian survivors served the interests of an intersecting set of local and global actors whose attempts to game the international trade in diamonds and other resources long predated the violence and, in many ways, caused it. While the most obvious entrepreneurs of the conflict include political leaders within the country and without—most notably Sankoh in Sierra Leone and Charles Taylor from neighboring Liberia—as well as local and international diamond traders, weapons dealers, and a whole host of other war-zone opportunists, the list could easily also include IMF and World Bank theorists, cold war engineers, and development specialists whose efforts before the war to better integrate the country into the formal networks of neoliberal global capital in many ways destabilized it and pushed it further into global capitalism's dark underbelly.

For a brief moment between January and April 1993, a nationwide grassroots public art campaign sought to mobilize popular dissent against both the RUF/SL and the underlying structural conditions that fueled it by visually imagining the country in control of its relationship to the forms of economic and political power that had left it in ruin. Inspired by the successful military coup nine months earlier that put Valentine Strasser and the National Provisional Ruling Council (NPRC) in power, the proponents of the arts movement believed that the conditions for the radical transformation of Sierra Leonean society were ripe (Opala, "*Ecstatic Renovation!*" 4). Shortly after the coup, in an effort to fulfill what they saw as their civic obligation to a state that was finally going to deliver its protections to them, Sierra Leone's long-standing urban neighborhood organizations and other newly formed youth groups launched a campaign to clean up the city.[20] Clearing away years of accumulated rubbish quickly gave way to whitewashing public building exteriors, which, in turn, led to more fanciful decoration and mural-making. By late January 1993 the city's muralists established the portrait format as their dominant mode of expression. John Williams's portraits (figure 1.1), located on a street-side wall on Wilkenson Road in Freetown's west end, provide a sample of the scale and organization of the portraits. Because the art movement was carried out neighborhood by neighborhood, each community association selected and painted its own collection of portraits (Opala, "*Ecstatic Renovation!*" 6–7). As a result, a pattern emerged with a subset of historical and military figures such as *Amistad* leader Sengbe Pieh and coup leader Valentin Strasser repeated in neighborhood after neighborhood across Freetown's elongated expanse and across the other cities to which the

Figure 1.1. Freetown wall paintings by John Williams, 1993. (Photo by Konrad Tuchscherer)

art movement quickly spread. Images of anticolonial and antiapartheid icons such as Bai Bureh and Nelson Mandela, the biblical figure Moses, the NPRC leadership, reggae heroes Bob Marley and Lucky Dube, local educators and artists, and, of course, *Amistad* leader Sengbe Pieh formed a narrative of immanent national redemption long thwarted by the slave trade, colonialism, and postcolonial chicanery.

That the youth artists' campaign to assert their ethos was carried out in the public arena on the outdoor walls shared by all should come as no surprise. Political historian Mamadou Diouf has argued that the "logics of exclusion based on tradition, like those of the postcolony's treatment of the young, render public space as an adult territory off limits to youth at the same time that it denies them a private space" (226). Moreover, the physical aspect of the city—its buildings, urban planning, its condition of upkeep or disrepair—functions according to a logic of social ordering and carries with it a textual history. Allessandro Triulzi writes, "It must be remembered that the contemporary African city is, by definition, the visual space of the political. It is also the 'site of memory' of colonization" (81). The urban landscape, then, operates as a text through which power is made visually recognizable and legible. Architecture and city planning function as organizing signifiers of modern postcolonial subjectivity and constitute a mnemonic apparatus for recollecting the operations of and challenges to power as well as the everyday struggles to get by. Any intrusion into this significatory ordering has the effect of altering its logic. Thus, Diouf argues, the painting of city walls functions to reorganize a city's spatial ordering and along with it, its hierarchies (226).

During the two-and-half decades leading up to the 1993 art movement, Sierra Leonean public sphere organizations were controlled largely by an elite concerned primarily with self-enrichment and funded in significant part by off-the-books diamond export and rice import contracts, all of which effectively shut the door on youth participation in civil society. Thus, Sierra Leone's late-century youth culture took shape as the product of an alienated and manipulated relationship with the state and the middle- and upper-class communities that benefit most from it (Abdullah et. al., "Lumpen Youth Culture" 46). Like their counterparts elsewhere in West Africa coming of age in the 1970s, 80s, and 90s, the generations of youth in Sierra Leone that followed independence faced the foreclosure of the promises of self-rule that sustained their parents' generation. As a result of the consolidation of authoritarian control on the part of '60s-era leaders, combined with the neoliberal IMF-imposed evaporation of civil service jobs in the 1980s, the cadres of educated and working-class youth forged social identities on the political and economic margins of society.[21] For these reasons, many of the young men at the forefront of the art movement found themselves caught between the competing claims of global capitalism and the state with few opportunities for security other than through work in the informal economy, migration, or hiring themselves to the war. Even while largely immobile, this population came to occupy a transnational space by virtue of its contingent, liminal relationship to the state.

When Freetown's youth took it upon themselves to lead clean-up crews, repair roads, and dramatically paint the city's public walls, including some of its most important government buildings, they sought to refashion one of the primary symbols of their age-class oppression under the old political regime: the physical aspect of the postcolonial city as the visual space of political hierarchy and economic stratification. With their paintbrushes, they invested familiar landmarks with a new set of memories, rewriting the common associations with the Public Works Department, for example, as a locus of power for both the oppressive colonial regime and corrupt postindependence autocrats, by painting the images of resistance heroes along its exterior walls.[22] Artists also delighted in the ironic refashioning of those institutions with which they had historically confronted state power most directly, in one case by painting a portrait of Malcolm X on the side of the Criminal Investigation Division of the municipal police offices (Opala, "*Ecstatic Renovation!*" 19). In their efforts to transform the appearance of Freetown, they aimed to insert themselves not as the liminal figures they had long been but as the principal actors in a new social order based on their ideals. The new territoriality they worked hard to form with their visual reordering of the city embodied the expectations—naïve perhaps—for the emergence of new practices of citizenship based on their youthful cosmopolitan ethics. Importantly though, they forged a public space that, far from being antigovernment, reflected what they defined as the necessary imperatives of the postcoup leadership. The public art detailed at once an explication of the country's present reality and a vision for an alternate future fashioned after the young male painters' own image.[23]

To comprehend the contents and contours of that alternate future, I return now to the painters' treatment of the *Amistad* slave rebellion leader Sengbe Pieh. Given the RUF/SL's obvious desire to take control of the diamond-rich regions of the country, Sengbe Pieh's success in resisting an insidious form of global capitalism—represented by the trans-Atlantic slave trade—made him a unique symbol of resistance for Sierra Leoneans at this particular historical juncture. The youth regularly linked Sengbe Pieh visually to NPRC leader Captain Valentine Strasser, thus intimately connecting past and present, telling their audiences that Strasser, like Sengbe Pieh, led an honorable and just revolt against tyranny. As Josee Lahai would later recollect:

> After reading about the *Amistad* revolt, we knew that Sengbe Pieh was one of those people who actually fought for his freedom. He also was suppressed because they caught him and tried to bring him to Cuba, you know, to sell him as a slave. He thought of an idea to break free, break loose the chains and set his other colleagues free and they attacked the captains of the ship. So, reading about Sengbe Pieh, I saw what he did, you know, as a young man, and he was that young, just like some of us at that time. And looking at the men who had just taken over, like Valentine Strasser, Saj Musa and the others, we kind of related, we tried to put these people together. (Lahai, interview)

By associating the two men, the painters explored how to remember and construct useful meaning most effectively from a national history in which slavery, forced labor, colonialism, racism, postcolonial despotism, and rebel terror loom large. Sengbe Pieh's prominence also amplifies the complex engagement of the young artists with the problems of the violence of nation-state-based subjectivity and transnational modernity in postcolonial Africa.

The youth artists' fashioning of the *Amistad* leader reveals much about how they understood their relationship as postcolonial Sierra Leoneans to global capital and transnationalism. Every artist who depicted Sengbe Pieh modeled his image on the U.S. painter and antislavery abolitionist Nathaniel Jocelyn's 1839 portrait, which was commissioned in support of the legal battle to free the mutineers (figure 1.2).[24] Jocelyn's majestic and noble figure served Sierra Leone's public artists well by giving them an immediately recognizable iconic image open to nearly endless significations. And resignify they did, rarely leaving the original unadulterated. Common changes included replacing the white toga in Jocelyn's original with the blue-and-white-striped country cloth common in Sengbe Pieh's Mende homeland and replacing the bamboo pole with chiefly walking sticks or spears (figure 1.3). The immediate effect of these revisions was to repatriate the hero of what the historical record had turned into a

Figure 1.2. "Joseph Cinque," portrait by Nathaniel Jocelyn, 1839. (Courtesy of The New Haven Museum & Historical Society)

Figure 1.3. "Sengbe Pieh," wall painting by Josee Lahai, 1993. (Photo by Tim Waites. Courtesy of Sierra Leone Adult Education Association)

distinctly American slave rebellion. Moreover, it was to remind Sierra Leonean audiences that a local man could navigate and impact the global circuits of power, which was no small claim at a moment when the global diamond and arms trades were undermining the stability of their country. As a hero for their utopian longings, Sengbe Pieh simultaneously reflected their immediate dystopic wartime realities, which is reflected in his frequent depiction as a warrior in the battle against the worst forms of violence and exploitation. And like playwright Charlie Haffner, whose *Amistad* leader inspired many of their own and who insisted that he be called by his Mende name, artists drew their viewers' attention to the name 'Sengbe Pieh.'[25] It was in this effort to name their hero that the artists made their most complex arguments about their transnational realities and about their vision of a utopian future.

First though, it is important to comprehend how the artists used Sengbe Pieh to allegorize the slave trade. The painting team of Amadu "Degool" Tarawalie and Mustapha Lawal Turay, for instance, explicitly identifies Sengbe Pieh as a model warrior for the fight against the most pernicious forms of contemporary globalized warfare. In their painting on Jones Street in the middle-class neighborhood just west of downtown Freetown, Sengbe Pieh's fight for freedom against enslavement and an earlier mode of dehumanizing global capitalist exploitation helps frame the meaning of the contemporary conflict as a similarly just battle against illegitimate global economic forces (figure 1.4). By virtue of how the portrait and the flags are framed by the masonry, they work together as a single image. Bordering the left side of the portrait are the green, white, and blue stripes of the Sierra Leonean flag, and to the immediate right of the flag are the names and flags of the five member nations of the West African regional peacekeeping force, EGOMOG. ECOMOG was based in Sierra Leone at the time of the public art movement to fight Charles Taylor's insurgency in neighboring Liberia but it was increasingly deploying soldiers and weapons to contain the rebel militia in Sierra Leone itself.[26] By linking ECOMOG's peace-keeping efforts with the slave trade and slave rebellion, the artists suggest that no matter how contained the contemporary war was within the geographic boundaries of the nation-state and the recent past, it was fully implicated in the networks of global capitalism and extraterritorial forms of sovereign power dating back to at least the era of the Atlantic trade. In other words, the painting suggests to its audience that the violence of the current moment, fueled by war-zone entrepreneurs like Charles Taylor, was deeply rooted in the violent

Figure 1.4. Sengbe Pieh and ECOMOG, wall painting by Amadu Tarawalie and Mustapha Lawal Turay, 1993. (Photo by Tim Waites. Courtesy of Sierra Leone Adult Education Association)

history of slave trading. Simultaneously, with the spear in his hands, Sengbe Pieh serves unambiguously as a model—if not a patron saint—for the confrontation against the agents of a war so deeply implicated in the global trade in diamonds, arms, and other resources. Like Sengbe Pieh, who had to battle a global panoply of corrupt African slave catchers, Portuguese and Spanish merchants, U.S. jailers, international trade law, and the patronizing racism of his erstwhile abolitionist supporters, contemporary Sierra Leoneans would have to approach the civil war with a similarly global perspective.

The young artists' fascination with Sengbe Pieh resided at least as much in his status as a transnational subject as it did in his specific attributes as a warrior battling the dehumanizing forces of economic globalization. At a moment when the nation-state was teetering on the edge of collapse, Sengbe Pieh provided rich material for the young men to reconsider the promises of postcolonial nationalism and to comprehend their own compromised citizenship. In other words, in their assessment of the black Atlantic slave rebel, the artists contemplated the possibilities and limits of a new kind of transnational citizenship that might resuscitate the dreams of decolonization but also dramatically refashion the forms of political identity championed in the 1950s and 60s. Recall Josee Lahai's argument on this point that I cited in my introduction. He explains the young Sierra Leoneans' fascination with Sengbe Pieh precisely because of his allegorical salience to those for whom transnational migration offers opportunities that residence in the postcolonial nation-state does not. What we see in Lahai's remarks and in the artists' treatment of Sengbe Pieh is an effort to reconcile persistent nationalist longings with transnational realities.

Nowhere is the effort to sort out the contradictions inherent in this reconciliation clearer than in Alusine Bangura's treatment of the *Amistad* leader's two names—his birth name, Sengbe Pieh, and his slave name, Joseph Cinque (figure 1.5). Unlike Lahai or Tarawalie and Turay, Bangura avoids revising the visual elements of Jocelyn's original to make his social

Figure 1.5. "Sengbe Pieh, or Joseph Cinque," wall painting by Alusine Bangura, 1993. (Photo by Tim Waites)

commentary; Bangura reproduces Jocelyn's more or less faithfully. Instead, by adding a simple line of text to the bottom of the painting—"Sengbe Pieh, or Joseph Cinque"—he emphasizes how Sengbe Pieh embodies the fracturing and hybridizing of black transnational subjectivities.[27] Intentionally or not, by juxtaposing the two names as he does with the conjunction "or," Bangura raises the thorny ontological problem of how to understand the interconnected subjectivity between continental and diasporic Africans. As a conjunction, "or" lacks the definitiveness of its counterpart "and." On the one hand, it grammatically allows for synonymy, thereby enabling Sengbe Pieh and Joseph Cinque to exist as equally descriptive alternate names for the same person. On the other hand, depending largely on context, the word "or" also indicates difference and inequality. Whereas "Joseph Cinque" is a product of Western historical forces that transformed Africans, through enslavement, into subjects of a racially stratified capitalist modernity, "Sengbe Pieh" is a part of a Sierra Leonean national identity that attempts to apprehend its own history of dependency, exploitation, and resistance. These are two different historically determined figures, and without contextual referents, the indeterminate "or" in Bangura's painting compels its viewers to question what the conjunction signifies and, consequently, the commensurability of the subjects "Joseph Cinque" and "Sengbe Pieh."

By virtue of raising this question, Bangura's painting, like Tarawalie and Turay's and like Lahai's commentary about his own, suggests that to the young painters Sengbe Pieh names the difference or hybridity that Stuart Hall claims is emblematic of diaspora. As Hall argues, "The diaspora experience . . . is defined, not by essence or purity, but by the recognition of a necessary heterogeneity and diversity; by a conception of 'identity' which lives with and through, not despite, difference; by *hybridity*" ("Cultural Identity and Diaspora" 31). For Hall, to understand diaspora as a modality of difference and hybridity rather than as a sign of origin is to circumvent the narrow particularisms of racial and national essentialisms that undermine the project of conceptualizing an "open-ended and contingent politics" ("Old and New Identities, Old and New Ethnicities" 41). Moreover, according to Brent Hayes Edwards, when diaspora is taken as a sign of difference and hybridity rather than as a "recourse to origins," it becomes available as a category of political identification to African communities who were never physically dispersed by the slave trade (13).

At the time of the movement, the young Sierra Leonean artists were not diasporic in the sense of being physically displaced from Africa, nor does the available evidence indicate that they used the word *diaspora*, but clearly the difference, hybridity, and contingency symbolized by the diasporic figure Sengbe Pieh defined their ideals for a new society. For them, the NPRC military coup was nothing less than a revolution in which their values, predicated on their urban, transnationalized material conditions, triumphed after decades of corrupted nationalism.[28] Their responsibility, according to Lahai, was to carry out the revolution by visually articulating the new values for a new Sierra Leone (Lahai, interview). What we see with the centrality of Sengbe Pieh's image, therefore, is an attempt to politicize their transnationalism by fashioning a politically liberating form of diasporic or transnational citizenship as national citizenship. The exuberance and idealism with which the young artists attacked the country's public space with their paint brushes and images of Sengbe Pieh reveals their hopefulness that embracing this kind of transnationalism might rectify the failures of the older nationalist elite and save the state itself.

Four months after the frenzy of the art movement began, the youths' energy for reinventing the nation sputtered. Perhaps the most challenging hurdle the young male artists faced was the one they did not foresee, the one that would destabilize the very idea of national citizenship: state collapse. Strasser did not turn out to be the great revolutionary the youth expected. In short time the young leaders decamped to Freetown's largest, most ostentatious home where they lived virtually the same corrupt lives as their predecessors. Moreover, the chaos instigated by the rebel militia escalated, and the government lost control of its own soldiers, who grew increasingly indistinguishable from their rebel counterparts. Quickly, the government existed in name only, and the artists found it impossible to maintain their enthusiasm or support. In the face of corrupted leadership and renewed violence, Josee Lahai turned his attention to the abuses of the military regime in editorial cartoons and quickly ran afoul of the leaders he once supported (Lahai, interview). Most, however, stopped painting and quietly returned to the challenges of survival in wartime.

Even if the coup leaders brought a quick end to the war and ushered in a new democratic regime like they promised, the artists' vision for a new transnationalized citizenship would not likely have produced the kind of utopian future they envisioned. First, there was the problem of their reliance on narratives of heroic masculinity. As any number of scholars of modern nationalism have made clear, the gendering of public-sphere nationalism produces various kinds of gendered hierarchies and exclusions in national life. To the extent that the art movement resignified public space as a way of making it available to the country's youth, it did so almost exclusively for male youth. Furthermore, the artwork itself offered little perspective on how women would fit into the utopian future. The second problem was that not a lot of thought was apparently given to how embracing a transnational subjectivity might reproduce the very modes of global capitalism that had made Sierra Leoneans so vulnerable in the first place. For all the ways that the *Amistad* slave revolt leader actively resisted his enslavement, artists such as Josee Lahai ultimately saw him as a model for managing and surviving more than as a model for resisting and reshaping the global order. Maybe that is all that Sengbe Pieh could do at the time, but there was no next step taken to theorize larger political and economic conditions. The war itself short circuited that step, of course, as did the coup leaders' unwillingness to make real change, and Lahai complained to me that the young men in his neighborhood were keen to celebrate their paintings with drink and parties but not to do the harder work of envisioning and implementing new kinds of civic political practices.

The artists' faith in the libratory potential of diasporic and transnational subjectivities, like we also see in Magee's and Mason's writings, would not disappear. Nor, however, would it go uncontested, least of all in Steven Spielberg's much-publicized cinematic study of the *Amistad* history, to which I will return in chapter 3.

2

Cannibals in the Postcolony

Charlie Haffner's Amistad Kata-Kata *and the Moral Economy of Global Consumption*

According to testimony given by Sengbe Pieh, he and forty-eight of the other captives aboard the *Amistad* schooner rebelled after a slave belonging to the ship's captain gestured that their Spanish-Cuban captors intended to kill, dismember, and eat them (Jones, *Mutiny on the Amistad* 24). The specter of cannibalistic consumption would hardly have surprised the captives after the months of capture and forced marches in West Africa, the pestilential holds of two slave ships, sadistic beatings, compulsory exercise, and a fattening-up regimen outside of Havana prior to sale on the auction block. It did, however, motivate them to forcibly reclaim their liberty. With the misinformation about their fate, the recently enslaved Africans unshackled themselves with a nail pried loose from the ship's woodwork, took up the cane knives stored alongside them, and stormed the deck, where they killed the captain and the slave and forced two deck hands overboard. *Amistad Kata-Kata*, Sierra Leonean playwright and songwriter Charlie Haffner's 1988 historical drama about the 1839 *Amistad* slave rebellion, magnifies the rebels' fear of cannibalism and transforms it into a metaphor for the confrontation between Africa and the West during the slave-trade era. Setting much of its action in 1980s Sierra Leone, Haffner's play also evokes cannibalism's prevalent contemporary connotation of the material excesses carried out by local authorities. Coupling the two significations into a single trope, *Amistad Kata-Kata* stages the contestations depicted in the play among African slave traders, the American White House, the U.S. judiciary, the British government, Cuban plantation owners, proslavery advocates, and numerous antislavery abolitionist factions over the bodies of the African mutineers as a reflection of the postcolonial nation-state with its own intertwined intra- and international competition over political, economic, and natural resources. As the work engages dialogically with two prior Sierra Leonean *Amistad* texts—published by the Sierra Leonean president's office and the U.S. Department of State—*Amistad Kata-Kata* employs the cannibal trope as a politically charged hidden transcript to expose, discredit, and disrupt the imbricated relations of power at work in Sierra Leone during the late 1980s just prior to its descent into civil war.

Previously unknown in Sierra Leone to all but a few academics, the *Amistad* narrative emerged in the late 1980s as a key modality through which meanings of Sierra Leonean nationalism and claims to state power were contested. In *Sierra Leonean Heroes* (1987) and *The Amistad Revolt: An Historical Legacy of Sierra Leone and the United States* (1987), Sierra Leonean President Joseph Momoh and the United States Information Service respectively sought to benefit from the potential popularity of the revolt's narrative of triumph over tyranny. In an apparent effort to circumvent growing scrutiny of his corrupt management of the national economy, Momoh published *Sierra Leonean Heroes* as a way of cloaking his presidency in the mutiny's veneer of moral authority and populist resistance. Just a few months later, the United States Information Service produced its own pamphlet on the revolt that, according to the U.S.I.S. director, could make America really "shine" for its Sierra Leonean readership (qtd. in Opala, interview). These official histories intervened directly in the popular imagining of a Sierra Leonean postcolonial national community, intending to bolster each office's hegemonic power over the state and the national imaginary. Challenging the narrative authority of each of these government-sponsored texts, Charlie Haffner staged the commercially and critically successful English-language play *Amistad Kata-Kata* a year later, the first in a series of *Amistad*-themed plays and visual art pieces to be produced by Sierra Leoneans during subsequent years. So important was the play that many of the artists featured in the previous chapter organized groups to perform a song from it to explain Sengbe Pieh's historical significance to their viewers. In its simplest articulation, *Amistad Kata-Kata* raises questions of representational authority and the politics of historical narration to contest the self-serving claims over the *Amistad* history made by the president's office and the U.S. Department of State. However, Haffner worked in a climate of heavy-handed government censorship of the arts, so any critique of the government, its allies, or its official national narratives had to operate through well-veiled doublespeak. With the *Amistad* revolt, Haffner could safely appear to advance the president's and United States Information Service's agendas while simultaneously masking a critique of the two governmental texts and of the larger interrelations of state and international power in the diamond-rich country that the two represented. I argue that this hidden transcript operates primarily through the cannibalism trope.

Though integral to Western "inventions of Africa" (Mudimbe 49–50), the language of cannibalism has long provided Africans themselves with a tool for dissecting the economic underpinnings of Western modernity. As evidenced in the writings of Mungo Park, Quobna Ottobah Cugoano, and Olaudah Equiano, vast numbers of Africans captured into slavery and transported to the plantations of the Americas believed their white captors to be cannibals, and for those left behind, cannibalism evolved into a powerful metaphor for the economics of exploitation that consumed enslaved African bodies and decimated the African communities from which they were stolen (Rice, "Who's Eating Whom"; Shaw, *Memories of the Slave Trade*).[1] For Africans faced with the Atlantic world slave trade that so violently remade social contracts, cannibalism easily evoked the terrors associated with excessive consumption, domination, exploitation, and death. In the context of postcolonial African political struggles, the language of inequality continues to revolve around the metaphors of eating and, by extension, cannibalistic consumption. As a symbol for the economic exploitation, material accumulation, and violent coercion carried out by postcolonial elites cannibalism has, in fact, come to dominate African political discourse. Quoting anthropologist Jane Guyer, postcolonial theorist Achille Mbembe declares that "because the postcolony is characterized, above all, by scarcity, the metaphor of food 'lends itself to the wide angle lens of both imagery and efficacy'" (Mbembe 131). Similarly, noting that the rush for the spoils of hegemony is often described in vernacular terms as "eating," political scientist Jean-François Bayart portrays the postcolonial African state as being fueled by a "politics of the belly" (Bayart 235). Not surprisingly, accusations of cannibalism feature prominently in postcolonial Africa's "occult economies," where the elite grow ever wealthier—and more obese—as if by magical means (Comaroff and Comaroff, "Occult Economies and the Violence of Abstraction"). In Sierra Leone and elsewhere, accusations of cannibalism are often deployed to subtlety undermine authority by exposing and disrupting the acts of excessive consumption and the hubris underlying corrupt power (Ferme 183).

The Krio-language word *kata-kata* in the title of Charlie Haffner's play intimates this kind of disruption. The word translates loosely as revolt, but according to Haffner, it is also intended to connote "trouble, disturbance, riot . . . pandemonium" (Haffner, interview). *Amistad Kata-Kata* couples cannibalism as a name for the excesses carried out by local authorities with cannibalism as a description of the dehumanizing consumption of enslaved African labor within the Atlantic slave system to form a key or legend for translating the century-and-a-half-old slave revolt into a discrediting, disrupting critique of the complex interrelationships between global capitalism and the practices of excessive elite accumulation in the postcolony. Like Zita Nunes who takes cannibalism as a central trope in the literatures of the Americas for the way "race relations in a democracy are apprehended and theorized" (xi), I argue that the concept provides a critical framework for the West African playwright to account for the historical reverberations of the trans-Atlantic slave trade in the operations of contemporary global capitalism. The trope's connotations come to fullest light in play's dialogic engagement with the works by Joseph Momoh and the United States Information Service, therefore I begin my analysis with an examination of two governments' texts.

One year before *Amistad Kata-Kata*'s 1988 premiere, President Momoh's office published *Sierra Leonean Heroes: Thirty Great Men and Women Who Helped to Build Our Nation* (1987).[2] The collection of biographies was the first major attempt to incorporate the *Amistad* revolt and Sengbe Pieh into the nation's standard historical narrative.[3] Based on a Freetown newspaper article by the long-time American resident of Sierra Leone and Fourah Bay College lecturer, Joseph Opala, the three brief paragraphs that make up Sengbe Pieh's entry in *Sierra Leonean Heroes* sketch the key events that led to and resulted from the shipboard revolt. Despite the biography's economy of words and factual emphasis, two character attributes are pronounced. First, with its repeated references to rice farming, Sengbe Pieh is made to represent a rural, agricultural past, a world that had come to signify an alterative to the corruption of urban modernity and political power. Second, the biography's conspicuous refusal to explicitly describe Sengbe Pieh's motivation for organizing the slave uprising graces the rebellion leader with an unambiguous moral authority. Without a second doubt or moment of self-reflection, the modest rice farmer reverses his state of subjugation. The absence from the entry of any mention of African complicity in the slave trade, especially by King Manna Siaka from whom Momoh's predecessor Siaka Stevens proudly claimed direct lineage and who is believed to have brokered Sengbe Pieh's sale to Portuguese slave traders (Abraham, *The Amistad Revolt* 1), also contributes to this depiction of the rural past as a place of uncomplicated and uncorrupted purity. Sengbe Pieh's ineffable opposition to injustice thus stands without distraction or moral ambiguity.[4]

Opala, a member of the editorial board that authored *Sierra Leonean Heroes* on behalf of the president, originally wrote the biographical sketch with the intent of helping foster patriotic pride in a country beset by what he regarded as low national self-esteem (Opala, interview). As a whole, the book purports to do the same by highlighting the themes of everyday courage and resistance to illegitimate authority and by celebrating Sierra Leone's legacy of political, military, and intellectual leadership. A. K. Turay, chair of the editorial committee that produced the book and minister of state for presidential affairs for Momoh at the time, declared that *Amistad*-revolt-leader Sengbe Pieh was conceived as one of the central figures around which these themes would pivot (Turay, interview).[5] Yet by concluding *Sierra Leonean Heroes* with biographies of living governmental functionaries, including Momoh's immediate predecessor, Siaka Stevens, the book inserts figures such as Sengbe Pieh into a teleological lineage that culminates with President Momoh and his All People's Congress (A.P.C.) political party, the country's single ruling party from 1968 to 1992, thereby legitimating and strengthening Momoh's and the party's authority. Whether or not any individual entry in the book, including Sengbe's, was written with the explicit intent of bolstering Momoh's authority—and arguably many were not—the book's teleological narrative and its association with the president's office perforce enlist each biographical sketch in this project.[6] Opala's original pro-Sierra Leone message was thus co-opted into a pro-Momoh statement.

Sengbe Pieh's value to a political figure such as Momoh stemmed from his populist veneer and his unambiguous moral authority. Two years into office, Momoh could claim neither despite his campaign slogans proclaiming "Constructive Nationalism" and a "New Order."[7] As the handpicked successor to the widely reviled and deeply corrupt Siaka Stevens, and as the only candidate running in a single-party election, the public treated Momoh with deep skepticism. Over the course of a seventeen-year reign, Stevens carefully engineered the unofficial transfer of state resources from government coffers to the private accounts of a small cadre of governing and business elite, creating a very powerful and deeply loyal constituency. Momoh, it was assumed, would pursue Stevens' *modus operandi* faithfully. With *Sierra Leonean Heroes* and with Sengbe Pieh as its celebrated centerpiece, Momoh (or, more correctly, his minister for presidential affairs, A. K. Turay, who chaired the book's editorial committee) sought to mitigate that perception. The book itself revived his campaign slogan promising a constructive nationalism, and, by cloaking himself in Sengbe Pieh's populist veneer and morally unambiguous authority, he endeavored to shed his shroud of moral and political corruption.[8]

By identifying himself with the leader of a violent rebellion against tyrannical masters, Momoh sent a second message to Stevens's established elite. By 1987, Momoh had begun displacing Stevens and his clique, who had attempted to keep a tight grip on him, and strengthening his own hold over the informal economy (Reno 156). Of the more intriguing examples of this agenda, Momoh welcomed International Monetary Fund loans with their stringent conditions as a way of neutralizing Stevens and his cronies even though those same stipulations chipped away at his own authority and the nation's sovereignty (Reno 160–61). Not surprisingly, his attempts to displace Stevens' elite led to a coup attempt in March 1987 (Conteh-Morgan and Dixon-Fyle 125). While work on *Sierra Leonean Heroes* commenced before the thwarted takeover, its populist, nationalist message and its emphasis on resistance to tyranny signaled Momoh's attempt to maintain public support while marking his rebellious independence from an entrenched elite. Altogether, *Sierra Leonean Heroes* employs Sengbe Pieh's rebelliousness to shore up Momoh's fragile political identity.

Shortly after *Sierra Leonean Heroes*' release, the United States Information Service (U.S.I.S.) staked its own self-aggrandizing claim to the rebellion by publishing *The Amistad Revolt: An Historical Legacy of Sierra Leone and the United States*. Written by Sierra Leonean Arthur Abraham and edited, again, by Joseph Opala, the pamphlet was produced in celebration of the bicentennials of the founding of Freetown and of the U.S. Constitution (Abraham, inside cover page) and was distributed to a limited audience of participants attending U.S.I.S.-sponsored events and to visitors to the U.S. ambassador's home (Opala, interview).[9] To its credit, by quoting the African mutineers' words from the historical record and reproducing in full the letters they wrote, the pamphlet privileges the African mutineers' voices more than any other account of the rebellion and casts them as the principal agents responsible for forcing the American judiciary and general public to confront the dubious legal rationale used to support enslavement. Yet, Opala, who pitched the idea of the booklet to the Freetown director of U.S.I.S. as part of his larger project to popularize symbols of Sierra Leonean national pride for Sierra Leoneans, points out that the director embraced the project immediately because of its potential to make the United States "shine" (Opala, interview). Despite Abraham's authorship as a Sierra Leonean and as a respected historian of Sierra Leone, the U.S.I.S. director's response forces us to recognize how *The Amistad Revolt*, like *Sierra Leonean Heroes*, has to be read in large part as a political exercise on the part of its producer. As the propaganda arm of the U.S. Department of State that supports "American foreign policy and promotes the national interest" (United States Department of State website), the U.S.I.S. and its director in Freetown sought to promote the United States's self-fashioned image as the world's defender of freedom, sovereignty, and democracy.

Though *The Amistad Revolt* dwells on the failings of the United States to live up to its ideals of freedom and democracy during the slavery era, its underlying message highlights a vision of a country whose citizens stand up freely to tyranny and support the efforts of those like the *Amistad* mutineers to do the same the world over. This message comes across most clearly in the way that the *Amistad*s American supporters are credited as much for Sierra Leone's successful struggle against British colonialism in the post–World War Two era as they are for their efforts in 1839. The pamphlet highlights the activities of the small group of American missionaries under the oversight of the American Missionary Association who accompanied the Africans on their return. Theirs was the first Christian mission upcountry, and, over the course of the following hundred years, the original mission merged with a United Brethren of Christ mission, added posts throughout southern Sierra Leone, and established the prestigious Harford School for Girls and Albert Academy in Freetown, a secondary school for upcountry boys (21). *The Amistad Revolt* describes the principal outcome of this "American missionary activity in Sierra Leone, with all its positive consequences," as the creation of "a nationalist elite which pressed for independence" (22). Among the members of this elite the pamphlet identifies "the first Prime Minister Dr. (later Sir) Milton Margai, and the first Executive President of Sierra Leone, Siaka Stevens" (21–22). Failing to mention either missionary complicity in the colonization of Sierra Leone in the 1880s or Siaka Stevens' decimation of the country's democratic constitution, the American missionaries, as representatives of the United States, are thus associated not with colonial rule and dictatorship but with the cold war myth of American freedom and democracy. In the pamphlet's representation of the past, the American missionaries ensure only the independence of the Sierra Leonean people, not their subjugation.

As the cold war came to an end in the late-1980s, such messages remained as important as ever to the U.S.I.S. While Soviet influence in the Africa was a diminishing concern, the perception that the United States sought to extend its imperium through the policies of international aid organizations like the International Monetary Fund and World Bank remained. For most African nation-states, stringent IMF structural adjustment loan conditionalities called into question the very notion of independent, national sovereignty so fundamental to American rhetoric (Nyang'oro 266), which is perhaps why the pamphlet codes U.S. missionary activity as leading to postcolonial independence rather than to British colonialism. At the very historical moment when the U.S.I.S. published *The Amistad Revolt,* Sierra Leoneans were themselves struggling to counter the immediate impact of renewed IMF conditionalities on both daily economic survival and the integrity of the sovereign state (Reno 160–61). Although the narrative of *The Amistad Revolt* does not in any obvious manner allude to this IMF intervention, its celebration of rebellion and independence can be read as an effort to mitigate the perception that the U.S. sought to undermine the sovereignty of countries such as Sierra Leone. The actual effectiveness of this message was likely limited by the narrow scope of the pamphlet's audience, made up mostly of visitors to the U.S.I.S library and guests at embassy social functions. Nevertheless, the U.S.I.S. pamphlet shaped the terms of the discourse to which playwright Charlie Haffner, who was one of those guests, would respond.

Against the backdrop of these two official narratives, Charlie Haffner premiered his play *Amistad Kata-Kata* with his theater troupe, the Freetong Players, at the British Council auditorium in Freetown a year later, in 1988. With the cannibalism metaphor at its center, *Amistad Kata-Kata* calls attention to the Sierra Leonean and U.S. governments' immorally voracious appetites, challenges the authority of their official narratives, and offers in their places a popular history that celebrates the legacy of struggle against enslavement and practices of colonial and postcolonial domination. The play's historical subject matter and concise narrative form departed significantly from the *telenovela*-style theatrical productions that defined Sierra Leonean theater during the decade leading up to its debut. With tortuously convoluted romantic intrigues and little if any direct social commentary, some ran twelve hours or more and had to be staged over successive evenings.[10] *Amistad Kata-Kata*'s realist aesthetic harkened back to the theater of social commentary by playwrights such as (Pat) Yulisa Amadu Maddy, Sarif Easmon, and Juliana John prevalent in the late 1960s and early 1970s and proved very popular with the audiences who saw *Amistad Kata-Kata* staged in auditoriums, schools, and public parks in Freetown and elsewhere in the country. The play's national success catapulted Haffner and the Freetong Players to international prominence with invitations to the 1992 National Black Arts Festival in Atlanta, Georgia, and to other U.S. and British venues.

At about the same time Joseph Opala began prosletyzing the *Amistad* narrative to the Sierra Leonean and American governments, he introduced the story to Charlie Haffner, who was a student of his at Fourah Bay College. Opala's involvement in the production of all three *Amistad* texts suggests just how deeply intertwined national and international hegemonies are in a postcolonial African nation-state such as Sierra Leone. As a member of the *Sierra Leonean Heroes* editorial committee, project editor for the U.S.I.S pamphlet, and Haffner's university instructor who oversaw the writing of the first draft of *Amistad Kata-Kata*, Opala functioned as a conduit interconnecting the individual producers and entangling their agendas in ways that implicated each in the others' projects and that simultaneously sought to impart his own vision for Sierra Leonean national culture. A more cynical critic might excoriate Opala for securing some neocolonial agenda of his own. Not only would that be unfair to Opala's record as an advocate for the country, but it would ignore the ways in which Opala himself might have been used in larger contestations over influence and power. Moreover, Opala's involvement in the production of each text complicates any easy distinction between Africa and the West and between oppressor and oppressed within the postcolony.

Haffner began writing *Amistad Kata-Kata* in 1986 but only completed it and staged it after the publication of the Momoh and U.S.I.S texts. The gap reveals much about Haffner's evolution as a politicized artist and about Sierra Leone's postcolonial political climate. Haffner entered the university with the goal of exposing "the APC for what it's doing to [the] country" but was discouraged from lacing his plays and songs with explicit attacks on individual public figures for fear of likely imprisonment (qtd. in Opala, "*Ecstatic Renovation!*" 29).[11] Instead, he was encouraged to let his art envision alternative social and political possibilities (29). Taking a page from Bertolt Brecht, *Amistad Kata-Kata* does this by depicting a place and time other than 1980s Sierra Leone, in which individuals stand up to injustice. Moreover, staging the play only after the two governmental texts were published also permitted Haffner to maintain the appearance of promoting the agendas of President Momoh and the U.S.I.S. even while resignifying the political meanings of their texts. Thus, by reproducing an official narrative, Haffner seized an opportunity to embed a hidden transcript, a politically charged form of double-speak (Scott 19).

Achille Mbembe argues that the subaltern classes in the postcolony lack a definitive vocabulary or set of discursive tools for dismantling the master's house. At best, he suggests that they can disrupt authority without actually overturning it. His claims rest on three assertions. First, he contends that the rulers and ruled are "inscribed in the same epistemological field" (14), lacking recourse to autonomous spaces of agency and thus sharing the same semiotic tools, as it were. Second, he points out the "postcolony is characterized by . . . a tendency to excess and disproportion" (2), which he associates with the obscenity, vulgarity, and grotesquery inherent in displays of "grandeur and prestige" (12). Third, he proposes that the postcolony's ruled classes target the grotesque, all-consuming body of the ruler, not as a form of resistance as Bakhtin argues, but as a way of "ordinary people bridle, trick, and actually *toy* with power instead of confronting it directly" (22). Insofar as Haffner manipulates the same set of symbols and discourses as President Momoh and the U.S. State Department, his decision to stage the *Amistad* story exemplifies the way that struggles over power play out in shared epistemological arenas. And, with its evocations of obscene cannibalistic consumption, *Amistad Kata-Kata* makes the visible markers of morally corrupt accumulation a primary target of address. But where Mbembe suggests that such forms of engagement can do little more than toy with power, Haffner's play attempts to condition its audiences to assume the mantle of Sengbe Pieh and the other *Amistad* mutineers and fulfill the original goals of the 1839 uprising. Much of the play's narrative tension stems from how effectively it can harness dominant narratives to undermine them.

Like President Momoh's and the U.S. government's texts, *Amistad Kata-Kata* tells the story of the rebellion in a relatively straightforward, linear narrative. Beginning with Sengbe Pieh's kidnapping, the plot concludes in the United States' Supreme Court chambers in Washington, D.C., with the court's favorable ruling reliberating the African mutineers. Haffner departs from the governmental texts and places his own aesthetic fingerprint on the *Amistad* narrative in two ways. *Amistad Kata-Kata* signals its first difference by framing the core plot with a secondary narrative. Featuring a grandmother upset by her grandson's late-twentieth-century historical education, the frame narrative draws its audience's attention to the politics of historical memory and, obliquely, to governmental corruption, thus giving the *Amistad* history an identifiable contemporary context.[12] In its second departure, *Amistad Kata-Kata* makes the mutineers' determination not to be cannibalistically consumed a defining trope for the Africans' confrontation with Western modernity and for the play's own critique of the intertwined local and global hegemonies at work in Sierra Leone. While audiences encounter the frame narrative first, it and the cannibalism trope mutually inform each other, with the meanings generated by the cannibalism trope retrospectively informing the frame narrative as much as the frame prospectively conditions the audience's reading of cannibalism.

Cannibalism first emerges as an important metaphor in the play when Celestino, a slave belonging to the *Amistad*'s Spanish-Cuban captain, gestures with rudimentary sign language to Sengbe Pieh and some of the others that their fate is to be eaten by the white Spanish plantation owners who have just purchased them in Havana. Sensing their imminent arrival to an as-yet-unknown destination and ominous fate, Sengbe corners Celestino above deck during a brief period of exercise. Translating his words with hand gestures, Sengbe demands, "Celestino, what is the white man going to do to us?" Taking clear pleasure in the torment he is about to inflict on Sengbe, Celestino replies, "(in cruel jest, grinning) Upon arrival in Puerto Principe (indicating with his fingers) the Spaniards plan to kill you, chop you up into pieces, dry you up and eat you. (He bursts out laughing and hurries out)" (AKK 8).[13] Despite Celestino's laughter, Sengbe Pieh fails to grasp the humor and dishonesty in the other slave's cruel joke. Sengbe Pieh's misinterpretation stems from more than just the linguistic barriers that separate him from Celestino, the narrative proposes, because Celestino's revelation follows in quick succession a series of terrifying developments for the Africans aboard the ship, including the drastic reduction of their food and water rations and being forced to witness the brutal punishment of one of their own, who suffered both a whipping of sixty lashes and the application of a mixture of gunpowder and alcohol to his torn flesh. The possibility of being hacked up, dried, and eaten comes as just one more horror in a mounting agglomeration of previously incomprehensible human indignities to be suffered in the social world of the slave ship.

In a way that the general state of captivity cannot, *Amistad Kata-Kata* suggests that the fear of cannibalism induces Sengbe Pieh and, in turn, the others to rise up in revolt against their captors. With the knowledge of their impending fate as meat for the Spaniards' cooking pots adding to the accumulating experiences of psychological and physical terror, Sengbe Pieh reveals to his fellow captives that they can break loose their chains with a spike he has pried from the ship's deck. Exhorting his fellow captives to take up arms, Sengbe Pieh repeats again and again the haunting specter of cannibalistic consumption by the white men:

> Sengbe: My brothers, this is our fourth night on the ship. We have just learned that the white man is going to eat us. We don't know where they are taking us to be eaten . . .
>
> Others: (variously) It's true. You are right . . . the white men want to eat us . . .
>
> Sengbe: It is possible for us to return to Africa . . . There are fifty-three of us and only seven of them, including the two slaves of the captain . . . So we may as well die trying to free ourselves than to be killed and eaten . . . Whether you join me or not, I am ready to fight the white man, single-handed. I was not born to be a slave—let alone to be killed and eaten." (9)

Gabro, another of the captives, takes up Sengbe's refrain and even more explicitly identifies the intent to commit cannibalism as a declaration of war on their bodies: "You are right, Sengbe. Death is death. Whether we are killed and eaten or we are slain in battle—it's all the same death. It is for us, now, to choose an honorable death" (9).[14] With each repetition of the words "eaten," "death," and "free" Sengbe and Gabro draw the commitment to resistance of more and more of the fifty-one other captives—forty-eight adult men, three young girls, and a boy in all—until each takes the oath led by Sengbe: "I swear that I will never surrender to the white man. None of us will be left in slavery. We rather die fighting

[sic]. God be with us" (10). With that oath they take possession of a cache of cane knives stored in the transport hold, storm the deck, kill the captain and Celestino, and take command of the ship.

Celestino's joke marks a critical moment of recognition for the characters in the play just as it did for the original mutineers in 1839, but a subtle semantic shift in Sengbe Pieh's speech suggests that he may have registered the threat of cannibalism as a metaphor for the impending psychological-subjective effects of enslavement as much as he understood it literally. In Haffner's hands, Sengbe replaces the word "cannibalism" in his oath with the word "slavery," thereby associating the two terms not around the notion of physical death but around that of indenture, labor, and subjugation. Celestino's reference to cannibalism comes to function quickly for Sengbe as an exaggerated description of how their bodies are to be consumed by their masters' insatiable appetite for labor. Celestino's cruel joke thereby exacerbates the *Amistad* Africans' experience of enslavement as a social death, comprising one of the principal scenes of subjection in their overall constitution as slaves. As Orlando Patterson argues, enslavement is a process of dehumanization—a social death—that strips the enslaved individual of his or her human subjectivity; and following Patterson, Saidiya Hartman underscores how the process is marked by sudden shocks to the psyche, occurring in primal scenes such as what Sengbe Pieh and the others experience with Celestino's revelation of their fate as cannibal fodder (Hartman 5). In this case, the psychic blow does not inure Sengbe Pieh further to his enslavement but jolts him into action in resistance to it.

Later in the play, Sengbe Pieh defends himself from a corollary form of cannibalizing incorporation when his Spanish captors and abolitionist allies alike attempt to rename him Jose Cinquez, which the abolitionists anglicize as Joseph Cinque. As explained in the previous chapter, 'Joseph Cinque(z)' was not the *Amistad* leader's given name, of course, but the one his Spanish captors slapped on him in their effort to circumvent legal restrictions dating to 1807 against the importation of newly captured Africans to the Americas. As Cinquez, the rebel leader would appear to import agents and colonial bureaucrats more likely to have been born in the Spanish Caribbean. In *Amistad Kata-Kata*, the rebellion leader repeatedly resists this reinscription by insisting that people call him "Sengbe Pieh." This demand comes at the moments in his captivity when he is most in danger of cannibal-like depersonalizing subjugation by the three primary institutional structures that fought over the control and meaning of his body: the first instance comes at the slave auction house in Havana, the second during meeting with U.S. abolitionists (*AKK* 17), and the third in a U.S. courtroom (21).[15] Sengbe's claim to his birth name is one act among many in the play to fight the forms of social death so critical to the successful operation of enslavement, as well as to resist interpellation by the Christian abolitionists and the state. With his name intact, Sengbe Pieh retains a kernel of his Mende self, independent and autonomous of the chattel slavery machine that included not just the plantation but also the abolitionist movements and the legal apparatus itself. We can see in Sengbe's insistence on his birth name an effort on Haffner's part to imagine the inner life of a figure who exists historically as little more than a vague outline and almost exclusively in the archival records of the three institutions that competed for his body and soul. A Sengbe who would refuse one of enslavement's fundamental forms of social death is, after all, consistent with the Sengbe in the historical record who took up a cane knife to prevent his physical enslavement.

For Haffner, Sengbe Pieh's insistence on the use of his birth name held a distinctly contemporary significance as well. Haffner has pointed repeatedly to the incredulous responses his play received when he first staged it in Sierra Leone, an incredulity he felt was born out of the failures of the educational system to undo the psychological damage of colonization and, significantly, out of the practical difficulty of recognizing the ethnic Mende farmer under the Western name (Opala, "*Ecstatic Renovation!*" 30; Osagie 106). For many viewers, it seemed impossible that a man with the foreign name 'Cinque' could be of Mende ethnicity and, therefore, come from Sierra Leone. Haffner understood this inability to recognize the rebel leader's local roots as just one more of the cannibalistic erasures produced by the trans-Atlantic slave trade and the colonial and postcolonial regimes that followed it, erasures that left Africans in the Americas equally cut off from their African past. Those scenes in which the *Amistad* leader insists on the name Sengbe function, then, to show his contemporary Sierra Leonean audiences the *Amistad* leader's "Sierra Leoneaness" as they are for giving a fuller inner life to the historical figure. With that not-so-subtle reminder that the *Amistad* leader was a home-grown hero, Haffner helped his fellow Sierra Leoneans see more clearly how they were implicated historically in the broader geopolitical networks that shaped the modern world.

The classificatory fictions produced in the West to legitimate racially stratified slavery and colonization have long relied on binaries opposing cannibalism and savagery with civilization (Mudimbe 49–50), and the Amistaders discover quickly that they themselves are as likely to be labeled cannibals by their white captors as they are to be metaphorically consumed by them. As the *Amistad* rebels are marched in shackles to a Connecticut prison after their recapture by the U.S. Navy, an angry white mob shouts, "Stop the pirates!! Capture the cannibals!! Save the white race!! Down with savagery!!" (*AKK* 13).[16] In their effort to reassert white privilege in a slavery-based racial hierarchy, the whites use "cannibal," and its counterpart "savage," to denigrate the mutineers and to deflate any pretensions of power or equality that they might have acquired in taking control of the ship. Finding themselves castigated as cannibals, the *Amistad* mutineers undergo a replication of the dehumanizing process critical not only to enslavement but also to racial hierarchy more generally. Thus, having been inspired to rebel in fear of cannibalistic consumption only to be labeled the same by other whites, the *Amistad* mutineers find themselves as much in a rhetorical as a physical battle over bodily integrity and social agency.

In depicting this rhetorical contestation, *Amistad Kata-Kata* deploys the cannibal trope to encapsulate the issues of power, exploitation, domination, and resistance that have defined the economy—both racial and monetary—that has made Africa central to the West's capitalist networks for the past four centuries. But the rhetorical underpinnings of the mutual accusations of cannibalism also characterize the contestations among the Sierra Leone president's office, the U.S.I.S., and Charlie Haffner over the meanings of the *Amistad* rebellion. The West, in this case represented by white Americans, projects the label of "cannibal" onto those Africans it wants to subordinate, thereby disavowing the cannibalistic underpinnings of its own racially stratified economic organization. Even though the mutineers articulated their critique of the West's brand of cannibalism in the voice of violent rebellion, the chains that bind them on their march to the jailhouse signify their lesser representational authority—vis-à-vis the white West—to shape the narratives that define global power relations. In other words, the competition over representational power is not unlike the U.S.I.S.'s attempt to dictate a pro-America narrative of rebellion and liberty with its booklet *The Amistad Revolt*. Politicizing the cannibal trope as it does, the play confronts the American government's text with the contemporary implications of the terms with which the pamphlet represents the *Amistad* revolt's history of exploitation. And by contextualizing the cannibal trope within the history of American racialized global dominance, *Amistad Kata-Kata* disrupts the sanitized, pro-America rhetoric voiced in the U.S.I.S. pamphlet.

Without directly naming its target, *Amistad Kata-Kata* marks and quickly discredits Momoh's *Sierra Leonean Heroes* no less forcefully. From its opening scene *Amistad Kata-Kata* raises broad questions about representational authority. In the play's frame narrative, set in contemporary Sierra Leone, a grandmother steeped in historical oral traditions chastises her university-enrolled grandson for his uncritical acceptance of the published narratives about Sierra Leone's history, books she views as being untested by the verifying rigors of oral debate: "If it is a lie," she tells him, "you can still write it down" (*AKK* 1). In response to the young man's complete lack of knowledge about who Sengbe Pieh really was, she takes him a *tenjamei* ancestor veneration ceremony for the *Amistad* rebellion leader. The chief priest leading the ceremony echoes the grandmother's sentiments about the authority of the written word, especially with regard to the available texts about the *Amistad* history: "Tell us Sengbe, what happened. Stories have come and stories have gone, yet we do not know who to trust. Our children want to know and we cannot tell them. Help us Sengbe. Let us right our wrongs, once and for all" (3). Until the play's 1988 premiere the Momoh and U.S.I.S. texts were the only widely circulating histories of the revolt in Sierra Leone, and the events were little known outside a small circle of academics, thus the chief priest implicitly identifies these works in his skepticism of the available historical record. Moreover, the chief priest, represented by the voice of his herald, declares that the improper memorialization of Sengbe Pieh in these earlier works has produced specific and commonly recognizable experiences of misery:

> [To Sengbe Pieh's ancestral spirit:] We are at your graveside, for sickness is threatening us . . . Poverty comes as rain and calamity engulfs us as flames . . . Hearts are unclean. Evil plotters multiply like mosquitoes in open swampland . . . Layvay informs us that we have wronged our great ancestors and we have, ourselves, condemned their spirits to remain on Earth and be haunted by them. We have come to beg, to pull the curse inflicted upon us, so that we can, hereafter, live in peace, prosperity, and unity once more. (*AKK* 2)

These references to the sickness, poverty, and calamity that the country suffers from as a result of not paying Sengbe Pieh his dues explicitly evoke the traumas of daily life in Sierra Leone under Momoh's presidency, and the mention of evil plotters alludes, perhaps, to the country's leadership. Far from interpreting Sengbe Pieh as an ancestor in President Momoh's direct political lineage, as Momoh's *Sierra Leonean Heroes* does, the grandmother and the chief priest recast Sierra Leone's historical trajectory to suggest that the current leadership is anything but glorious. In citing the relationship between prior *Amistad* narratives and the country's corruption-induced poverty, *Amistad Kata-Kata* targets *Sierra Leonean Heroes*' and *The Amistad Revolt*'s self-serving accounts of Sengbe Pieh's rebellion as a cause for many of the country's problems.

By calling attention both to cannibalism as politicized trope and to the relationship between memorial practice and suffering, Haffner's *Amistad Kata-Kata* invokes complex Sierra Leonean discourses about excessive (mis)use of power by local authorities. Accusations of cannibalism are often made to discredit greedy, corrupt leaders. Such accusations are not made capriciously, but with a consideration of the all-consuming hubris that leads an official to disrespect and exploit his or her inferiors (Ferme 183). Moreover, the political discourse on cannibalism situates these local acts of excessive consumption within the broader networks of global capitalism. As scholarship on modernity in Sierra Leone reveals, cannibalism has long functioned as a discursive category in daily Sierra Leonean life to articulate the problems of extreme economic inequality, domination, and bodily exploitation arising out of the social transformations brought on by modernity. Anthropologist Rosalind Shaw argues that contemporary discourses on witchcraft and cannibalism bear the traces of their historical formation in the trans-Atlantic slave trade when elite Africans discovered that accusing less powerful community members of witchcraft and cannibalism more easily justified their expulsion from the community and sale to slave traders (213). Simultaneously, she notes, the socially weak members of the community—those most vulnerable to such accusations—constructed counterdiscourses in which the wealthy elite were identified as the true cannibals to explain how their seemingly magical accumulation of new wealth corresponded to the disappearance of neighbors and kin (222).

Kept alive throughout the slave-trade era into the colonial period and reinvigorated after independence, Shaw notes that this counterdiscourse now evokes images of affluence associated with the modernity of global capitalism. For her informants, the wealthy Sierra Leonean businessmen and government functionaries accused of partaking in this cannibalistic "occult economics," enjoy exclusive access to "a prosperous [witch] city where skyscrapers adjoin houses of gold and diamonds; where Mercedes-Benzes are driven down fine roads; where street vendors roast 'beefsticks' (kebabs) of human meat . . . and where witch airports dispatch witch planes to destinations all around the globe" (202). The saturation of these images with references to unacceptably excessive consumption needs no underscoring. Luxury cars, skyscrapers made of precious metals, and global travel resonate deeply in a country of crumbling and unpaved roads, high infant mortality rates, and conspicuous consumption by a wealthy microminority fueled by the profits of diamond mining and import contracts and also where European and North American cities "represent inaccessible urban landscapes of wealth, power, commodities, technology, and mobility" (209). This provenance of witches bespeaks the power of wealthy local men, the same men who, either through their partnerships with government leaders or through their own positions in office capitalize on their political access to global markets to privately accumulate vast material resources while the general population languishes in poverty.

Amistad Kata-Kata plays on these meanings when slave traders are said to be cannibals conspiring to eat the Africans in their control, when it shows the white Americans hiding their voracious appetite for black bodies behind the disavowing taunts of "cannibal" and "savage," and when the captives themselves take up arms to prevent their consumption by white men. *Amistad Kata-Kata* locates the confrontations over cannibalism at the cultural and economic interstices of the highly profitable Atlantic slavery-based economy, where profits go not strictly to white or Western capitalists but also to the fellow Mendes who are shown kidnapping Sengbe Pieh and to a regional king who is said to have brokered Sengbe's trade to the Europeans (*AKK* 6), the same king to whom President Momoh's predecessor proudly claimed direct lineage. In the play, as in the history of everyday life in Sierra Leone, accusations of cannibalism are wielded strategically by the powerful to condemn the weak to servitude and simultaneously deployed tactically by those who lack authority to challenge the excessive and obscene accumulation and exploitation of power under which they suffer. In the play, as in the daily life of its audiences, confrontation takes place where accusations of cannibalism made by each group intersect. The play thus shares a lexicon with the language of the everyday world of Sierra Leone in which cannibalism evokes the conflicts of human relationships as they are integrated into political and economic structures, which are themselves incorporated into a nexus of global power networks. Through the cannibal trope, *Amistad Kata-Kata* crystallizes a language of inequality that is deeply familiar across West Africa but that has not always been clearly legible.

To translate that language into a structural critique and a viable praxis, however, is not an easy task, as is exemplified in one of the few other major West African literary texts on the slave trade, Akínwùmí Ìsòlá's 1966 Yoruba-language classic *Efúnsetán Aníwúrà*. Like *Amistad Kata-Kata*, Ìsòlá's historical play places the discourse of slaveholding-as-witchcraft at the center of an incipient slave rebellion plot, but it suggests that the enslaved were never able to turn the discourse into an effective structural critique. *Efúnsetán Aníwúrà* details the triangulated conflict in nineteenth-century Ibadan between the male slaveholding elite and Efúnsetán, an unusually powerful female rival who is known as much for excessive cruelty to her slaves as for her unusual political and economic authority, and between the slaveholders, male and female alike, and the city's enslaved population. In Ìsòlá's hands, according to literary critic Adélékè Adéẹ̀kọ́, the male leaders drive Efúnsetán to suicide in order to deflect a broad-based slave rebellion that Efúnsetán's cruelty has fomented (150). So scared are the male elite that a rebellion would destroy the entire slave-based economy from which their power emanates that they devise a campaign to brand Efúnsetán a witch. Adéẹ̀kọ́ argues that by individuating Efúnsetán's cruelty with the language of corrupted supernatural power, the male chiefs successfully redirect her slaves' resistance away from their nascent structural critique and, instead, toward destroying her as a morally monstrous individual. The chiefs' plot succeeds because the slaves themselves had already begun to identify Efúnsetán's sadistic treatment of slave bodies, and the social death that it produced, as a form of witchcraft (155). In Adéẹ̀kọ́'s analysis, Ìsòlá is careful to highlight that Efúnsetán's methods differ from those of her male counterparts only in proportion; in fact, Adéẹ̀kọ́ notes, the *oriki* praise poetry that Ìsòlá incorporates throughout the play acclaims the men for their blood-thirstiness and for occupying the "crossroads to heaven," just one step removed from divine sovereignty (153). The only reason that the male slaveholders deflect witchcraft accusations is because they more effectively deploy the discourse itself. In *Efúnsetán Aníwúrà*, as in *Amistad Kata-Kata*, the language of life-consuming witchcraft sits at the intersection of elite strategies to dehumanize their fellow community members and of subaltern tactics to comprehend and disempower that process. But unlike *Amistad Kata-Kata*, the subaltern remains just that, unable to effectively deploy political discourse to its advantage. Adéẹ̀kọ́ proposes that Ìsòlá's unwillingness to imagine an alternative result is because he ultimately privileges the political intrigues between the male chiefs and Efúnsetán over the narrative of the slaves. But whatever the reason, *Efúnsetán Aníwúrà* serves as a powerful reminder of the challenges and limitations of politicizing the cannibal/witchcraft discourse.

Attentive to such limitations, Charlie Haffner's *Amistad Kata-Kata* labels neither President Momoh nor the U.S.I.S. a cannibal; nevertheless, it associates them both with the trope and with its underlying political significations. In this way, *Amistad Kata-Kata* disrupts their claims to power. If *Amistad Kata-Kata* deploys the cannibal trope to identify and toy with specific practices of contemporary domination, it does so in the context of a narrative that is above all about armed rebellion. Resisting enslavement by Spanish landowners and persevering through an extended legal battle, Sengbe Pieh revolts against the West's usurpation of his body and spirit. Collecting this insurgent energy at its conclusion, *Amistad Kata-Kata* refashions Sengbe Pieh's rebelliousness to issue what amounts to an oblique call to arms, a declaration of rebellion against the tyranny symbolized by President Joseph Momoh's All People's Congress political party. In the play's penultimate scene, the mutineers break into song, celebrating their victory in the U.S. Supreme Court and their imminent return to their West African homeland. The song repeats the lyrics "Back to Sierra Leone/Back to Sierra Leone/The land of the rising sun."[17] Given the play's self-defined political context, the lyrics encode a politically charged double meaning. On the one hand, they express the mutineers' joy about returning to their homeland; the rising sun refers metaphorically to the direction of West Africa. But the rising sun also evokes the ubiquitous logo of President Momoh's A.P.C. political party: a red sun rising on the horizon.[18] Sung in celebration of the triumph over America's seemingly omnipotent all-consuming, cannibalistic political and economic system, the song targets, ominously, the exploitation and excess consumption of the country's own profiteering A.P.C. leadership. Efficiently, if obliquely and coyly, it invites the prospect of mounting a revolt in the mutineers' homeland against President Momoh's A.P.C. political machine as ferocious as the one carried out against the institution of slavery in the West.

By turning the *Amistad* revolt over to those who suffer as a result of Sierra Leonean and American ruling bodies' actions and policies and by proffering rebellion as a viable alternative to the subjugating violence of postcolonial exploitation, *Amistad Kata-Kata* disempowers the Sierra Leonean and American governments of their narrative authority over the rebellion. Moreover, *Amistad Kata-Kata* deploys the cannibalism discourse embedded in the *Amistad* Africans' impetus to revolt to disrupt the machinations of Sierra Leone's governing elite and simultaneously to address the complicity of the West, particularly the United States, in the postcolonial political and economic crises of the 1980s. *Amistad Kata-Kata* evokes the kind of asymmetrical power relations in globalization that allowed President Momoh, for example, to manipulate IMF loan conditions to extract evergreater capital and labor from Sierra Leonean citizens even as those stipulations chipped away at the sovereignty of the nation-state over which he presided. Moreover, the play demonstrates that political power in Africa has been integrated into Western economies since the beginning of European contact. And whereas colonialism skewed political perceptions to equate domination with Great Britain, it reminds its audience that America, too, has also played an integral role in the processes that shape daily life in Sierra Leone. In the *Amistad* revolt, Haffner recognizes a narrative for articulating and engaging with this new historical framework.

By way of concluding this discussion on cannibalism, the *Amistad* revolt, and elite hegemony, I would be remiss to suggest that *Amistad Kata-Kata* resolves any significant contradictions or tensions of postcoloniality. Haffner's play certainly goes a long way toward addressing the shift in postcolonial geopolitics from European to American dominance, and it evocatively captures the imbrication of local and global hegemonies. Likewise, it makes fascinating use of the language of eating and cannibalism to frame its political interventions. Its emphasis on violent rebellion and its replication of the trope of heroic masculinity, however, call into question the relationships among gender, globalization, and postcolonial nation-state subjectivity. Narrations of nationalism often feminize the nation, inscribing new gendered regimes of dominance that turn women into the symbols of the body politic. As the standard-bearers for morality and the nation's ideals, women citizens, thus, find their range of possible actions severely circumscribed. Haffner's symbolic deployment of the grandmother as the embodiment of the oral tradition in order to mask counterhegemonic constructions of national identity renders the play ambiguous on this account. However, in its attention to physical, violent rebellion as a site for political struggle, *Amistad Kata-Kata* bespeaks a masculinist construction of political action and a masculinist construction of political subjectivity that is no less implicated in the production of gendered hierarchies. Moreover, the nation-state itself remains unproblematized in relation to Sierra Leone's postindependence conflicts.

As an avowed nationalist, Haffner wants his plays and songs to foster a Sierra Leonean national pride strong enough to inspire its citizens to act in its name and on its behalf, especially against the corruption of its own leaders. Yet, as a colonial inheritance in an era of globalization and transnational migration, the nation-state form generates hierarchies and exclusionary practices of its own and simultaneously lacks the capability to address others.

I raise these thorny issues at the end of the chapter not to marginalize their importance to my larger argument, but to raise some of the implications that *Amistad Kata-Kata*'s treatment of nationalism and the intersecting hegemonies at work in the state provoke. Haffner moves his audiences away from vertical binary conceptions of political power divorced from horizontal or diagonal mediations. To open up the political to multilocational imbricated hegemonies, as Haffner does, is to open it up also to the power dynamics generated by structures of gender, class, age, ethnicity, and the urban-rural divide. Few texts, especially dramatic works with their time and staging constraints, can address each of these issues in detail; but if, like *Amistad Kata-Kata,* they show a commitment to unpacking the relations of power that shape the postcolony in globalization, the challenge becomes how to acknowledge the overlapping regimes of dominance without obscuring other differentiated power relationships and without reproducing the relations of domination that make them significant political problems in the first place.

3

Neoliberal Masculinity, Black Transnationalism, and the United States' Disappearing Borders in *Amistad* and *Echo of Lions*

In the final weeks before the December 2007 opening of Steven Spielberg's historical drama *Amistad*, media buzz turned from whether Spielberg could capture the public's fascination with the slave trade as successfully as he did with the Holocaust in *Schindler's List* to questions of representation and ownership. At issue were not the usual suspects of stereotype and racial paternalism (these would surface after the movie's theatrical release) but of copyright. African American writer and sculptor Barbara Chase-Riboud brought a $10 million suit against Spielberg and his nascent movie studio, DreamWorks, on charges that the film plagiarized significant portions of her 1989 *Amistad* revolt-themed novel, *Echo of Lions*. In particular, Chase-Riboud highlighted the striking similarities between *Amistad*'s African American abolitionist, Theodore Joadson, and *Echo of Lions*' character Henry Braithwaite, whom she fabricated for her narrative. In support of her claim, Chase-Riboud's injunction noted that David Franzoni, *Amistad*'s screenwriter, had been employed prior to Dreamworks at Punch Productions, where he was listed as the principal screenwriter for a film adaptation of *Echo of Lions* (*Chase-Riboud v. DreamWorks* 4). Chase-Riboud's lawyers maintain that two months after Punch let its option expire, DreamWorks hired Franzoni to head up its *Amistad* project (5). About the same time, Chase-Riboud says a law firm on behalf of an anonymous bidder contacted her about optioning the film rights to the book. Chase-Riboud rejected the offer (5). Whether the anonymous bidder was DreamWorks is unclear, but the studio obviously went ahead with its project. DreamWorks, meanwhile, maintained in court and in the press that neither Spielberg, Franzoni, nor co-producer

Debbie Allen had ever seen or read *Echo of Lions* (Weinraub B11; Eller, "Novelist Urges Court" D11; and Eller, "Spielberg Lawsuit" D5). Whether as a tacit acknowledgment of guilt or to get the controversy out of the way, DreamWorks and Spielberg settled the case out of court, paying Chase-Riboud an undisclosed award.

Conspicuously absent from the public posturing that typically attends such high-profile legal fights was any mention of race or of the politics of racial representation that had dominated cultural debate during the previous two decades and still enjoyed significant currency. The closest either camp came to invoking the rhetoric of political correctness was when a Spielberg representative declared that the historical past remains freely available to everyone (Eller, "Novelist Urges Court" D1, 11), hinting at the popular claim made by cultural conservatives that no one individual or group can lay sole claim to narratives about specific racialized communities. Apart from this one potentially coded statement, Spielberg's team carefully steered clear of the polarizing rhetoric of the culture wars. For her part, Chase-Riboud strictly limited her public comments to the details laid out in her legal claims. Spielberg's and Chase-Riboud's reluctance to embrace a battle over narrating the history of slavery and slave rebellion suggests that they perceived a culture war fatigue and, as mass market culture producers, were unwilling to alienate any potential paying audience that might not want to hear any more about political correctness or might not share a similar viewpoint on it—though, as we will see, critics and commentators were all too happy to parse *Amistad*'s politically correct credentials. Spielberg and Chase-Riboud's retreat from the language of race and representation to fight over a story about race and representation is certainly ironic enough. But, if their refusal to employ the culture wars rhetoric points to the escalating exhaustion of the arguments over who can speak and which histories are worthy of memorialization, it points too to the broader ways that the evolving hegemonic authority of neoliberalism impacted the discursive struggles over the meanings of race and citizenship. After all, Spielberg's and Chase-Riboud's practiced respectfulness and carefully inoffensive media posturing gesture toward the financially motivated color-blindness and commoditized multiculturalism embraced by many prominent neoliberals during the 1990s.

As neoliberal rationalities and their corollary forms of global capitalist accumulation gained broader popular consent in the United States during the period Chase-Riboud and Spielberg produced their *Amistad* works, Ronald Reagan's racialized neoconservative rhetoric gave way to a putatively deracinated market-oriented individualism and to a market-friendly brand of multiculturalism.[1] Part and parcel of the emergent neoliberal state's task of ensuring efficient market operations, securing private property rights, and generally promoting market solutions to political problems included freeing the competitive potential of the individual by shrinking the state, its regulatory sweep, and its so-called hobbling social services; in short, to protect "the private sphere from state incursion" (Goldberg, "Racisms without Racism" 1713). Disdain for state institutions and bureaucracies is central to neoliberal conceptions of citizenship, for neoliberalism's market-oriented, antiwelfare-state imperatives seek to shift the burden of public welfare from the nation-state to the self-supporting individual, who, as a choice-making consumer, bears responsibility for making appropriate decisions over his or her life.[2] Included among these privatized personal preferences are matters of race and racism. In neoliberal thinking, racial discrimination only competitively disadvantages the discriminator and undermines market efficiency, thus making racism a matter of individual choice. Hence, neoliberalism justifies its claims to color blindness. In turn, neoliberalism's growing hegemony might explain Spielberg's and Chase-Riboud's retreat from the language of racial representation.

By privatizing racial preference, neoliberal rationalities also moved to commercialize narratives like the *Amistad* rebellion and racialized cultural formations generally. So, rather than obscuring racialized histories and denigrating black cultural practices as had been the preference of many neoconservative culture warriors, neoliberalism's proponents hoped to subject them to the competitive consumer logic of the market. Or, as Spielberg's suspiciously neoliberal iteration of President John Quincy Adams puts it, "the side that tells the best story wins" (*Amistad*). In other words, neoliberalism coopts the multiculturalism so derided by cultural conservatives.[3] While the progressive antiracist imperatives that initially gave rise to multicultural political projects would appear to grate against neoliberalism's individualist ethos, communities of color proved to be lucrative markets with equally profitable commodifiable cultures and histories, including the *Amistad* rebellion.[4] Whatever their political inclination, as mass-market culture producers, Spielberg and Chase-Riboud alike benefited by capitalizing on this brand of multiculturalism.

Celebrating as it does a cultural difference stripped of the structural inequalities that produce those differences in the first place, neoliberalism actively erases the language of racism while entrenching and exacerbating racisms.[5] *Chase-Riboud v. DreamWorks* emblematizes the challenge of checking neoliberalism's appropriation of racial discourse and the difficulties it poses for generating a critical analysis of race. For good reason, Chase-Riboud expected the court to protect her intellectual property and, thus, competitive viability against a more resource-rich competitor that was allegedly willing to disregard basic property rights. The evidence, after all, pointed in her favor. On the one hand, Chase-Riboud's eventual success settling out of court served as an important reaffirmation of the hard-fought right of African Americans and other racially marginalized communities to hold legally respected property claims over their own cultural productions. On the other, however, Chase-Riboud's recourse to the court simultaneously, if unintentionally, affirmed the fundamental neoliberal tenet that the state's legal apparatus functions primarily to ensure the efficient operation of the market. Where, in an earlier generation, demanding legal protection would have contributed to the larger civil rights project of forcing the liberal democratic nation-state to ensure the equality, welfare, and basic security of all citizens regardless of race, under neoliberalism, such demands register as the simple market calculus of an entrepreneur protecting her market share. Moreover, legal protection facilitates the commoditization and privatization of cultural difference and risks depoliticizing any counterhegemonic critique texts such as *Echo of Lions* may contain. Given neoliberalism's refined technologies of appropriation and containment, Chase-Riboud is made to look, wittingly or not, like a stakeholder in the neoliberal state. For even the most politically committed of writers, neoliberalism's market-based rhetoric significantly complicates the effort to sustain critiques of racialization or to forge any sort of oppositional space.

Neoliberal global capitalism also entangles older discourses of Pan-Africanism and black nationalism with a new discourse on immigration and citizenship. The flexible production and accumulation models that characterize this period of late capital, in which factories and service centers constantly relocate in search of ever-cheaper labor pools, produced corollary globally mobile management and labor classes, themselves in regular motion across nation-state borders either scouting or following new production sites. Holding multiple allegiances and facing suspicion, if not outright hostility, by longer-standing populations, these mobile workers would shape racialized forms of flexible citizenship and diasporic practices at odds with the unitary nation-state subjectivity so central to the United States' immediate postwar conception of itself. The restrictive immigrant social services, English-only, and antiaffirmative action measures on California's and other states' ballots in the 1990s, as well as the building of a wall at the U.S.-Mexico border the following decade index the degree to which conservative hostility toward new immigrant populations was hitched to the profound global reorganization of economic and political power after the collapse of European empire in the 1960s and the attendant liberalization of U.S. immigration policy in 1965. Certainly, anti-immigrant nativism characterizes American political life at least as far back as the influx of Irish immigrants in the 1840s and the writing of various Asian exclusion immigration laws beginning in the nineteenth century. Repeatedly, efforts over the past century and a half to define a homogenous (white) nation-state subject cast racialized noncitizen immigrants, especially from Asia and more recently Latin America, as the destabilizing inassimilable other against which its own homogeneity is constituted; even, as Lisa Lowe so expertly argues, their labor proved indispensable for the state's capitalist production (4–5).[6] To the neoconservative generals organizing the foot soldiers in the culture wars of 1980s and '90s, but also to a large swath of the general population that benefited from the postwar economic expansion, the flexible citizenship and diasporic public spheres engendered by neoliberal global capitalism converged with the specter of home-grown race and ethnic nationalist movements to produce a phantasmagoria of monstrous transnational alliances corrupting and weakening the U.S. nation-state.

Latin American and Asian immigrants were the primary targets of this cultural panic, but the increased visibility of newly migrated Africans generated only slightly variant anxieties. Where apprehension about Asian and Latin American immigration questioned whether those communities would remain insufficiently incorporated as they maintained allegiances to their countries of origin, concern about African immigrants focused on whether they would overly identify with the civil rights grievances of African American communities who traced their ancestry back through the slave trade. More often than not, cultural commentators suggested that, in fact, African migrants did not, but the question almost always defined discussion. Certainly Barack Obama's 2008 presidential bid brought these anxieties to the fore. In a *New York Times* article published in tandem with the 2008 Democratic convention, "Is Obama the End of Black Politics?" Matt Bai pointed to perceptions that, without the historical experience of slavery, Jim Crow, and segregation, African immigrants tend to shy away from African American civil rights claims, thereby undermining efforts to battle persistent racial inequalities. In a similar vein, a 2004 *New York Times* article highlighted that as many as two-thirds of Harvard University's black students were either African or Caribbean immigrants (or their children) and cited Henry Louis Gates Jr. and Lani Guinier's concerns that those black communities disadvantaged by generations of segregation and racism and for whom affirmative action programs were designed to assist were again being excluded from higher education (Rimer and Arenson). While these are more recent examples, as early as 1994 the *Los Angeles Times* called attention to the economic and educational advantages enjoyed by African immigrants in relation to traditionally defined African American communities and the tensions and mutual suspicions that resulted (Aubry J12).[7] The underlying assumption linking these observations is that the shared fact of blackness should somehow naturally align African immigrants with African Americans to reinvigorate a powerful pan-Africanist black nationalism. Whether or not the groups forge political alliances, one concrete outcome has been that popular conceptions of blackness have now intertwined with those about immigration in a way unfamiliar to America's dominant black/white binary discourse on race, and, consequently, have moved in closer alignment with end-of-the-century racialized discourses on Asian and Latin American immigration.

Given how implicated Chase-Riboud and Spielberg are in an emergent neoliberal regime of power, it should come as little surprise that their respective thematic treatments of the *Amistad* rebellion narrative reflect popular anxieties about the resignification of race and citizenship in this moment. Spielberg and Chase-Riboud alike underscore the potential for transnational alliances like those between the African mutineers and Americans of different class and race subject positions to reshape fundamental U.S. national values. While the example set by the *Amistad* mutineers, as depicted in both texts, is shown to renew the foundational American myths of liberty and liberal democracy, the Africans' fierce Mende allegiances and provisional status within the U.S. nation-state borders evoke anxieties akin to those raised by neoliberalism's denationalization of production, flexible models of accumulation and citizenship, and opening of borders to mobile workforces. As a black male "body in dissent," to borrow Daphne Brooks' formulation, that refuses incorporation into the body politic and that simultaneously offers African Americans a transnational mode of affiliation, *Amistad* revolt leader Sengbe Pieh reinvigorates a specter of black nationalism, but in a fashion that has as much to do with early 1970s militancy as it does with the new transnational diasporas forming in the 1980s and '90s.

Despite their plot similarities, *Amistad* and *Echo of Lions* differ radically in their narrative treatment of the forms of transnational diasporic identification that the destabilizing and threatening foreign other Sengbe Pieh makes available to Americans. In *Amistad*, the traumatic rupture of the Middle Passage and plantation slavery are suggested to have so fundamentally alienated African Americans from their African roots that no form of trans-Atlantic pan-African identification is possible, or necessarily desirable. Once the *Amistad* mutineers return to their homeland, having revitalized (white) America's commitment to freedom, their absence from the American nation-state effectively precludes any trans-Atlantic linkages among black men that could radically politicize African Americans to fight for their own liberation or to imagine forms of racial identification that reject state borders. Through its containment, and ultimate expulsion, of Sengbe Pieh's contaminating presence, the narrative reinscribes a monolithic nation-state and a monologic national citizen. In sharp contrast, *Echo of Lions*' African American protagonist draws on his and the larger communal reserve of experience in dealing with white America's systematic racial subjugation to help Sengbe and his fellow mutineers resist the social death of enslavement. The African revolt leader, in turn, offers the African American the example of his as-yet unenslaved African subjectivity as a reminder of the empowered autonomous selfhood available to blacks outside of the seemingly totalizing regime of slavery. Although the two men part ways at the novel's end, their commitments persist, and a younger generation is shown to embrace a transnational blackness that neither privileges nor devalues any one nation(-state) over another. While the novel celebrates the distinctly American promise of liberty and equality, it refuses to secure the nation's borders against long-term diasporic and transnational social formations in the way that *Amistad* does.

By no means, however, should *Amistad*'s closed borders and monologic national subject be taken as a repudiation of the globalized social formations of neoliberal global capitalism. For all of its neoconservative-tinged nostalgia for an uncomplicated homogenous America, the movie trades in a deracinated individualism fully in keeping with a neoliberal ethos. Nor should *Echo of Lions*' open borders and its author's recourse to the court's protection of her market share be understood as an indication of Chase-Riboud's uncritical embrace of neoliberal market rationalities, for her novel equally articulates a practice of diaspora in resistance to global capitalism's propensity to trade in human flesh and deconstructs the unfettered manly individualism that underpins neoliberal ideology.

What each text reveals, but neither satisfactorily solves, then, are the tensions and contradictions neoliberal global capitalism poses to black transnationalism and its diasporic social formations. In revealing these contradictions, the two texts simultaneously point to the enduring stakes of transnational identification as a counterhegemonic practice.

Neither Steven Spielberg nor Barbara Chase-Riboud is typically identified as a participant in cultural debates over global capitalism, neoliberalism, or transnationalism, yet the way their works reveal these unresolved contradictions shows no less an engagement with and intervention in the cultural politics of neoliberal global capitalism and black transnationalism. For this reason, and for the fact that Steven Spielberg's power as a marquee director and studio head to structure dominant readings of the historical past (not to mention that he and Chase-Riboud together reach audiences of at least double- or triple-digit multiples to all the other *Amistad*-focused writers and artists combined), *Amistad* and *Echo of Lions* provide a fascinating lens through which to consider the cultural operations of a U.S.-centered black transnationalism and mainstream American understandings of neoliberal global capitalism generally.

Amistad tells the story of the 1839 rebellion as a neoliberal parable in which the nation-state secures the freedom of the mutineers but in which true liberty for enslaved Africans and free whites alike is only achieved outside the encumbering purview of the government. As *Amistad*'s narrative unfolds, and the mutineers' fight for freedom moves from the slave ship to the American courtroom, Cinqué's liberty is shown to be constricted as much by a hobbling, inefficient state as it is by his putative slave masters. By the film's end, Cinqué's longing to "function without state assistance or supervision as self-disciplining, self-sufficient, responsible and risk-averting individual," as Laurie Oullette has described in a different context as the idealized neoliberal citizen (232), all but surpasses his commitment to resist bodily enslavement. From his unequivocal rejection of any obstacle to his personal liberty to his "irritability in face of bureaucracy" (Yarborough 39), Cinqué commands a cool self-authorizing individualism fully in keeping with a neoliberal ethos. The film's depiction of Cinqué as having been torn violently from a state of ennobled radical freedom, his unstinting effort to return to that state, and its structuring of his every action naturalizes the neoliberal subject attributes of privatized self-care and self-responsibility freed from government intervention. It is with this example that he liberates his white male allies to achieve the full potential of their individual authority.

Amistad produces this neoliberalized iteration of the slave rebellion leader through an overdetermined racialized and gendered cinematography familiar to audiences of other Spielberg movies such as *The Color Purple*, *Schindler's List*, and *Saving Private Ryan*.[8] From the opening sequence in which the movie enlists the troubling racialized trope of subordinated violent black masculinity, *Amistad* characterizes the rebel leader as being more authentically free than his white counterparts. *Amistad*'s expository scene depicts Cinqué prying loose a spike from the ship's deck and unlatching his shackles. The close-up shot frames his manacled limbs, bloodied fingers, shivering upper torso, and straining face—all illuminated intermittently by flashes of lightening so that his glistening black skin dissolves into the slave ship's black floorboards. The film then launches directly into the revolt sequence, which ends with a shot of Cinqué slowly plunging a sword into the captain's chest. Nostrils flaring and eyes bulging, Cinqué lets out a rageful primal scream over the dead white man's body. The primacy of Cinqué's brute physicality is all the more emphasized by the fact that nearly ten minutes pass before he speaks at all, and forty-five go by before his Mende is subtitled into English, thus making him, for non-Mende-speaking viewers, an emblem of both unrestrained animalistic physicality and instinctual purity.

Given DreamWorks' massive prerelease marketing campaign, which included the distribution of school study guides in addition to the usual print and electronic media advertising, this troubling racial representation of the rebel leader was not entirely decontextualized. In the prerelease blitz, Spielberg indicated that he and cinematographer Janusz Kaminski aimed to give their treatment of the slave trade a haunting Goya-esque aesthetic (Spielberg et. al. 54)—not to mention that he made *Amistad* as a tribute to his adopted African American son's racial heritage[9]—but their depiction of Cinqué's body shares as much with Robert Mapplethorpe's hypermasculine and hypersexualized portraits of African American men as it does the Spanish chronicler's depictions of bodies brutalized in war. Like Mapplethorpe, Spielberg and Kaminski simultaneously evoke and disavow late-twentieth-century racial phantasmagoria of the black male body as a source of inexplicable violence. Moreover, the shots make a spectacle of the mutineer's painful physical subjugation in the hands of white men, a long-standing representational practice that Elizabeth Alexander argues provides a not-so-subtle reminder about the consequences of defying white authority (Alexander 105).

If the opening scenes call to mind Hollywood's unsavory history of representing the black male body, they also structure the film's conception of his autonomous self-authorizing freedom. Beginning with this opening sequence, the film's racial representation plays off primitivist discourses dating to the nineteenth century that construct black men as more authentically masculine, more instinctually motivated, more sexually virile, and thus, radically freer than their white counterparts, whose material privilege and administrative labors have rendered them complacent and feminine (Bederman 19).[10] Unencumbered by the same corrupting decadence of excessive financial wealth or the debilitating self-questioning of Enlightenment modernity that plague the middle- and upper-class whites, black men and many lower-class whites are argued to retain the full complement of their masculine attributes. In other words, they enjoy a liberty and understanding of truth that their white counterparts do not. Even if, in the racist logic underlying this discourse, black men are still cast as being incapable of the self-care and personal responsibility so crucial to the neoliberal ethos, their primitivist freedom serves as a necessary precondition to achieving those goals. Unfettered by civilization's complexity of rational thought or by an overreaching and hobbling government, *Amistad*'s noble savage, Cinqué, acts in the opening scene and throughout the film with a freedom and purity of motive almost unrecognizable to his attorney, Roger Baldwin, or his advocate, John Quincy Adams, America's rightful, but failed, leaders. As Gail Bederman so compelling argues, the corrupting feminization of white men such as Baldwin and Adams puts nothing less than the nation-state itself at risk, a circumstance only redeemable by the efforts of elite white men to reassert their "natural" masculinity.[11]

If *Amistad*'s audiences fail to appreciate the visual representation of Cinqué's radical, if disturbingly racialized, freedom, they would be hard-pressed to overlook the reminder midway through the film when, in front of an immense bonfire around which the Africans are celebrating an unexpected legal victory in the district court, their attorney Roger Baldwin arrives with the dispiriting news that the decision has been appealed on the president's orders. The appeal comes at a moment when the government has already revealed the depths of its bankruptcy. Had the decision been handed down in the Cuban plantation owners' favor, as originally expected, President Van Buren conspired to prevent an appeal by secretly dispatching a ship to New Haven that would immediately ferry the mutineers to Cuba where they would be handed over to Spanish authorities. (Van Buren's unconstitutional interference would, incidentally, provide the Supreme Court with its primary justification for liberating the *Amistad* mutineers later on.) When the White House's hand-picked district court judge unexpectedly rules that the mutineers were not and had never been slaves, and furthermore that the president was obligated to return them to Africa, both the district attorney and the Spaniards Montes and Ruiz filed appeals based on technical points of the decision. Baldwin can only feebly explain an appeals process that unnecessarily blocks the mutineers' rightful liberty, weakly justifying the government's morally corrupt behavior to the rebellion leader. At one point, the frustrated Baldwin states, "What I should have said . . ." to which Cinqué's translator indignantly—if somewhat comically—replies that the Mende language does not contain the word *should.* "You either do something or you don't," he asserts, underscoring a neoliberal brand of self-responsibility-in-liberty that is second nature to the noble savage and severely circumscribed by the U.S. government even for the putatively free white attorney (*Amistad*). In a rage, Cinqué strips naked to express his contempt for Baldwin's impotent capitulation to an overreaching and inefficient government too willing to abrogate the rightful private liberties of America's inhabitants. The fire, Cinqué's nudity, and his rage at Baldwin's fallibility signal the depth to which his character is inscribed with a primal, uncorrupted masculinity utterly lacking in the would-be American statesman and that naturalizes neoliberal ideologies of the self.

It is important to note that despite the homoerotic threat Cinqué's naked body poses in this scene and the gendered discourse of emasculation that *Amistad* so freely indulges, the film carefully steers clear of inscribing Cinqué with the fraught sexual motivations that plague a work such as William Styron's *The Confessions of Nat Turner*. In Styron's hands, Nat Turner experiences enslavement as castration, and those feelings, in turn, manifest themselves in a constellation of sexual insecurities and rape fantasies. His slave rebellion, consequently, takes shape out of a desire for sexual union with white women as much as it does from his Old Testament conception of deliverance. Sexually neurotic and irrationally hateful, Styron's Nat Turner embodies the racial and sexual phantasmagoria that much of white America at the time of the novel's 1967 release associated with the nascent black power movement. Spielberg's team seems to have learned the lesson from the blistering critique directed at Styron for this depiction, for *Amistad*'s Cinqué is eminently sexually respectable.[12] To the extent that Cinqué expresses a sexual identity at all, he does so in a brief flashback to the moment just prior to his capture when he looks fondly into the distance at his wife and son. Depicting the rebel leader as a loving, monogamous paterfamilias, the scene assures its audience's of Cinqué's safely bourgeois heterosexuality. Moreover, the brief scene reinscribes the neoliberal conception of the heterosexual nuclear family as the primary unit of privatized production.

Cinqué's steadfast masculinity, his respect of power,but contempt for government, and his unquestioning self-reliance exert a transformative, almost philanthropic effect on the men around him. As *Amistad* screenwriter David Franzoni declares, Cinqué's inherent moral and psychological fortitude liberates attorney Roger Baldwin and former president John Quincy Adams to achieve the growth they need to fix America's ills:

> We wanted to tell the story of Cinqué and the Africans, not the story of slavery. Cinqué was not a slave and had never been a slave. He doesn't bend, he doesn't equivocate. Because he has that kind of power, he becomes—even while in prison—the freest man on earth.
>
> When any country imposes an unjust system on any members of its society, all members of that society are affected. Metaphorically, when Cinqué arrives in this country, it's America that's in chains, not him. The thread was to have Cinqué free John Quincy Adams, free Roger Baldwin, free the abolitionists. (Spielberg et. al. 38)

Cinqué, it would seem, is imagined as an ideal hero for a neoliberal age. As the person who is himself most free from governmental authority—the individual most independently sovereign even while shackled—he enables the Americans he encounters to achieve full potential of their citizenship and, thus, to produce the most just society. That *Amistad* casts an individual like Cinqué as the most effective agent of societal change smacks of the neoliberal imperative to outsource philanthropy, which is to say to privatize the obligations of the liberal state by shifting them into hands of NGOs, civic groups, and individual citizens.[13] Indeed, by playing the philanthropic black sidekick to Roger Baldwin and John Quincy Adams in the tradition of the popular cross-racial buddy films of the 1980s and '90s, Cinqué helps the two men realize their own measure of neoliberal selfhood. Baldwin, especially, evolves from an (grossly mischaracterized) ambulance-chasing lawyer who clutters the courts with frivolous lawsuits and otherwise bogs down the efficiency of the market, to a principled individual who puts his will to fighting government interference.[14]

Of course, the unjust system Franzoni identifies is legally sanctioned chattel slavery, and to suggest that the example Cinqué sets should not inspire an equal commitment to liberty and equality would be cynical at best. And to be fair, *Amistad*'s neoliberal leanings are balanced at times by its nostalgia for the liberal democratic state. In one of their more playful moments, the filmmakers cast the liberal Supreme Court stalwart Harry A. Blackmun to play Justice Joseph Story. However, given the movie's depiction of the White House's interference in the judicial process and its suggestion that authentic freedom, individual potential, and self-responsibility are best achieved outside the purview of the political apparatus, it is difficult to view the chains shackling America in Franzoni's metaphor as signifying anything other than the government itself. Perhaps more Clinton- than Reagan-era, *Amistad*'s neoliberalism nevertheless overshadows its liberalism. It is important to note that Cinqué's healing touch does not, however, extend to the film's African American abolitionist, Theodore Joadson. I will return to this point later because, where self-care-based privatized philanthropy threatens to produce racialized transnational alliances, *Amistad* reveals the tensions and contradictions at the nexus of nationalism, neoliberal global capitalism, and race.

On the surface, Chase-Riboud fashions her rebellion leader in similar terms, but to signal a very different configuration of self and community in the transnational interstices of the Atlantic slave economy. *Echo of Lions* represents the rebel hero like *Amistad* does as physically powerful, utterly self-confident, unquestionably heterosexual, potently virile, and altogether self-authorizing. To emphasize the measure of Sengbe Pieh's manliness, the novel's opening paragraphs highlight "perfection of his body," his capability "of severe exertion under great privation," and his ability to "hunt, walk, or fight until he dropped" (*Echo* 18). Moreover, the initial pages detail his exemplary discipline, responsibility, and self-sufficiency as indexed by descriptions of his wealth, rice-farming acumen, two wives, and children (*Echo* 17). Sengbe's unassailable manliness, in turn, grants him a measure of social and political power disproportionate to his relatively young age, as for instance, when his impassioned testimony at a trial before what is depicted at the Mende analogue of the U.S. Supreme Court ensures his family's legal victory. Physically powerful, sexually virile, unselfishly honorable, and eminently patriarchal, Sengbe's exemplary manliness renders him a statesman and Mende patriot. Like *Amistad*'s Cinqué, *Echo of Lions*' Sengbe Pieh's manliness will serve as the standard against which others are measured. But unlike Cinqué, who remains a static monolith, Sengbe's archetypal masculinity will also mark his own descent into the horrors of enslavement. In contrast to his cinematic counterpart, *Echo of Lions*' rebel hero proves to be susceptible to self-doubt and the traumas of subjugation. More significantly, Chase-Riboud's Sengbe can only survive the racial terror of the Americas by recognizing his contingency and dependence on others. By no means is he the freest man as *Amistad* imagines him.

Echo of Lions depicts Sengbe Pieh's psychological experience of enslavement primarily as a process of racial emasculation but denaturalizes the equation of masculinity and liberty reproduced in *Amistad* and thus reveals the untenability of neoliberal individualism as the film projects it. Although the novel and film follow the same narrative trajectory, Chase-Riboud puts the slave revolt leader's racialized masculinity to a significantly different set of tests than does Spielberg. In *Echo of Lions*, Sengbe Pieh encounters the subjective displacement of enslavement—a topic completely elided in the film—through the categories of race and, especially, gender. For Sengbe Pieh, enslavement comes to be experienced in large measure as a loss of the manly privilege and power that had come with that coherent subjectivity he enjoyed before his capture into Western slavery. The unequivocal, unassailable male in full possession of his dignity, integrity, and humanity that we see at the novel's opening serves thus as a measure against which the brutality and degradation of enslavement will be marked. In keeping with his gendered experience of enslavement, Sengbe Pieh develops a resistance strategy that both utilizes the masculine attributes of self-denial and aggressiveness and restores patriarchal authority. However, Chase-Riboud also draws attention to the disproportionate gendered privileges Sengbe Pieh gains by manipulating the public image of his manliness. In so doing, she underscores the mutability of gendered identity in making claims to independence and power. Sengbe Pieh derives authority from his masculinity, the novel informs us, but not because the two are inherently connected. Rather, the relation is a privileging social construct to which he, as a heroic male revolt leader, has access. Thus, she denaturalizes the gendered concepts of emasculation and castration, thereby deconstructing the central tenets upon which white patriarchy ensures it hegemonic power.

On the slave ship, Hortence Spillers famously declares, "[O]ne is neither female, nor male" (72) and Sengbe Pieh's social death in enslavement takes immediate gendered form. In the first days of his capture, Grabeau, the man who will serve as second-in-command during the revolt, tells Sengbe, "You think they will hold you for ransom? And your father will come and get you, little boy?" (*Echo*, 24). Grabeau's chiding awakens Sengbe Pieh to the depth of his familial alienation; but, in a manner that would be unthinkable in the film *Amistad*, it serves too to destabilize his gendered identity. Only twenty-four hours prior, he had enjoyed the gamut of manly privileges from marriage and fatherhood to economic success and community respect, all of which secured his ability to take the kind of personal responsibility that Spielberg's film registers as innate. After the moment of capture, his status is reduced, in Grabeau's words, to that of a "little boy." Furthermore, the suggestion that his father might redeem him from his captors indicates a second level of dispossession of manly power in that he lacks the capability for self-defense. Later, after the seeming finality of his capture sets in, he reveals that he

> saw himself as a prisoner of war. The fear of whiteness and its evil connotations had not altogether left him. He thought of himself as being in the *palihun*, the deep—neither here in the "new" world nor home in his own. The sole emotion he felt was deep, abiding fear, and an even deeper shame of this fear . . . But Cinque felt helpless to control it. It was as if he were a child, and he was no child. Too often now tears of frustration welled up. Even the name of his mother rose to his lips. That he should die was one thing. That he should die despised, a criminal, a prisoner in a strange and hostile white world, was another, this world in which he could not even protect his children. (*Echo* 154)[15]

Finding himself in but not of the "new" world, he experiences his relative powerlessness, in part, as a state of liminality, and he discovers that his powerless status gives whites free reign to disrespect him; but what is even more significant, it strips him of his masculinity, turning him into a child, and dispossesses him of his patriarchal power to protect "his children." The independent, manly Sengbe Pieh is, thus, transformed into the enslaved Cinque, as the novel will call him throughout the remainder of his ordeal in the Americas. With this passage, Chase-Riboud hauntingly captures how Africans caught in the Middle Passage "were literally suspended in the 'oceanic,' if," in Spillers' formulation. "[W]e think of the latter in its Freudian orientation as an analogy for undifferentiated identity" (72).[16]

Sengbe Pieh's feelings of infantilizing emasculation are only magnified in the Americas and, thus, underscore how the novel identifies self-care as a function of male privilege, rather than as a matter of personal choice as neoliberals and the movie *Amistad* would have it. In his infantilized state, Cinque lacks even the defenses to protect himself from white children, leading him to a particularly strong sense of degradation in relation to women: "From heroes we have become wards and paupers; children white boys ride out to harass and taunt . . . When I think of it, I am more and more ashamed to face any woman" (*Echo* 248). At another point, when he finds himself frustrated simultaneously by his dependence on an attorney to speak for him and his inability to communicate in English, Cinque yells at his friend and interpreter James Covey, "I want, I need to be able to speak, to defend myself and my men. I shall not be treated like a child" (*Echo* 168). Elsewhere, Chase-Riboud writes, "In his broken English, which he himself realized resembled the speech of a young child, he told Dr. Gibbs that he was a full-grown man, sanctified by Poro ritual, who was being treated as if he were an infant"; moreover, "Until he and Covey spoke again in Mende, he remained in this childlike state, irreparably diminished" (*Echo* 201). Sengbe's reference to Poro ritual underscores his feeling of puerile powerlessness, but it also points to how gender is culturally coded and constructed. For the Mende, the Poro society defines and arbitrates Mende masculinity. Initiation into the society features as one of the, if not the, single most important events of the Mende man's life, and his entire social identity is determined by his membership. Once a boy passes successfully through the initiation ritual, he gains the rights and responsibilities of an adult man and can no longer be treated as a child. Hence, Sengbe Pieh's infantilization explosively ignites his pride.

The gendered logic by which Cinque comprehends his failure to lead the other mutineers home to West Africa suspends him in a dangerous and unsustainable Manichean binary not unlike that by which the racial order of the slave trade itself operated, nor, for that matter, unlike that which so many black nationalists of the late 1960s and 1970s fell prey. The deeper Cinque sinks into "impotent rage" (90) the more emphatically he claims absolute authority. As the middle ground between the poles of the racial castration of enslavement and the authoritative freedom of patriarchal power slips away, Cinque is accused by a fellow captive of becoming "more a white devil than the white devils we are fleeing" (87). And Cinque himself comes to view his authority over the other mutineers as total, not as the owner of chattel, but hauntingly close. Similarly, in Cinque's New Haven prison cell, the *Amistad*'s Mende translator James Covey describes Cinque as "a clever, hard-nosed African tyrant, quick to anger, sure of his physical and mental superiority, arrogantly stoic as befitted his role" (153). Covey believes that these attributes keep Cinque "intact" throughout the ordeal of enslavement and incarceration (153). But Cinque's rigid adherence to absolute patriarchal authority traps him in a disabling binary. Cinque's rigidly gendered response to enslavement is one that has burdened generations of black men in the Americas for whom "the 'racial' power exercised by the white male slave master was the denial of certain masculine attributes to black male slaves, such as authority, familial responsibility and the ownership of property" (Mercer 137) and for whom the slogan "I AM A MAN" appealingly equated manliness with social power and valorized the fit, fierce figure idealized in the leather jacket–garbed Black Panther.[17]

If, like so many black nationalists to come, Cinque's only two options are absolute masculine power or absolute feminized subjugation, the reality of his incarceration can lead nowhere but annihilation, as it nearly does during a voyage by barge from their prison cells in New Haven to a Hartford courtroom when the other mutineers take up a lament. Cinque can only comprehend "his men's chant [as] a subtle challenge to his authority" (155). Under the double pressure of captivity and this sign of his failed authority, Cinque can contemplate nothing other than to jump "over the side of the barge and swim until he sank or the rifle of one of the guards killed him" 156). If he remains intact, as Covey claims, he does so only tenuously. Cinque's gendered self-conception helps sustain him in the short-run, but its delimiting binary logic proves to be a liability over time.

Far from adopting Spielberg's naturalizing representation of the unequivocal black African male or from allowing her narrative to lapse into a conservative reinscription of patriarchal power, Chase-Riboud lays a foundation for understanding how Cinque's masculinity is both socially constructed and, at times, strategically performed. By doing so, Chase-Riboud begins, if only tentatively, a process of deconstructing the race-gender categories that have authorized white patriarchal hegemonic power in the United States as enacted under the sign of neoliberalism. As her revolt leader discovers, the independent self-authorizing agent proves to be a construct predicated on structural race and gender hierarchies. In no way can the self-sufficient, self-disciplining, self-responsible autonomy so central to neoliberal conception of the self stand up to the pervasive technologies of an economic system predicated on slave labor. If *Echo of Lions*' Sengbe Pieh begins as a similar figure to his cinematic successor, his transformation to Cinque leads him to a very different subjective state.

Where *Echo of Lions* and *Amistad* begin with ineffably manly heroes, they also align at the point where the rebel leader's response to the terror of enslavement leads him to forge transformative friendships and alliances with his American supporters, relationships that are not reflected in the historical record. Unlike Charlie Haffner's *Amistad Kata-Kata*, *Echo of Lions* and *Amistad* highlight these fictionalized relationships to such a point that they all but dictate the texts' narrative arcs. Again, however, the narratives quickly reveal different treatments of black transnational formations. Given the context of the texts' production in the late-twentieth century, this divergence suggests significantly different ideological approaches to the pressures placed on U.S. nation-state nationalism by the racialized transnationalisms that are so much the product of neoliberal denationalization. Where *Amistad*'s Cinqué's unequivocal commitment to a neoliberal-inflected justice and freedom transforms the white men around him, it will neither produce the same results in the African American abolitionist who appears in nearly every scene set on U.S. soil nor reciprocally alter Cinqué's own sense of self. *Amistad*, therefore, stakes a claim to a market-friendly multiculturalism at the same time that it shies away from embracing the broader economic and political implications of the neoliberal ethos it otherwise celebrates. Additionally, the U.S. nation-state remains the sole beneficiary of the West African's labors, without suffering the threat of a black transnationalism eroding its hegemonic nationalist discourse. In contrast, Sengbe/Cinque's survival in *Echo of Lion*s will depend on his ability to recognize the contingency and mutability of his subject position and to acknowledge his dependency on others. On the one hand, this characterization reiterates the limits of self-sufficient, self-disciplining, and self-responsible autonomy so central to neoliberal conception of the self. On the other hand, it casts black transnational social formations as Fanonian "zone[s] of occult instability" that destabilize the hegemonic nationalisms that the film's gendered constructs ratify.

The figure at the center of ideological contest is the African American abolitionist Chase-Riboud fabricated for *Echo of Lions* and that she contends the DreamWorks' team plagiarized for *Amistad*. The fictional abolitionist as imagined in the two works reflects several African American antislavery leaders active in public life at the time, including Robert Purvis and James Forten, the Philadelphian who commissioned Nathaniel Jocelyn's famous portrait of Sengbe Pieh, though none played as central a role in the *Amistad* case as Chase-Riboud's Henry Braithwaite or Spielberg's Theodore Joadson.[18] In both works, the character is a well-to-do Connecticut printer and Underground Railroad agent, and in both, he interacts extensively with the revolt leader, his translator James Covey, and the other mutineers. Only subtle outward details differentiate the two. Where *Echo of Lions*' Henry Braithwaite is the descendent of a long line of free northern blacks, *Amistad*'s Theodore Joadson escaped enslavement in Georgia. And where Braithwaite functions as a supportive bystander in the legal fight, Joadson plays a central part in supporting the legal team and in convincing former president John Quincy Adams to defend the mutineers. For all their similarities, however, Joadson and Braithwaite respond to Sengbe Pieh as differently as the two works portray the revolt leader himself.

For as proud and principled as *Amistad* portrays the African American abolitionist, the film denies him any form of identification with Cinqué that would privilege a transnational racial identification over his American loyalities. *Amistad*'s final shots succinctly encapsulate this refusal. In a textual postscript that follows what initially appears to be the final fade, the film explains that after the Supreme Court ruling freed the *Amistad* mutineers, Cinqué returned home to find his village destroyed and his fellow villagers sold into slavery. The text reveals, too—and with a note of triumph—that the slave rebels' defense attorney, Roger Baldwin, would subsequently ascend from an ambulance-chasing attorney to the elite ranks of American statesmen to become governor, and later senator, of the state of Connecticut. Cut between each text frame are Civil War battle scenes and a depiction of the destruction of the slaving barracoon on the African coast that launched the *Amistad* mutineers on their trans-Atlantic odyssey. Ever the cinematic master of the emotional idiom, Spielberg concisely and unambiguously summarizes in these final shots the film's theme of redemption in its individual, national, and greater moral iterations. Baldwin gives up his crass, cynical materialism to become a selfless public servant. The United States, wracked by both slavery and the cynical abdication of moral leadership by men such as John Quincy

Adams, becomes truly dedicated to the principles of liberty and equality laid out in the Declaration of Independence. And the British navy turns its guns on the slave dealers it once protected. The tragic hero responsible for all this redemption is, of course, Cinqué, a man valorous, morally and ethically uncorrupted, and in no need whatsoever of redemption himself. Cinqué's healing touch (uncannily akin to the glowing finger of E.T., that other great Spielberg foreigner accidentally washed up on U.S. shores) does not extend, however, to Theodore Joadson. Joadson remains beyond Cinqué's redemptive powers, not because he too is so uncorrupted as to be without need of redemption. Nor does he remain untransformed for Cinqué's lack of effort. In their final encounter, which punctuates Cinqué's repeated failure to elicit Joadson's identification, the African gives Joadson his lion's tooth as a talisman to keep him safe. With it in hand, Joadson backs away frightened, speechless, and uncomprehending, too scarred even as a free black by the psychic violence of the institution of slavery to recognize the self-defining authority in himself that he sees in the majestic African warrior.

Any other response by the African American would risk shifting his loyalties from his white abolitionist colleagues to the West African. In neither of the two scenes where Cinqué implores Joadson for some acknowledgment of their shared history can Joadson muster more than a confused mumble or frightened stare. In a scene midway through the film that foreshadows the failed connection at the end, Cinqué describes his heroic response to the lion attack on his village that earned him the tooth he gives Joadson. Although Cinqué's story comes in response to a question posed by his attorney, Roger Baldwin, he addresses much of his tale directly to Joadson, fingering the well-to-do African American's coat lapel as he tells of receiving the most prestigious country cloth as a reward for his feat. Cinqué looks deeply into Joadson's eyes, pleading with him to show some sign that he, with his sartorial trappings of wealth and power, recognizes himself in the African revolt leader. The most Joadson can do in response is back away uncomprehending, as he will again at the end when Cinqué offers him the tooth. Taking a charitable approach to these scenes, *LA Weekly* cultural critic Erin Aubry argues, "Joadson did not recognize himself in Cinque, in any of the Africans. The Africa-America link has been a long time broken . . . Cinque had much more to say to the likes of attorney Roger Baldwin and John Quincy Adams because they understood power, having assumed it at some point themselves; Joadson, and his millions of descendents, stood haplessly on the outside looking in" (Dargis et. al. 38). Fair as Aubry's position may be, the film's liberal multicultural nationalism precludes any other possibility. Cinqué cannot transform Joadson because the African's virile, hypermasculine commitment to liberty raises the unwelcome specter of the militant black nationalism of the 1970s, and his unmitigated Africanness reverberates uncomfortably with the new diasporic social formations of the 1990s.

In nearly all of Joadson's major scenes, *Amistad*'s filmmakers take special care to erase any possibility that he be suspected of such militancy or transnational allegiance by fashioning him as the consummate U.S. citizen, so much so that he cannot even speak from a racialized perspective as an *African* American. Meeting with former president John Quincy Adams, Joadson exhibits a moderate and all-encompassing political vision that contrasts sharply with the moral dogmatism shown by Lewis Tappan, the wealthy white abolitionist benefactor of the Amistad Defense Committee. In their successive appeals to the aging former president, Tappan makes his appeal as an abolitionist for the cause of abolition, whereas Joadson makes his as an American for the cause of ending slavery, a subtle but telling difference. Far from espousing a radical abolitionist stance or black nationalist rhetoric, Joadson shows himself to be a dedicated student of the American dream and its promise of liberal equality.[19] Moreover, when Adams asks Joadson later in the film for the personal narrative that defines him, Joadson finds himself unable to articulate the faintest description of life for blacks in antebellum America. His silence is likely supposed to signify the tragedy of his trauma, but it simultaneously leaves little fear that Joadson might ever command a violent rebellion against white men for equal rights. Just as important, Joadson's silence on matters of racial subjectivity also reveals a man who identifies himself exclusively as American, making no claims politically or culturally as an African American, let alone as part of a transnational black diaspora. Furthermore, Joadson's sadly inarticulate psychological morass privatizes the trauma produced by institutionally sanctioned class-race-gender hierarchies in the best neoliberal fashion to an experience of individual psychological damage.

While eminent *Amistad* historian Howard Jones—along with nineteenth-century U.S. historian Eric Foner and even conservative critic George Will—argued that the film's historical liberties did not fundamentally alter its success in "revealing the essential truths of a compelling story" (Jones, "Letter to the Editor" A20), Spielberg's fabrication of Theodore Joadson drew sharp contempt from some neoconservatives who viewed Joadson's presence as the worst form of affirmative action.[20] Reducing Joadson's fictionalized appearance among eminent white political and legal leaders to a matter of racial quota, *Commentary* contributor Gary Rosen scornfully declared, "*Amistad* is a major artistic offensive in the current debate over race. It is, in fact, an extraordinary example of racial preference, giving blacks a prominence and importance they did not have while distorting or denying the role of whites," adding, "and, while being 'only' a movie, it is conveniently far removed from the remedial reach of a referendum-wielding electorate or the various courts that have recently struck down similar policies of 'affirmative action'" (Rosen 50). Similarly, in *The New York Review of Books*, Eric McKittrick dismissed Joadson's character as compensatory, "for no such person of the bearing and dignity depicted by Mr. Freeman would have been allowed to exist in the America of 1840" (qtd. in Newman 219).

What these critics fail to grasp is that while the film identifies cynical disregard for the ideals of the revolutionary age as the nation-state's chief threat, it carefully forecloses the opportunity for that cynicism to engender forms of identification and allegiance in competition with a brand of American nationalism very sympathetic to their own. Joadson's second-class citizenship could easily breed a cynical contempt that far surpasses Baldwin's or Adam's and ally him politically with Cinqué or to take up arms as the rebel leader did. But it does not, and Joadson complacently relies on the largesse of white America to live up to the Revolution's egalitarian promise. That Cinqué empowers Roger Baldwin, John Quincy Adams, and the United States to rediscover the liberal democratic ideals defined by the founding fathers, but is denied a transnational affiliation with the African American community and is himself expelled from the rigidly bounded U.S. nation-state at the film's end, precludes any possibility whatsoever for forms of black transnationalism that would destabilize the nationalism of the film's facile cultural pluralism. Whereas such transient and contingent subject formations the two men might form are fully compatible with neoliberal political rationalities, they grate harshly against the nationalist nostalgia in which the film so unapologetically trades. Thus, the threat posed by Cinqué, like the corollary threats of contemporary black nationalism and the practices of flexible citizenship and transnational identification, must be contained as it is with Joadson. A slave rebel and immigrant simultaneously, Cinqué's presence is thus crucial for reinvigorating the nation's ideals but completely incommensurable with the nation-state's operating logic.

That nationalist logic is not, however, entirely consistent with the neoliberal ethos articulated in Cinqué's character. After all, by prioritizing market rationalities and individual liberties over state regulation and collective obligations, neoliberal global capitalism has done more to antiquate nationalism than perhaps any other force. At the same time, though, neoliberal globalization "reinvigorates nationalism (as a response to the perception that the nation is embattled)" (Apter 69) insofar as it instigates reactionary responses from individuals and communities unwilling to relinquish older models of political organization and political subjectivity. As we saw in chapter 2, Ronald Reagan was particularly adept at marrying neoliberalism with the neoconservatism that still celebrated a monolithic nation-state nationalism. Spielberg's color-blind ideal is celebratory where Reagan's was contemptuous, but in his hands, Cinqué is no less able to energize American nationalism by leading its would-be leaders to personal redemption and by failing to forge a bond with Joadson than he is to demonstrate the virtues of neoliberal individualism.[21] But by reinvigorating U.S. nationalism through the example of his neoliberal ethos, Cinqué reveals a logical contradiction that the film never fully resolves. It is, after all, the neoliberal rationality of globalization that helped produce the ontological crisis underlying the film's brand of nationalism in the first place.[22] Fortunately for the filmmakers, the historical material provided a convenient, if not entirely satisfying, resolution to this contradiction: immigrant, noble savage, black buddy, and guest worker Cinqué goes home.

In an essay on *Echo of Lions*, Trimiko Melancon argues that Chase-Riboud's novel depicts Cinque as the "natally alienated or 'stranger' on the margins of society . . . who 'clarifies' the boundaries of the white nation-state" (850). Chase-Riboud herself indicates that one of her primary artistic goals is to reveal the fictions of race and nation that have underwritten "the 'purity' of the founding narrative in American identity" (Chase-Riboud, "Slavery as a Problem in Public History" 828). In its attention to the reinscription of racialized national borders, *Echo of Lions*' plot unfolds like *Amistad*'s. Cinque's interactions with his white and black allies compel them to reflect on the contradictions of revolution and slavery. Where *Amistad*'s John Quincy Adams learns by Cinqué's example to shed his cynicism, *Echo of Lions*' former president has to confront the haunting truth that he, too, "was the president of a slave-holding republic" (*Echo* 301). In both instances, the African outsider's will to liberty compels the former president to assess his commitment to the founding ideals of the revolution and, thus, to assess the cultural, philosophical, and racial boundaries of the American nation-state. By no means, however, does Melancon suggest that the novel's rebel hero functions as the expendable guest worker that he does in *Amistad*. Quite the opposite, in fact, because Melancon's attention to Cinque's outsider status and the processes of racial Othering that his presence disrupts reveals an important way that *Echo of Lions* preempts Spielberg's brand of color-blind neoliberal nationalism. In Melancon's analysis of the former president's arguments in the novel, "Adams argues that a verdict against the Amistaders would situate America within the paradigm of 'Otherness' typically associated with blackness. Moreover, the politics of difference between America and Africa . . . collapsed. The United States, while generally conflated with whiteness and civilization, becomes paradoxically the antithesis of modernity" (852). In other words, Cinque and his fellow mutineers provoke a national ontological crisis that no amount of individualist self-actualization of the kind that Spielberg's white protagonists achieve can address. And the crisis will remain long after Cinque returns to Mendeland, ensuring, too, that Cinque himself will remain in the United States, if only spectrally, as long as America's racial injustices persist.

One has to be careful also not to overstate Cinque's outsider status because Cinque's transnational labors in the novel produce more than a simple accounting of the erasures of American history and of the racial Othering that shapes the nation's history of self-representation. Cast almost immediately after his incarceration in Connecticut as the nodal figure in a transnational diasporic network of African American and black British communities, Chase-Riboud's Cinque is not merely a mechanism by which the hegemonic center recalibrates itself. Rather, by making the rebel leader's closest allies a free African American male landowner and a free West Africa–born Black British sailor and by foregrounding the uneasy intersections of race, masculinity, citizenship, and legal status in those friendships, the novel highlights the practices of black transnationalism as productive of a Fanonian "zone of occult instability" (Fanon 227) that destabilizes both the bounded, monologic nationalism and the neoliberal individualism that Spielberg's film's gendered constructs ratify. Far from exploiting the *Amistad* history to "clarify the boundaries" of the nation-state as *Amistad* does, *Echo of Lions* narrates the history to contest their hegemonic authority.

For Fanon, a zone of occult instability describes a state of perpetual emergence that works in opposition to the fossilizing imperative to fix cultural and/or social forms in a delimited time or place. *Amistad*'s effort to naturalize a neoliberal conception of the self in the primitivized body of the African revolt leader is an example of this fossilization, as is the movie's reification of an America defined by the founding fathers. Fanon had the radical potentiality of anticolonial nationalism in mind, but a politicized transnationalism holds much the same potential to destabilize the structurally hierarchical state forms and the modes of capitalist production that underwrite them. We see this potential when the novel's African, African American, and black British characters remain fiercely loyal to their respective nation-states—or ethnolinguistic community, in Sengbe Pieh's case—yet privilege the shared racialized experience of enslavement as a basis of identification when politically advantageous for undermining the slave trade's structural bases. Provisional, contingent, and liminal, their transnational alliance stands perpetually at odds with the insular, monologic nationalism celebrated in Spielberg's film and concedes little to the neoliberal global capitalism that would threaten to coopt it. Moreover, inasmuch as Spielberg's nationalism and neoliberalism alike are predicated on a primitivist, racialized masculinity, *Echo of Lions* suggests that black transnationalism remains counterhegemonic only insofar as masculinity itself is deconstructed.

Chase-Riboud began her artistic career in the 1950s as a sculptor, work for which she has earned critical praise and that she continues to produce (most notably of late, *Africa Rising*, the official monument at the African burial ground in lower Manhattan), and cites as a primary influence the Italian futurists of the 1930s like Umberto Boccioni (Spencer 754).[23] In the deconstructive tradition of the futurists, Chase-Riboud claims that she endeavors to "destroy the substance of objects through the use of mixed materials, which is substituting reality with materials more real than reality" (755). The result of this kind of deconstructive practice, Chase-Riboud contends, is to "make a new reality" (755). *Echo of Lions* demonstrates an analogous narrative approach with a similar end. The novel entwines its fictional imagining of the interior lives of Cinque and the other participants in the *Amistad* saga with an assemblage of diary entries, newspaper accounts, visual art, and court records reproduced from various historical archives. Like other postmodern novels with which it shares its pastiche aesthetic, *Echo of Lions* highlights the voice traces of the mutineers and reads the dominant print archive contrapuntally to deconstruct the hegemonic historical narrative of slavery and resistance, which at the time Chase-Riboud began research on her *Amistad* rebellion, still too infrequently told the history of enslavement and resistance from the slaves' perspective. In a similar fashion, Cinque's experience of capture, Middle Passage, armed rebellion, and recapture is cast as a deconstructive process that fragments parts of his identity, dissolves others, but also incorporates new knowledges to produce a new reality, which is to say, a new transnationalized and racialized subject.

For Cinque, so battered by the psychic violence of enslavement, reconstruction into a new reality comes with his first lesson in the politically transformative possibilities of transnational identification. He learns that lesson from the African American abolitionist Henry Braithwaite, who teaches him to recognize the mutability and performativity of gender. Under Braithwaite's tutelage, Cinque undergoes a refashioned Poro initiation ritual. In its own way, the earlier initiation in West Africa naturalizes, and fixes, a Mende construct of masculinity. What Cinque requires, and what Braithwaite helps him achieve in a moment of transnational affiliation, is to recognize that that construct is not entirely appropriate to the demands of life in the diaspora. Braithwaite instructs:

> A man . . . can never be a slave if he doesn't *know* he's a slave. You are a man apart for this country because you are not lost: you have brought the essence of another continent with you intact, undiluted, pure, free. You frighten. You are frightening because you are still attached to your ancestors. You have an identity, a lineage, you are specific. Not like those of us who are brotherless, sisterless, fatherless, motherless, wifeless, and childless. (*Echo* 225)

At first, Braithwaite's insistence on Cinque's untainted Africanness confuses the revolt leader because of his feelings of powerlessness, alienation, and dehumanization in captivity. But quickly, his thoughts stray to his own Poro initiation:

> I think of the Mabolesia imploring the sacred stones and invoking the spirits of the Poro on my behalf, praying, "Father Siaffa . . . These children, whom we are pulling from the Poro today, let nothing harm them; let them not fall from palm trees; make their bodies strong; give them the wisdom to look after their children; let them hold themselves in a good way; let

> them show themselves to be men!" I think of standing bound with thread and moss to the other initiates so that I may be as strongly attached to my society as I am to them. (*Echo* 225)

Despite Chase-Riboud's rather fanciful imagining of the Poro initiation, the Mabolesia's invocation during this earlier Poro ceremony parallels Braithwaite's in its emphasis on manliness, family, and community. But, where Braithwaite draws the rebel leader's attention to the various gendered negations that produce the diasporic subject, he effectively shows Cinque how to adapt his Mende manliness to his transplanted circumstances. Cinque comes to understand his encounter with Braithwaite as a reinitiation. One result of this recognition is that he is forced to acknowledge that definitions of manhood are contextually determined and that his Mende manhood has to be reimagined and redeployed in the Americas. What Cinque also discovers is that gender performances can be manipulated and deployed tactically. As the months of captivity multiply, and the seduction of psychological capitulation intensifies, Cinque will fashion a praxis for resisting social death in enslavement that is predicated on destabilizing his white captors' own assumptions about gender and race.

Cinque is not the only character whose transnational affiliations condition such disruptive forms of social and political contingency. In fact, *Echo of Lions* underscores the enabling libratory potential of black transnationalism for nearly every major African and African diasporic character. The *Amistad*'s Mende translator, James Covey, and his fictional fiancée, Vivian Braithwaite, are prime examples. Mende born, Covey was captured into slavery as a young child and liberated by the British navy's antislavery patrols. He would eventually apprentice as a ship's boy and become a seaman. Covey was drawn into the *Amistad* ordeal when he encountered the mutineers' supporters roaming New York City's dockyards shouting Mende words in a desperate search for a translator. In Chase-Riboud's hands, Covey is profoundly orphaned, alienated from the land of his birth and, by virtue of his interrupted Middle Passage, disconnected from the diaspora communities in the Americas. Vivian is equally alienated despite her entrenchment in a powerful northern black community. As a child, she survives a vicious antiblack mob that set fire to her multiracial school. The restrictive constraints of antebellum northern femininity, combined with the danger of speaking publicly against whites, however, compel her to repress her trauma, thus stripping her, too, of a secure sense of place or belonging. Covey's and Vivian's divergent experiences of diaspora prove intoxicating, and the two fall in love. Covey's psychic transformation is inaugurated prior to meeting Vivian. He is initially transnationalized, as it were, when he "become[s] Joseph Cinque" through the act of translation (155). But he only gains a fully awakened "sense of wholeness" (175) in contact with Vivian Braithwaite and the "continuity and coherence" (197) she represents, and like Cinque who is resurrected by the diasporic Poro initiation rite, Covey "dies and is reborn" in his romance with Vivian (192).[24] For her part, Vivian's longing for Covey is "more like a fatal enchantment for an entire unexplored continent" (257), the metaphoric continent of another human being, but also the continent of Africa and the promise of wholeness it holds for her. Like Covey, Vivian too is awakened to a new, liberated self and to a world of possibility previously foreclosed by America's institutionalized racism. Repeatedly in the novel, black transnational affiliations liberate characters from their alienation, from mental enslavement, and from the multiple restrictions enforced by the global slave economy.

If, as we saw earlier in the chapter, strict masculinist nationalist ideologies threaten to destroy Cinque and his black compatriots, multidirectional and provisional racialized affiliations across state borders save them. And they do so by destabilizing the nationalist binaries so critical to Spielberg's nationalism as well as to America's neoconservative culture warriors. What Cinque, Covey, and the Braithwaites effectively create is a nineteenth-century diasporic public sphere, an imagined transnational community produced by and in response to global capitalism's traffic in African bodies, nationalism, and racism. Their diasporic public sphere is different of course from Arjun Appadurai's conceptualization of the term insofar as it is formed exclusively by the forced migrations of enslaved African bodies rather than through the multiple flows of media, ideology, bodies, and capital.[25] Moreover, the characters' affinities are produced less through shared claims to a distant homeland than they are for the contemporary communities that Appadurai describes. In fact, Cinque, Covey, and the Braithwaites remain fiercely loyal to their respective polities and, with the exception of Covey and Vivian Braithwaite, never fully trust one another. Covey's British loyalties remain an affront to Henry Braithwaite only one generation removed from the Revolutionary War, and Covey's and Braithwaite's shared Western appearances draw Cinque's suspicions about their convictions. In this respect, Chase-Riboud carefully resists the essentializing lure of "the family romance" that has hobbled so many Pan-Africanists (Hartman, *Lose Your Mother* 76).

Through their shared experience of alienation, double consciousness, and contingent claims to a nation-state, they refuse to let the state make absolute claims on them either. Rather, they tactically articulate a temporary, provisional diasporic community within but in resistance to the predatory U.S. nation-state. Articulation, as Brent Hayes Edwards, following Stuart Hall, uses the term, signifies the linking of discrete units not into a unitary ineffable whole, but rather into an affiliatory collectivity marked by various forms of difference (Edwards 11–12). Diaspora-as-articulation destabilizes hegemonic nationalism's binaries and monologism in two important ways: first, because the impermanence and contingency of this form of collectivity challenges modern nation-state nationalism's teleological unitary narrative of an "immemorial past" leading to a transcendent future (Anderson 11), and second, because its intrinsic heterogeneity challenges nation-state nationalism's demand for a singular subject. As such, the diasporic public sphere temporarily formed by Cinque, Covey, and the Braithwaites gestures toward the "zone of occult instability" described by Fanon as a space of a radical transformative potentiality capable of unmaking bourgeois nationalisms altogether.

For as much as Cinque's insertion in a radicalizing nineteenth-century diasporic public sphere reactivates his commitment to liberty, the space of black transnationalism as a "zone of occult instability" does not, however, provide the rebel leader a viable praxis for the radical action necessary to secure that liberty. From their position of relative powerlessness, Cinque, the other mutineers, the Braithwaites, and the community of free blacks are simply not in a position to disarticulate American nationalism from its institutionalized racism nor to remake the state in the image of transnational diaspora. Thus, subject to an unyielding white male nation-state and its nationalist ideology, Cinque is compelled to fashion a practice of resistance attentive to the gendered and racialized logic of his indenture that nevertheless refuses to concede its authority. It is at this point that he puts his lesson about the mutability and performativity of gender to productive use. Like generations of enslaved Africans in the Americas and especially of anticolonial nationalist movements worldwide, Cinque crafts a public persona that performatively reproduces dominant forms of social organization and power separate from a fiercely protected private-domain spiritual and cultural core. As historian Partha Chatterjee notes in his work on anticolonial nationalist movements, this tactic of bifurcation produces "a 'modern' national culture that is nevertheless not Western" (Chatterjee 6). By forging "the 'essential' marks of cultural identity" as an inner, spiritual core, colonized or enslaved communities seeking independence, Chatterjee argues, create a "a domain of sovereignty" even while outwardly and selectively embracing imposed forms of social organization from above (6). Insofar as this tactic of splitting material and spiritual nationalisms denaturalizes the nation-state form, it disrupts and destabilizes the exclusionary nation-state formation that subjugates Cinque in Chase-Riboud's novel and that is so celebrated in Spielberg's film. But, given its continued reliance on the modular form adopted from the slave-owning and colonizing West, it remains perpetually at risk of reproducing a political sociality predicated on radical inequality.

Cinque has little other choice than to take that risk if he wants to endure the psychological toll of incarceration. Upon completing his refashioned Poro initiation under Henry Braithwaite's tutelage, Cinque immediately launches his project of crafting an outward public persona that reproduces the same masculinity of the nationalist constructs seeking to subjugate him. At its center is a warrior hypermasculinity. Cinque vows "to spend [his] days building the morale of soldiers [and] to continue the war of the *Amistad*" (*Echo* 226). In his effort to turn the other men back into the warriors they were on ship, he substitutes "military words for our everyday actions" and imposes "military discipline" (226). To this end, he becomes almost tyrannical in his role as martial commander forgiving no "failure of nerve," abhorring "all sentiment" and responding to homesickness with "cruelty and derision" (226). Cinque leaves the men room neither to doubt his authority nor to question the requisite tactic for resistance. And, as if to emphasize the public performativity of this warrior masculinity, Cinque reveals that he will become "cold and unfeeling, masking my own despair" (226). Cinque's goals are, in part, of course, psychological. He recognizes that their opponent is not so much a physical enemy as it was during the shipboard revolt as it is the psychological assault of alienation and incarceration: "For if America breaks our spirits, saps our will, perverts our memories," he reflects, "we will never make the Return" (226).

While Cinque adopts the gendered style of his captors for public display, he simultaneously delineates a private spiritual domain resistant to the degradations of enslavement. In an internal monologue he reveals that one of the group's resistance tactic is to shield the inner core of their individual lives and cultural identities from the missionaries, lawyers, journalists, and other visitors to their prison cell. He thinks to himself:

> I and my men have taken a sacred Poro vow to reveal as little of ourselves as possible and as little of our lives before this place as we can. We have vowed to tell the white man only what he wants to hear. When they ask of our religion, we tell them we were too young to have participated in the sacred rites. When they ask us about war we say there had been peace. None of us would tell a foreigner who we aren't even sure is a *human being* of our Ki'aya, or our mother, or our sister, or the secret society of the Poro or the smooth tattooed skin of our wives. Could I imagine telling a stranger about Bayeh Bia and her beautiful black-dyed hands? Or the Poro marks of the "Spirit teeth" on my back? (292)

The parts of their lives that Sengbe Pieh identifies as the most critical to protect—family, marriage, and especially the Poro initiation rites—are the typical elements that anticolonial nationalists designate as essential and different from the outer material world of the West. By concealing these elements, Sengbe Pieh struggles to safeguard much of what has been assailed during captivity. In the process, they fashion a sovereign domain for themselves.

Over the short term, Cinque's tactics fuel his and the others' resistance to subjugation. Long term, however, such tactics tend to produce new hierarchies and forms of violence. As R. Radhakrishnan notes, "by mobilizing the inner/outer distinction against the 'outerness' of the West, nationalist rhetoric makes 'woman' the pure and ahistorical signifier of 'interiority.' In the fight against the enemy from outside, something from within gets even more repressed, and 'woman' becomes the mute but necessary allegorical ground for the transactions of nationalist history" (192). For all his recognition of the mutability of identity, Cinque does not quite learn this particular lesson. During his voyage home he relishes telling his son of his adventures but wants to keep particular details from his wife. He thinks, "I will tell him the whole story . . . just as it happened, sparing nothing, even to reliving it. I will hide the worst from Bayeh Bia" (*Echo* 369). After nourishing the spiritual domain of the captives, the Mende woman is denied access to the outer realm of Cinque's battle with his captors. She remains the mute, repressed signifier Radhakrishnan describes.[26] Cinque's plan comes to naught, however, because he discovers on his return that slave raiders captured his entire family and community and destroyed his village.

Cinque's difficulty in translating the provisional and performative transnational political subjectivity into a more broadly transformative political praxis points to bigger challenges of sustaining a politicized transnationalism. In the manner that splitting inner/outer risks reproducing the racialized and gendered binaries of the colonizing and slave-holding West's nationalist ideologies, transnationalisms can similarly retrench nationalisms. Inasmuch as transnationalisms are produced dialectically by and in resistance to nationalisms, transnational forms of identification and affiliation reinvigorate nation-states. One need look no further for an example than Spielberg's film, which would reach the public eight years after Chase-Riboud's novel and so vociferously claim the rebellion narrative for a nostalgic insular nationalist imaginary. By no means does *Echo of Lions*' brand of black transnationalism break the impasse of exclusionary nationalisms. For as much as the practices of black transnationalism sustain Cinque, Covey, and the Braithwaites, they do not fundamentally challenge the primacy of the nation-state and its enabling nationalist narratives. That is not to say that transnationalist practice is merely a balm for those individuals excluded from the privileges granted by hegemonic nationalisms or even that it is impotent in the face of such hegemony. Rather, black transnationalism provides a critical "corrective," refusing, and consequently, destabilizing, the totalizing narratives of the center.

As the next chapter highlights, the dissolution of the nation-state hardly offers a welcome alternative. While contests over the signifier "America" preoccupied U.S. cultural politics, a brutal and bloody civil war unfolded in Sierra Leone, revealing a very different kind of challenge to the nation-state under global capital. If Spielberg's and Chase-Riboud's treatments of rebellion show the power of nationalisms of dominant nation-states such as the U.S. to contain and manage the threat of global capital, works such as that of the Sierra Leonean playwright Raymond DeSouza-George lay bare how fragile nation-states such as Sierra Leone remain tragically vulnerable to the same forces. And like Barbara Chase-Riboud, DeSouza-George grapples with black transnationalism and the history of black Atlantic modernity to explore avenues out of the nationalist impasse.

4

Enslaving Globalization

Trans-Atlantic Slavery, Civil War, and Modernity in Raymond DeSouza-George's The Broken Handcuff

> To articulate the past historically does not mean to recognize "the way it really was" (Ranke). It means to seize hold of a memory as it flashes up at a moment of danger. Historical materialism wishes to retain that image of the past which unexpectedly appears to man singled out by history at a moment of danger. The danger affects both the content of the tradition and its receivers. The same threat hangs over both: that of becoming a tool of the ruling classes.
>
> —*Walter Benjamin, "Theses on the Philosophy of History"*

In the early 1990s, a pernicious form of global capitalism threatened to reduce Sierra Leone's most vulnerable subjects to a new level of dehumanization. To live in Sierra Leone at that moment meant to face the danger of a rapidly escalating armed conflict fought less over political power than over the spoils of a lucrative global mineral trade that revolved primarily around diamonds. Armed attacks on civilian refugee camps, small towns, and military posts began in March 1991 with cross-border incursions from Liberia by a Sierra Leonean militia whose leaders had trained in Libya and enjoyed support from Charles Taylor, the military commander who would soon topple the Liberian government. The Revolutionary United Front/Sierra Leone, as the militia called itself, fought a low-level campaign against government forces for nearly two years, suffering as many setbacks as advances, until an opportunity presented itself to take control of the country's lucrative diamond fields in the Kono District, which it did with a carefully coordinated attack in September and October 2002. For the next decade, the diamonds would fund the RUF/SL's arms purchases, and the social and political instability those weapons manufactured would help the RUF/SL to turn Sierra Leone into an international crossroads for war-zone entrepreneurs moving arms, drugs, and other contraband across the shadow networks of the global economy. While RUF/SL forces participated in two military campaigns on Freetown, its leaders seemed more interested in the spoils generated by perpetual instability than formal political power. The violence they instigated would eventually take upwards of fifty thousand lives and would radically undermine the security of the rest. For the civilian survivors, forced conscription, sexual violence, amputation, displacement, slave labor, privation, and simple, persistent fear became all-too-often daily realities.

The danger of Sierra Leone's armed conflict took an epistemological form as well. The country's civil war (1991–2002) has been described in one account as the result of a crisis of modernity (Richards *Fighting for the Rainforest*), because, by the late 1980s, it became clear that the expectations of a postindependence and postcolonial modernity defined by effective institutions, standard of living, and an inclusionary public sphere were not to materialize even as vast sums of mineral-derived hard currency continued to flow through the circuits of exchange controlled by the country's political and economic elite.[1] From the 1950s into the '70s in Sierra Leone, as across the African continent, decolonization was to be effected through the nation-state as a spatial and temporal organizer of modernization and of a modernity marked by its difference from that defined by the imperial West. As such, the nation came to be understood as the time and place that structures culture, and national culture, in turn, as the battleground for the epistemological decolonization that would accompany political and economic liberation (Gikandi 635). However, this discourse of decolonization failed to predict how global capital—freed from direct colonial control—would remake the patterns of production and consumption on which the nationalist premises had been based. While nation-states continue to this day to regulate citizenship and movement, "the transnationalization of primary production," the neoliberal imperatives of the IMF and World Bank and the globalized civil conflicts in Sierra Leone, Liberia, the Congo, and elsewhere undermined the ability of postindependence governments to follow the trajectory of development as it was defined in the 1960s and '70s (Comaroff and Comaroff, "Millenial Capitalism" 302). That is, of course, if the individuals leading those governments had been consistently committed to that trajectory—for political figures like Sierra Leone's president Siaka Stevens who presided over the country during the 1970s and early '80s, the rhetoric of national development provided little more than a convenient cover for consolidating his authority over the state and its resources.[2] As the nationalist narratives of development in places like Sierra Leone consequently collapsed, the anticipated epistemological decolonization all but ceased to offer any hope for liberation. Quite simply, the material conditions of the postindependence nation-state dangerously threatened postcolonial nationalism and its attendant discourses of modernity.

Walter Benjamin writes that the task of the historian is to capture the image that flashes up in such moments of danger as a way of protecting both the content of the memory and its receiver from becoming agents of dominant power. To capture that image as it flashes up, to articulate—or conjoin—the two moments, is to protect that past as Benjamin indicates, "from a conformism that is about to overpower it" (255). But it is also to reanimate a spirit of restorative justice represented in the recollected image from the past against the forces responsible for the danger in the present. Thus, according to Benjamin, the historian fans the flame of hope that the enemy will not prevail in its drive for complete domination. Among all the *Amistad* texts produced in the late 1980s and early 1990s, writer Raymond DeSouza-George's 1994 play, *The Broken Handcuff*, makes the most explicit attempt to develop a postcolonial critique of globalization to account for its history in the trans-Atlantic slave trade. But it is also the most explicit in delineating the limits of postcolonial critiques that overly privilege colonization as the principle framework for modernity in Africa. Produced at a point in the civil war's escalation when the sense of crisis was most acute, his *Amistad* text reassesses the discourses of modernity to renew the longstanding critique of colonial governmentality so important to postcolonial literary study and to the theoretical inquiry into postcolonial nationalism. However, in his effort to make sense of the "crisis of modernity," DeSouza-George calls into question the discourses that associate modernity and postindependence political crises almost exclusively with the colonial encounter.[3] Turning to the more expansive cartography of the Atlantic world with its evermorphing circuits of exchange—of which colonialism represents but one spatiotemporal element—*The Broken Handcuff* brings a new focus to the residual traces of the trans-Atlantic slave trade's remaking of village social structures, practices of violence, and definitions of personhood. The focus on the daily, intimate relations of power that characterized the local slave-trade economy underscores how for at least three centuries prior to formal colonization and for nearly a century after Freetown's inauguration, West Africa was integrated into the networks of a burgeoning global modernity, which, through the trans-Atlantic slave trade, was transforming human bodies and human labor into alienable commodities and realigning the political organization of capital and social power throughout the Atlantic world.[4] Only with such a spatial and temporal remapping, the Sierra Leonean play suggests, can the postindependence crises begin to make sense or be resisted.

Drama has long been the predominant site of cultural production and political critique in Sierra Leone, and *The Broken Handcuff*'s author, Raymond DeSouza-George, has played a leading role as a writer, director, actor, and mentor for young theater professionals coming up through the Institute of African Studies at Fourah Bay College where he teaches.[5] As a founding member of the influential drama company Tabule Theater, DeSouza-George acted in a leading role in Dele Charley's *Blood of a Stranger*, Sierra Leone's official entry in the politically charged FESTAC '77, the festival of black arts held in Lagos, Nigeria, which saw the staging of now-canonical plays such as Ngugi wa Thiong'o and Ngugi wa Mirii's critique of neocolonialism *I Will Marry When I Want*. DeSouza-George's own scripts include the Krio-language play *Bobo Lef*, which was performed at the London International Theater Festival in 1983, and the English-language work *On Trial for a Wheel*, plays that take aim at the corruption of Sierra Leone's political leaders and the failure of the country's citizens to stop it. Like other Sierra Leonean playwrights of his generation, DeSouza-George has refused to assign external figures such as Euro-American slave traders and British colonizers sole blame for the country's ills, preferring instead to lay a portion of the responsibility in the hands of the country's own precolonial and postindependence elite (pers. communication, Eustace Palmer). DeSouza-George does not, however, propose that Africa has met the West on equal footing. Suggesting that Euro-American slave traders would not have been able to purchase slaves if there were not Africans willing to sell their fellow Africans, DeSouza-George asks, "[I]f the West came to Sierra Leone and wanted to buy [slaves] and the Sierra Leoneans didn't sell, who would they have bought?" At the same time, he nevertheless insists that slavery is only possible when trans-Atlantic economic conditions are defined by a stark "difference in levels of opportunity" (DeSouza-George, interview). One of the tensions giving his writing its richness stems from the challenge of representing that local culpability without losing site of the relative socioeconomic disadvantage structuring it.

Like DeSouza-George's most famous play, *Bobo Lef* (1983), *The Broken Handcuff* remains highly critical of the greed of the country's citizens, especially as it charts the activities of African slave catchers and dealers, but unlike the earlier text, *The Broken Handcuff* carefully historicizes the interaction of internal and external forces in shaping the apocalyptic situation of country. Staged with few props other than a large shackle against the back wall of the stage, the play revisits two histories: Sierra Leone's anticolonial nationalist movement and the trans-Atlantic slave trade, which is depicted through the lens of the *Amistad* slave revolt. Ambitious in its historical scope, the play is also ambitious in its production; more than twenty-five characters appear on stage speaking three different languages: English, Krio, and Mende.[6] Following just a two-night run at Freetown's British Council Auditorium for an invited audience of scholars, theater professionals, and potential sponsors, the play toured several western Canadian cities as part of the 1994 Canadian Fringe Theater Festival (DeSouza-George, interview). The play has not been staged since, nor has DeSouza-George attempted to publish it.

The Broken Handcuff never directly depicts the civil war, but its opening scene, which juxtaposes the funeral of a union organizer and the forced march of several shackled men against the commentary of a pair of Brechtian narrators, invokes a contemporary postindependence Sierra Leone beset by rampant enslavement of Africans by other Africans, a defunct labor movement, and a bankrupt nationalism, all with strong echoes of the intensifying violent conflict. This is a world where capital appears to have triumphed over both labor unions and nationalism and where slavery is not so much a vestige of early capitalism but, apparently, its logical late-twentieth-century outcome. In this opening scene, the play also claims for itself the authority and pedagogical task of the historian. As the scene concludes, Kakpindi, one of the play's two narrators, asks with regard to the enslavement he sees around him, "[I]s this thing happening all the time?" (*Broken Handcuff* 2). Implicit in his query is a fundamental inability to see, understand, or make sense of the exploitative and violent sociability around him. While Kakpindi plays the earnest but unknowing everyman to fellow narrator Lavalie's sagelike omniscience, he's not a blank slate. Therefore, the cognitive dissonance impeding his comprehension suggests that the interpretive frameworks available to him are insufficient to the task of explaining globalization and civil war. The mission the play claims, then, is to give Kakpindi and, by extension, the audience an interpretive framework and to give some sense of why Kakpindi lacks one in the first place. The play turns first to the historical legacy of colonialism and then to trans-Atlantic slavery, but not before fellow narrator Lavalie points Kakpindi in the direction the narrative will take. Hinting at the relative silence about African involvement in slave trading, Lavalie first posits that that inability or unwillingness to acknowledge enslavement "is how much of our history and culture were swept away" (2). Echoing Orlando Patterson's thesis that enslavement entails a social death, he proclaims that enslaved Africans on their way to the Americas "experienced the reality of living death through the ignominy of feeling and sometimes even accepting that they were less than human in the eyes of their fellow men. Is it any different among ourselves today?"(2).

With the setting of the civil war established in its opening scene, DeSouza-George's play looks back in time to retrace the nation-state's genealogy up to the onset of the armed conflict, attempting in the process to identify the underlying causes of the war. Given the way that colonization has been marked as a point of radical rupture in so many earlier African texts, the play's genealogy begins where we might expect: with Sierra Leone's colonization by the British, which the play dates to 1792 when John Clarkson was named governor of the Sierra Leone Company.[7] In scene 2, the lights come back up to reveal a confrontation, set in the ancestral world of the nation-state, between Clarkson and six anticolonial nationalists from Sierra Leone's colonial and early independence past. Taking in the subjects upon which Europe defined Africa's premodern otherness—language, dress, and avarice—the verbal battle between the anticolonial nationalists and the governor reads like a cataloguing of the physical and epistemological violence done by colonialism. Among other accusations, anti-colonial leaders Bai Bureh, Mammy Yoko, and I. T. A. Wallace-Johnson charge Clarkson with imposing new values and the English language in such a way that the colonized Sierra Leoneans come to denigrate their precolonial cultural beliefs (4–6). Unsurprisingly and unironically, the colonial governor insists on colonization's role in civilizing the continent, thus supposedly kick-starting Africa's progress out of a prehistoric timelessness.

As an early British outpost on the continent, Sierra Leone saw such Manichean colonial discourse take root early. While the capital city, Freetown, was founded by liberated slaves from the Americas in 1787, they were almost immediately joined by white British abolitionists such as Granville Sharp and William Wilberforce, who sought to make Freetown the laboratory where they could put into practice their Enlightenment philosophies about reason and governmentality. Initial attempts at forging a multiracial radical democracy quickly failed, however, so after only four years, a white British governor was installed. By 1807, the "Province of Freedom" was declared a crown colony under complete control of a British administration.[8] As such, Sierra Leone remained the locus of British attempts on the African continent to develop its ever-contradictory practices to civilize the "heathens" increasingly under its control. Model villages with names like *Hastings, Charlotte, Bathurst,* and *Regent* were established around Freetown's rural outskirts where Africans "would be moulded into obedient subjects of the Crown in an environment constructed to reflect the heart of England's countryside" such that they would become a "vanguard of civilization" to penetrate the interior of the continent (Kanneh 52). Subject to daily lessons in the Protestant ethics of industry and respectability, these Africans—the Krio—were to be the missionaries who would speed up the developmental evolution of their country folk, thereby catching them up to the so-called modern world. The imprint of colonial definitions of civilization and barbarity and of Africa's temporal lag, thus, has been deeper and, in some ways, longer lasting in Sierra Leone than elsewhere, such that well into the twentieth century, Freetown's Krio elite struggled against the stereotype of being black Englishmen, more English with their Queen's tongue, Anglican faith, and worsted woolen three-piece suits than the English themselves.[9]

A key conflict of DeSouza-George's narrative revolves around the contention that colonization marks a false birth into a corrupting modernity, with the consequence of eliding colonial modernity's historical formation out of the slave trade. In their confrontation with Governor Clarkson, the anticolonial nationalists end up deadlocked, unable to escape the binary relation of colonizer-colonized or to produce a useful critique of the root causes of the civil war. At the point when the anticolonialists' tactics appear to have reached their discursive limits, which is to say at the moment when the discourse of decolonization faces the danger of collapse, up flashes a memory that Walter Benjamin insists must be seized by the materialist historian if the threat is to be confronted. In this moment of danger, Sengbe Pieh, leader of the *Amistad* slave rebellion, steps out of the literal and symbolic shadow of Clarkson and anticolonial nationalists to authoritatively assert, "Brothers and sister, I think the governor has run out of time and words. His continued stay will be a distraction. He should be allowed to go," and, after ushering Clarkson off-stage, he goes on to say, "Well! We have been setting our eyes on the wrong targets all the time. When the stranger arrived he took our attention. We were distracted. When he was going did he ask us to give him our attention? He did not; but he made sure that he left our brothers holding the mirror so that we would continue looking at his reflection" (7). As literary critic Iyunolu Folayan Osagie argues, Sengbe Pieh's intervention here functions "to elevate the stature of the *Amistad* hero to national significance" (*The Amistad Revolt* 113). But no less important, his description of the postcolonial predicament of staring locked eyed at the colonizer's image underscores the binary logic that traps the narratives of decolonization in a reductive dialectic.

Sengbe Pieh's words here echo Obierika's lament to Okonkwo in Achebe's *Things Fall Apart* about the rupture to traditional life brought on by the arrival of the colonizers. Obierika states: "We were amused at [the white man's] foolishness and allowed him to stay. Now he has won our brothers, and our clan no longer acts like one. He has put a knife on the things that held us together and we have fallen apart" (176). In this most crucial of passages in Achebe's novel, Obierika credits formal colonization for unleashing the corrupting forces of Western modernity. Taken as a dialogic intertext, Obierika's comments amplify *The Broken Handcuff's* critique of this very periodization. The mirror that reflects only the image of the colonizer leaves the anticolonialists quite literally unable see beyond or around the structuring terms defined by colonizers such as Clarkson. This, Pieh suggests, distracts from other equally relevant histories. With his words and his physical presence among the anticolonial nationalists, Sengbe Pieh consequently opens up a space for alternative sites of memory, alternative temporalities, and alternative modernities than those defined exclusively by the colonial encounter. Those alternatives include, obviously, one rooted in the history of the trans-Atlantic slave trade.

At this point, the thesis put forward by Paul Gilroy and others that the Middle Passage and the practices of enslavement in the Americas are constituent of modernity—and, in fact, underwrite the Enlightenment discourse of freedom itself—is commonly acknowledged. Yet despite Achille Mbembe's recent declaration that "the [slave] trade was *the* event through which Africa was born to modernity" (13), trans-Atlantic slavery rarely, however, features in African discourses of modern space, time, or subjecthood. Instead, formal colonization, with the radical ruptures induced by colonial governmentality and education, tends to be taken as inaugurating modern conceptions of space, temporality, and individual personhood, not least because the colonizers themselves viewed their arrival as constituting year zero for their subjects. The reluctance, or inability, to challenge this conceptualization has to do in part with the difficulties for Africans to talk about African participation in the trade without reproducing colonial narratives of their own inhumanity or without seeming to absolve the West of its voracious consumption of African bodies. In Sierra Leone the problem is compounded by Freetown's central place in the formation of a distinctly colonial discourse of modernity as well as its history as a haven for liberated slaves, a history that can overshadow the active slave trading that was carried out just beyond the city's protective borders for nearly a century after its founding. The problem of theorizing trans-Atlantic slavery on the African continent also results from the way that in canonical works on the topic, like Gilroy's *The Black Atlantic*, the moment of terrifying rupture aboard a slave ship making the Middle Passage transit across the Atlantic is held up as the constitutive element of slavery's modernity, which effectively renders those who remained on the African continent spatially exterior and temporally prior to modernity.

To the extent that African writers and scholars have turned their attention to the modernity of trans-Atlantic slavery—and this community is quite small—two overlapping critical frameworks have emerged. One approach, found in Achille Mbembe's recent theorization of postcolonial subjectivity and in Adélèkè Adéẹ̀kọ́'s study of Yoruba oral narratives about the slave trade and slave revolts, extends Gilroy's Hegelian-informed theorization of black subject formation in slavery to the African context.[10] Another, more explicitly materialist, approach can be found in anthropologist Rosalind Shaw's provocative work on ritual memory of trans-Atlantic slavery among the Temne ethnic group of northern Sierra Leone. Shaw proposes that "modernity in West Africa was . . . born of globalizing commercial flows of foreign wealth, the growth of new elites based on that wealth, and various processes of enslavement through which, over the course of nearly four centuries, people were transformed into alienable commodities." Furthermore, Shaw argues, "both the Atlantic slave trade and the colonial legitimate trade that followed it . . . marked capitalist modernity as entailing the exchange of human life for wealth and power" (Shaw 17).[11] It is this latter approach, detailed by Shaw, that resonates most with the conception of slavery's modernity that takes shape in DeSouza-George's play.

In its third and longest section, *The Broken Handcuff* turns its attention to a seemingly isolated village, not unlike the one we see in *Things Fall Apart*, that is nevertheless networked into the vast web of the trans-Atlantic slave trade in a way that Achebe's is not. It is in this section, which details the conditions of Sengbe Pieh's capture and his eventual rebellion, where the play proposes that it is in the slave trade where we find the genesis of the forms of sociability underwriting the civil war and the global capitalism that fueled it. Sharing Shaw's argument that to be modern is to be subject to commodificantion and capitalist predation, *The Broken Handcuff* constructs a nineteenth-century village struggling against the commoditizing predations of the Atlantic slave trade. In the farming and hunting village—home to *Amistad* revolt leader Sengbe Pieh—personhood is defined relationally rather than individualistically, and the value of any one person is determined more in terms of social reproduction than of individually valued economic production. The first sign that this form of sociability is under pressure comes with the confession of a young woman to a friend that her husband, Brima, has undergone an unsettling transformation. Brima, she reveals, will no longer have sex with her, nor for that matter interact with her in any way at all (*Broken Handcuff* 11). The few times he is at home rather than out hunting, all he will do is lie on his mat and stare at the ceiling wrapped up in thoughts that he refuses to share. The confession comes while Miatta, the young woman, sits in her friend's compound, helping the friend prepare food for an evening meal. Embarrassed, her friend reveals that she has the exact opposite problem: her husband cannot seem to keep his hands off of her, desiring sex morning, noon, and night. On cue, the libidinous husband comes running in from the fields to carry his wife into his room, leaving Miatta alone to tend her friend's stew. Emerging a moment later, the sexually gratified husband promises to send Miatta and Brima a bag of rice after the harvest (12). The scene is played for laughs as a brief respite from what is an otherwise somber and emotionally difficult narrative, but it highlights the relational sociability and the gift exchange economy—the shared labor, the promise of rice, the lovemaking even—upon which the community defines personhood and, in fact, itself as a community, a relational sociability from which Brima seems to have retreated.

This is not to say that the community operates outside of the bounds of commodity exchange—Miatta refers to selling hunted game at a nearby market when the harvest is meager—but it would suggest that human labor and human bodies are not commodifiable in the same manner. As you might suspect, however, Brima's newly developed focus on himself as an individual signals a more ominous way that humans are being redefined as discrete commodity objects alienable from the web of relations that otherwise define them. Brima's hunting trips, as we discover in the next scene, have as their object commodifiable prey, but not in the manner that his wife believes. While he captures enough wild game to keep up appearances, Brima's real quarry are the young men and women he can sell to the traders moving human cargo to the slaving entrepots on the coast. On a legitimate hunting trip with a fellow villager, the two witness the capture of Sengbe Pieh, soon to be leader of the *Amistad* slave rebellion. Brima, concocting a story to tell the chief about why they failed to intervene on Sengbe Pieh's behalf, draws the fellow hunter's suspicion and is forced to reveal his slave-trading past and motivations. For Brima, other humans have become objects to be possessed; he divulges, for instance, that he sold the fellow hunter's sister into slavery because he could not possess her sexually (19). Moreover, humans have gained a commodity value; Brima tries to give his wife, Miatta, as a reward to the hunter in exchange for the sister he previously sold and for his silence—a form of exchange that the companion finds utterly incomprehensible (19). Of course, Brima cannot actually take that risk, so he sells the fellow hunter to his accomplices who have just captured Sengbe Pieh. But, as the social web unravels, spinning out discrete alienable individuals, Brima, like his fellow villagers, loses the protection afforded by the community. As a narrative comeuppance for his violations, Brima himself is betrayed by these slave dealers and is carried off as the commodity he has made of so many others. And, as if to emphasize the trans-Atlantic slave trade's redefinition of personhood and community, one of the slave dealers says to Brima, "The boat that goes out to the big seas tomorrow will make a good village for you" (20).

The Broken Handcuff magnifies the slave trade's impact on sociability by instrumentalizing the three languages used on stage. In the African context, decisions about language are never neutral or innocent. Gikuyu-language novelist Ngugi wa Thiong'o, for example, argues famously in *Decolonizing the Mind* that the imposition of colonial language on colonized

African communities constituted one of colonization's principal forms of epistemic violence. By rupturing the link between languages and culture, Ngugi contends, the colonizer masterfully alienated the colonized from his or her community and values, thus preempting effective resistance and ensuring the colonized's allegiance. To write in European languages, thus, is nothing less than an act of the deepest betrayal, perpetuating the work of the colonizer long after the colonizer returned to Europe. By no means have Ngugi's declarations gone uncontested, but his forceful arguments remain the standard against which other positions must defend themselves.[12]

The Broken Handcuff's configuration of indigenous, colonial, and creole trade languages suggests a more complicated, less rigidly binary dynamic and suggests that in West Africa, at least, indigenous languages and the trade languages dating to the fifteenth century bore traces of Atlantic capitalism long before the first colonial schools began teaching English. DeSouza-George's play freely mixes English, Krio, and Mende, but not in the interest of realism, which is to say as a representation of the linguistic code switching of everyday discourse in Sierra Leone. While individual passages of dialogue intermix the three languages, they do not do so in a manner that reflects common usage. Rather, the code switching is highly stylized, and each language carries symbolic weight. For instance, the chorus and only the chorus, which represents the general population, speaks Krio even when responding to English-language remarks by the narrators or English-language action. Likewise, only the West African slave catchers speak Mende, the dominant language of the region from which the *Amistad* mutineers were captured. The exclusive use of Mende by the African slavers would initially appear to challenge Ngugi's contention that indigenous languages necessarily authentically represent a culture and ensure its harmony. In fact, *The Broken Handcuff*'s Mende-speaking slave catchers are at least as corrupted by the Atlantic slave economy as are the colonially educated students Ngugi describes. At the same time and for that very reason, the play also reinforces Ngugi's argument by suggesting that transformative impact of slave trade, like colonization, was so profound that even indigenous languages were radically unmoored from their cultural bases and made to speak in the voice of the European slavers. European languages might themselves be corrupting as Ngugi argues, but African languages, at least in the slave-trading zones of West Africa, are suggested to have been thoroughly corrupted by the time of formal colonization. Moreover, Krio, like Nigerian Pidgin, developed as a trade language to facilitate interactions with European traders during slave trade and colonialism and now serves as the country's lingua franca, spoken by nearly 100 percent of the population. Thus, more than any other language, Krio bears the most explicit traces of the modernity of the trans-Atlantic slave trade. In this respect, the general population, represented in the form of the chorus, is always already marked linguistically by the modernity of the Atlantic slave trade.

DeSouza-George's depiction of African participation in slave trading is fascinating for the manner that it explores how forms of desire and practices of social control that existed prior to the inception of trans-Atlantic slavery were transformed and given new outlets as the trade shifted power to individuals such as Brima. As it is depicted, the unequal encounter between Africa and the West exerts a profound transformation on how desire could be manifested and acted upon, with the effect of radically reshaping the sociability and definitions of personhood of those who remained on the African continent—and remain still to this day. Brima's commodification of his fellow villagers and his own transformation into an alienable commodity, after all, serve to illustrate Lavalie's claim to his fellow narrator in the opening scene that the dehumanizing imperatives of trans-Atlantic slavery are the same imperatives that define contemporary social relations.[13] It is important to note that to make the claim that trans-Atlantic slavery is responsible for the commodification of human bodies, *The Broken Handcuff* comes dangerously close to romanticizing the relational gift-exchange economy, which itself has been suggested to be a historical product of three centuries of slave trading (Piot 71). Moreover, the suggestion rests uneasily with John Thornton's insightful historical arguments, especially in *Africa and Africans in the Making of the Atlantic World*, about the precontact commercial practices coastal Africans brought to the European trade and with which they often dictated the terms of exchange.[14] In this respect, DeSouza-George runs some of the same risks as other writers and filmmakers depicting the slave trade, including Anglophone novelist Ayi Kwei Armah and Francophone filmmaker Roger Goan M'Bala. Yet, whether the play's historical claim that the trans-Atlantic slave trade transformed social relations in precisely this way is correct is largely beside the point. After all, DeSouza-George is a creative writer, not a historian or anthropologist. And as Gayatri

Spivak cautions in *Death of the Discipline*, neither imaginative literature nor the work of comparative literature should be mistaken for social science. Rather, Spivak argues, we might approach comparative literature as a supplement to area studies by highlighting the ways that imaginative literature problematizes notions such as collectivity and modernity in ways that area studies cannot.

In that spirit, I argue that *The Broken Handcuff*'s insistence that the predatory, dehumanizing commodification of human bodies is constitutive of both the trans-Atlantic slave trade and contemporary wartime Sierra Leone raises a provocative set of questions about how to historicize the violence of global capitalism in postcolonial contexts like Sierra Leone. These questions, in turn, reveal challenging implications for the way that modernity has been theorized in recent postcolonial discourses of globalization. Moreover, to link the histories of trans-Atlantic slavery and the civil war of the 1990s poses the complicated consideration of how, if it is even possible, to reanimate the spirit of restorative justice found in the *Amistad* slave rebellion against the forces of exploitation fueling Sierra Leone's violent conflict.

Two questions in particular stand out. First, in what ways do theories of postcolonial subjectivity, with their emphasis on hybridity, liminality, and difference, have to be rethought in West and Central African contexts to account for the alienating processes of commodification that shaped subjectivity prior to colonization? Second, in what ways do the discourses of postcolonial nationalism, with their attendant emphasis on naming and representing a collectivity marked by its hybridity, liminality, and difference from the imperial West, have to be rethought to account for the ways that the social formations of colonialism are predicated on a modernity shaped by the slave trade? Given the context of state collapse in which *Amistad* texts such as DeSouza-George's were produced, the latter of these two related questions is especially compelling to consider. To propose that the modernity and subjectivity of the slave trade have been elided by the nationalist forms of epistemological and political decolonization is to suggest that the project of postcolonial nationalism is in a sense doomed from its inception. The violent sociability of slave trade cannot be counteracted if it is misdiagnosed a symptom of colonialism. Moreover, it is to suggest that the time and space of the nation are always already implicated in an extranational network of global flows that are at odds with nation-state sovereignty. Without recognition of these two factors, modern sociabilities rooted in the slave trade persist, undermining the state's ability to incubate liberated postcolonial subjects.

Such considerations point to intriguing implications for a key debate about modernity that has emerged in globalization discourse. Staking one position is anthropologist Arjun Appadurai, who proposes that the global flows of capital, human communities, ideologies, and cultural practices characteristic of late capital have destabilized the nation-state's privileged status as the principal organizing vehicle of modern space and time. This temporal disjuncture is significant for Appadurai because it signals the disruption of Eurocentric chronology and the center-periphery hierarchies that that chronology has underwritten, which makes it possible to recognize alternative modernities. Acknowledging the usefulness of global flows models proposed by Appadurai for critiquing overly schematic spatial rubrics of globalization such as are found in world-systems theory, literary critic and theorist Simon Gikandi nevertheless questions the claim that the disjointed global flows so central to Appadurai's framework disperse and undo Eurocentric time and its symbolic economies (636). Gikandi's reluctance to celebrate the demise of Eurocentric temporal hegemony stems from the overwhelming evidence he sees that a deep investment in the Enlightenment ideal of progress persists among the very transnational populations who are supposed to be exemplars of the new global time consciousness.[15] Like Appadurai, Gikandi calls for a fundamental rethinking of "global time itself." Yet, "the truth is," he counters, "we cannot speak of a new global culture without at the same time accounting for the forms of time consciousness associated with its genesis in modernity, a modern temporality that cannot be conceived outside colonial governmentality" (642).

It is precisely this sort of accounting that we see in DeSouza-George's text, yet the play challenges Gikandi's claim that modernity is rooted in colonial governmentality. The implications of DeSouza-George's rehistoricization of modernity for our thinking about global time and postcolonial nationalism stem from the claim that the trans-Atlantic slave trade redefined individual humans as alienable commodity objects. This alienation and commodification of the individual affects not just those made to suffer the Middle Passage and enslavement in the Americas but also the individuals who escaped the dragnets of slave dealers and remained on the African continent. That alienation, which is accompanied by the threat of removal from the community, complicates the primacy of a modern temporality that is rooted in the colonial governmentality that is so central to Gikandi's argument. Whereas colonial capitalism, for example, insisted on the notion of progress and endeavored to discipline African bodies to the sequencing of industrial temporality, with its so-called rationalized work shifts and pay periods, the slave trade, at least as it is portrayed in DeSouza-George's play, had already subjected individuals and communities to a new economy of time predicated on slavery capital's needs for a globalized work force.[16] At any point, an individual could be wrenched from his or her community and its temporal patterns of harvests, markets, ritual feasts, and so on, only to be thrust into a mysterious world an ocean away. Time is thus destabilized and reordered. It is, in every sense, globalized.

It is also a temporality that resonates deeply for contemporary Sierra Leoneans living in an era of global capital, globalized work forces, and a globalized civil war. To give one example, let me revisit the quote from Josee Lahai that I highlighted in my introduction. Lahai's original painting of Sengbe Pieh appeared several months prior to the first public staging of DeSouza-George's play. Like DeSouza-George, Lahai had explored the histories of both colonialism and trans-Atlantic slavery in his public paintings. And like DeSouza-George, he focused his artwork on the *Amistad* slave rebellion and its leader, Sengbe Pieh. I interviewed Lahai several years later after he had fled the violence in Sierra Leone for Atlanta, Georgia. Recall that he proposed:

> First of all, young Sierra Leoneans, most of us are ambitious. We are thinking you go to school, come to the United States, because the United States is like really the heaven where you come, educate yourself, and go back to Sierra Leone, get a good job, you know have your family, live well. So, now when we thought about Sengbe Pieh and the connection to the United States, we thought other Sierra Leoneans have come to the United States and have survived and succeeded. Sengbe Pieh was one of those, came to a country like this where he doesn't even know any law and he still, with the help of other people, survived and succeeded. So we youngsters thought the connection between Sierra Leone and the United States . . . we thought having this connection was a great thing that one day Sierra Leoneans would have easy access to the United States like the United States people have easy access to Sierra Leone . . . we thought if we have people who have come to the United States and lived here and worked here in the United States and survived and do it young, then any other Sierra Leonean could do it. So it was more like a morale booster for young Sierra Leoneans. (Lahai interview)

Lahai's remarks also call attention to a contemporary form of time consciousness that has its roots in the modernity of the trans-Atlantic slave trade. If the role model for the contemporary global worker is the enslaved African, then the temporality of the slave trade serves as model—if not an actual antecedent—for the contemporary experience of time in the global economy. The temporal patterns of contemporary life as Lahai describes them—school, university, work, family, economic success, living well—are radically disrupted, paused, and deferred into an indefinite point in the future, while the "ambitious" young Sierra Leonean migrates to what is supposed to be a higher wage zone in the United States. Effectively, the body, labor, and time are all indentured by and for the demands of global capital. In other words, Lahai's description of the temporality symbolized by Sengbe Pieh and experienced by the contemporary Sierra Leonean denies the nation-state—as the vehicle of development, progress, and decolonization—privileged ownership over time or, for that matter, space.[17]

Recall that for Walter Benjamin, to capture that moment of the past as it flashes up in the present functions in part to reanimate the spirit of restorative justice against the forces of danger in the present. As we have seen in the Sierra Leonean context, these forces of danger include the material threats of a civil war fought over and funded by the spoils of a global commodities trade and the epistemological crises that come with the attendant collapse of nationalist narratives of decolonizaton. In such an environment, the problem of restorative justice is paramount, and it is the problem at the center of the Sierra Leonean stories of the *Amistad* revolt. For as much as Raymond DeSouza-George's play attends to the trans-Atlantic slave trade's transformation of sociability and definitions of personhood, and for as much as it offers a metahistorical critique of colonial historiography, it is ultimately a play about violent rebellion as is Josee Lahai's artwork and the half dozen other major *Amistad* texts produced in Sierra Leone during the period. These are all texts fundamentally preoccupied with the question of how to successfully resist dehumanization and bodily exploitation. Among the historical rebellions available to DeSouza-George, Lahai, and their fellow writers and artists—the Haitian revolution, Denmark Vesey's and Nat Turner's slave rebellions, Bai Bureh's anticolonial uprising, and so on—the *Amistad* revolt proved to be particularly well suited to imagining the possibility of resistant restorative justice because the transnational quality of the danger that the *Amistad* mutineers faced so closely reflected the dangers facing Sierra Leoneans in the 1990s. Carried out on a slave ship in the extranational waters of the Atlantic Ocean, the *Amistad* rebellion powerfully symbolizes resistance against the networks of global capitalism past and present.

The point with which I want to conclude is that despite the opportunities the *Amistad* revolt provides to imagine radical action and radical alternatives, the forms of restorative justice envisioned by Raymond DeSouza-George and Josee Lahai are muted. For Lahai, the *Amistad* offers an example not of how to change and transform the structural conditions of global capitalist inequality, but more modestly of how to manage the displacement and temporal insecurity faced by transnational migrants operating from a position of disadvantage within it. Similarly, *The Broken Handcuff* displays more ambivalence about resistance than it does celebration. While Sengbe Pieh is shown to rally his fellow captives to armed rebellion with the promise of return to the relational sociability of the village, the results of their revolt are cast in a more despairing light. With an allusion to the subsequent *Dred Scott* decision issued by the same Supreme Court bench that ruled in favor of the *Amistad* mutineers, the main narrator, Lavalie, tells us, "Judge Taney got up . . . no it was Justice Story, he got up and read the verdict" (31) as if confusing the author of the *Dred Scott* opinion with that of the *Amistad*. Lavalie goes on to lament that on the day of the verdict "Down South, men were still being subjected to the atrocities of slavery" (31), conceding that the act of resistance had little effect in liberating any other slaves in the Americas or on impacting the Supreme Court in any way that would prevent it from further abrogating the rights of African Americans as it would with *Dred Scott*. The play's ambivalence about resistance is no less pronounced in the final page-long scene, which depicts Sengbe Pieh returning to his West African home village, which has been completely decimated by the ravages of the slave trade. Homeless and, according to Lavalie, "unable to put the bits and pieces back together" (32), Sengbe Pieh gets caught in the orbit of the Christian mission established by representatives of the American Missionary Association who accompanied the *Amistad* mutineers on their return voyage. It is there that he dies, lacking the kind of community he fought for. After battling so hard to preserve his dignity against the slave traders who sought to command African bodies, he dies in the presence of missionaries attempting to command African souls, missionaries his act of resistance ushered in and missionaries who would help lay the groundwork for colonization in subsequent decades.

Open-ended and bleak, the play's conclusion perhaps reflects the context of its production: three years into the civil war, there was no apparent end in sight for a conflict fought for the spoils of a lucrative trade in diamonds and other resources. And foreshadowing the flood of captivity and enslavement narratives to come, *The Broken Handcuff* seems to offer a forewarning of the seven additional years of violence facing the country. In the broader context, the reluctance in DeSouza-George's play (and in Lahai's remarks) to embrace the notion of resistance and to elicit an oppositional praxis from the *Amistad* revolt would appear to signal distress over the seemingly limited forms of resistance available against global capitalism's pervasive violence. There is simply little room made in *The Broken Handcuff* to imagine alternative social formations: its privileging of preslave-trade sociability refuses to naïvely propose a "return to the source"; the liberational potential of the postcolonial nation-state is shown lacking; and it utterly rejects the celebratory global village ideal espoused by some globalization proponents.

Yet, while DeSouza-George's play ends on a pessimistic note, it is important not to lose sight of the way that it challenges understandings of modernity and globalization in postcolonial West Africa. Rethinking, as it does, the temporal hegemony of colonial modernity to account for its roots in the slave trade, *The Broken Handcuff* calls attention to the limitations inherent in the prevailing discourses of modern time and space that have underwritten practices of epistemological decolonization, including postcolonial nationalism. Thus, the play makes available new historical frameworks for identifying the dangers of global capitalism facing places like Sierra Leone in the late twentieth century and for envisioning new forms of resistance to the not-so-new forms of global capital threatening to reenslave Africans living in war zones like Sierra Leone.

There is, more generally, much to be gained and much to be risked by linking the modernities of trans-Atlantic slavery and contemporary globalization. Beleaguered and threatened, postcolonial nationalism nevertheless stands to gain by such a rehistoricization of modernity, but only if it recognizes the previously elided violent sociability of the slave trade and that the nation-state alone cannot contain or account for the global quality of modern personhood. Linking the modernities of the slave trade and late-twentieth-century globalization also identifies globalization as only the most recent iteration of capitalism's long, messy evolution, thereby contesting the claims of some scholars that globalization is something new, that it is the product of a rupture from a quasimythical period when nation-states held exclusive sway over economies and subjectivities. I would also suggest that there is something to be gained politically by describing workers in the global economy as slaves. This might in fact be an accurate description in places where globalization's dark underbelly reveals itself, places like Sierra Leone's wartime diamond mines or the brothels of the global sex industry filled with what can only be called "captive" labor. But even in the more legitimate sites of global commerce, the rhetoric of enslavement can frame the moral economy of consumption and labor in such a way as to mobilize international communities of sentiment.

At the same time, while there is an inviting dramaturgy to the rhetoric of enslavement, one runs the risk flattening out the important differences between the two modes of production and of conflating distinct modes of subjectivity. In an era of flexible manufacturing, flexible capital, flexible workforces, and even flexible citizenship, workers exist in a very different relation to the source of labor than they do in the African coastal slave entrepot, slave ship, or plantation. Living with the insecurity of knowing that they can be easily replaced by any of the dozens of desperate job seekers outside of the factory gates or across nation-state borders, workers in the globalized workforce are disciplined, in a Foucauldian sense, quite differently from the enslaved person living with the prospect of bonded life-long labor. In this way, the modernity of the one is importantly different from the other, and to conflate the two risks reproducing Kakpindi's inability to properly recognize to the nature of exploitation. There is the risk too that in linking slavery and globalization too closely, colonialism can disappear altogether, when in fact these histories exist in complicated, overlapping, intertwined relations with one another. As a text that runs these risks, *The Broken Handcuff* nevertheless poses the vital challenge to rethink the meanings of modernity and the violence of globalization.

Conclusion

Rebellious Futures

I began this book with Josee Lahai's reflection on Sengbe Pieh's importance to his art and Ruchell Magee's adoption of the name 'Cinque' in order to evoke the valences that the *Amistad* rebellion offers writers, artists, and activists at the end of the twentieth century as they articulate critiques of nationalism, citizenship, and subjectivity under the regimes of global capitalism. In the intervening pages, I elucidate the allegorical treatments of the rebellion by Charlie Haffner, Clifford Mason, Amadu Tarawalie, and Mustapha Lawal Turay to interrogate the experiences of subjugation to the intersecting hegemonies of American and Sierra Leonean canniballike accumulation. I show too how writers and artists such as Barbara Chase-Riboud, Alusine Bangura, and Raymond DeSouza-George trace the historical genealogy of the resistant black transnational subject and redefine the violent sociability of civil war as a function of the modernity of the slave trade. Seizing hold of the image of an armed slave rebellion "which unexpectedly [appears] to man singled out a moment of danger," as we have heard Walter Benjamin assert, the creative artists I have highlighted endeavor to protect both "the tradition and its receivers . . . from becoming tools of the ruling classes" (Benjamin 255). Writing and painting in spaces of material and epistemological danger, from outside worlds of publishing and distribution deals (or, in the case of the African American writers, outside the respectable literary canon), and for audiences often excluded from intellectual and political debates over the processes of global capitalism and transnational formations, Haffner, Magee, Bangura, Chase-Riboud, and the others identify a usable past floating semiobscured at the margin of the black Atlantic's collective memory. By refashioning and reframing a shared memory rather than trying to speak the language of elite intellectuals, they seek to mobilize popular public spheres in which the genealogies of global trade, racialized exploitation, and successful forms of resistance and self-identification can be analyzed, debated, and, where appropriate, enacted.

Insofar as the *Amistad* texts examined here stand, like Walter Benjamin's angel of history, facing the past, the majority refuses to be blown "into the future to which [its] back is turned" (Benjamin 258). That is to say, without becoming transfixed and paralyzed by the past, they attend to the "unquestionable spirit of restorative justice" (Adéẹ̀kọ́ 1) to envision utopian futures. Idealistic in their desire to transform the world they and their audiences occupy, they reanimate a rebellious history to fashion a future in which the easy lures of market rationalities and temporalities, the commodification of human bodies, and rigid territorially bounded conceptions of citizenship lose their power to indenture African and African diasporic communities. The future they imagine is distinctly transnational, rooted in the nation-state and routed across its borders. Thus, far from dismissing the nation-state as an irrelevant artifact, they subject it to historical interrogation, as Raymond DeSouza-George and Barbara Chase-Riboud do. They challenge the nation-state to deliver the liberty and security it promises, as *Amistad Kata-Kata* does when it calls on its Sierra Leonean audiences to hold their country's political leadership accountable to the ideals of the nation-state form. They also seek to transform the nation-state for a global age and to remake its most exclusionary and debilitating elements, as Freetown's artists do with their articulation of a transnationalized practice of citizenship and as Ruchell Magee's campaign to dismantle the United States' prison-industrial complex does. But they transform it without losing sight of the traps laid by global capitalism, as Clifford Mason's novels warn when they intimate that African and African diasporic communities might be better off politically and financially in the future by following the resistant example of the *Amistad* leader rather than consenting to hegemonic methods of neoliberal capitalist accumulation.

Where the texts intervene in practices of historical representation in order to envision alternate futures, many of the *Amistad* rebellion's contemporary writers and artists invest an equal belief in the idea that their creative works will compel Sierra Leoneans and Americans to recognize the nineteenth-century roots of their mutually constituted present, and that through that shared recognition of their bond they will commit to a cooperative and just future. In other words, material transformation hinges on producing a direct cultural and political discourse across the Middle Passage with the *Amistad* history at its center. Josee Lahai is the most explicit in expressing this belief when he declares that greater recognition of the shared *Amistad* rebellion in Sierra Leone and the United States will ensure that "one day Sierra Leoneans would have easy access to the United States like the United States people have easy access to Sierra Leone" (Lahai, interview). For Lahai, giving the United States the knowledge that its historical development is as contingent on Sierra Leone as Sierra Leone's is on the United States, promises to level the uneven geopolitical terrain that so severely restricts Sierra Leonean mobility and opportunity. Idealistic and perhaps naïve, Lahai nevertheless identifies tangible transformations to immigration policy and general material well-being that can result from a trans-Atlantic engagement with the *Amistad* history. Nearly every writer that I have touched upon has sought to dialogue across the Atlantic, whether by performing Sierra Leonean plays for North American audiences, by hiring Sierra Leonean writers to consult for American movie productions, or by exchanging perspectives on memorializing slave rebellion at international symposia.[1] Such efforts to reach audiences across the Atlantic suggest the desire for a greater acknowledgment of the two countries' intertwined histories and, thus, of their present and future mutual obligations.

The impulse of the contemporary *Amistad* champions to transfigure the global cartographies of inequality suggests that the "past's future," to borrow a formulation from Jennifer Wenzel's illuminating reading of the nineteenth-century Xhosa cattle killing's cultural afterlives, has yet to be realized (*Bulletproof*). Wenzel contends that as "repositories of desire that things might yet be otherwise, incomplete pasts shadow the present and keep possibility alive" (198). That is, to attend to the *Amistad* mutineers' desire for freedom from slave catchers, plantation owners, and paternalist abolitionists—indeed, from the modernity of Atlantic capitalism—is to attend to a "projected past that *will have been* in the future" (198). In no way, do the *Amistad* authors suggest, should the effective homelessness of the *Amistad* mutineers or fraught establishment of a Christian mission upon their return be taken as the narrative's endpoint. Rather, by reanimating a critical episode in the history of antislavery resistance, writers and artists such as Haffner, Mason, Bangura, and Chase-Riboud declare that it is still possible, if not obligatory, to fulfill the ethical demands for justice and liberty made by Sengbe Pieh and his fellow insurrectionists when they took up cane knives to assert their freedom. Moreover, by inserting themselves as historical agents in the *Amistad* rebellion's longer narrative arc, the writers and artists endeavor to shape a conclusion that has yet to be written. To retell the story of armed rebellion in moments of escalating inequality, to advocate for transborder modes of resistance, and to seek out audiences across the Atlantic is to agitate for a future free from the multiple manifestations of violence that have defined African and African diasporic relationships to capitalist production and accumulation from the moment the first slave ship set sail from the African coast.

In these final pages, I look at a 2007 effort to add a new chapter to the *Amistad* narrative by bringing together Sierra Leonean and U.S. artists, museums, and governmental agencies in a direct trans-Atlantic dialogue about the lessons of the rebellion of the sort imagined by Josee Lahai. Expectations were high, if guarded, that the encounter would transform political practice at the national level, realign geopolitical relations between the two countries, and generate tangible economic and political benefits for Sierra Leone as it continued to rebuild from the wreckage of the civil war. In practice, however, the encounter was marred by incommensurable expectations for the outcomes of the event, inter- and intranational contestations over the meanings of the slave trade, and the incursion of neoliberal rationalities at odds with the critical interventions made by so many of the *Amistad* texts. I conclude with this episode for three reasons. The first is for what it reveals about the impulse to translate aesthetic practice into engaged trans-Atlantic political and economic practice and about the stakes and limits of that endeavor. Efforts to place the *Amistad* history at the center of such projects underscore the enduring obstacles produced by the political and economic asymmetries dividing Sierra Leone from the United States as well as by the different historical meanings of slavery in the two locations. The second reason is for what the trans-Atlantic activist effort reveals about the future challenges faced by the populations of both countries as they individually confront the proliferating hegemonic dominance of market-based neoliberal rationalities. The tangle of material conflicts and discursive traps that haunted the encounter forecasts very clearly the obstacles that will increasingly confront the *Amistad*'s proponents if they hope to translate the historical narrative into a progressive future. Third, I conclude with this episode to return to the creative texts themselves. As the encounter shows, aesthetic practice does not translate smoothly into governmental action or economic policy, nor should it have to. Expressive narrative is most effective at reshaping imaginaries, at envisioning alternate forms of collectivity, and thus at making the ethical demands on audiences that condition radical futures.

The encounter that brought so many artists, activists, and institutions together began when AMISTAD America, a nonprofit education organization based in Mystic, Connecticut, sailed a recreation of the *Amistad* schooner into Freetown Harbor on December 7, 2007. The landing commenced a two-week program of lectures, theatrical performances, symposia, and ship tours. AMISTAD America conceived of and took the lead for organizing the port visit. In the organization's words, the collaborative event was designed "as not only a commemoration of a significant moment in history, but as important symbolism as Sierra Leone achieves reconciliation, development and reclaims its rightful place among West Africa's leading democracies" (AMISTAD America, Inc. "Amistad Arrives in Freetown"). The Atlantic Freedom Tour, as the voyage was anointed, comprised a critical component of AMISTAD America's cultural pluralist mission to educate audiences around the world about the trans-Atlantic slave trade and the human will to freedom as exemplified by the *Amistad* mutineers and their abolitionist supporters and, thus, to

> promote improved relationships between races and cultures by acknowledging our common experiences and encouraging dialogue that is based on respect. The inherent lessons and legacies of freedom, justice, perseverance, cooperation and leadership arising from the historic Amistad Incident of 1839 are symbolized by the re-created Amistad . . . The vessel offers an important message for all Americans about our collective history and future. (AMISTAD America, Inc., "Mission Statement")[2]

To that end, AMISTAD America sponsored events in Freetown ranging from historical skits to a symposium on urban youth empowerment. The group's leaders also garnered support from the U.S. secretary of state, Condoleezza Rice, and the New York Public Library's Schomburg Center and worked with the U.S. Embassy's Cultural Affairs Section and the Sierra Leonean Ministry of Tourism to involve a wide cast of Sierra Leonean educators, activists, and arts professionals in the festivities. *Amistad Kata-Kata* author Charlie Haffner, for one, welcomed the forward-looking Americans and hoped that the expensive U.S. government-supported spectacle would mobilize his own government to recognize "the potential for any future historical, touristic, educational and economic cooperation and ties [to the United States and Spain]" (personal correspondence July

25, 2010). In other words, Haffner hoped that the collaborative encounter would transform governmental practice in tangible ways. No doubt the port visit's other sponsors envisioned it producing a better future, too.

The *Amistad* visit proved popular as thousands of Sierra Leoneans welcomed the vessel on its arrival and as many as three thousand spectators per day lined up to tour the deck and inhumanly cramped holds in an effort to gain an experiential lesson in the pedagogy of the ship as a machine of enslavement. In tandem, the Sierra Leonean national museum mounted an extensive exhibit about the legacy of the rebellion, the U.S. Embassy sponsored a well-publicized student essay contest on why Sierra Leoneans should admire the mutineers, and Haffner's Freetong Players performed their ballad about the rebellion at the schooner's official welcome ceremony on December 9 and restaged *Amistad Kata-Kata* at the British Council auditorium, where the play had premiered almost twenty years earlier.[3] If, however, as its press releases and blog postings suggest, AMISTAD America envisioned that the interweaving of its ship tours with other cultural events would generate intercultural dialogue, enhance mutual respect for each other's shared history of resistance to slavery, and materially advance Sierra Leone's postwar political and economic development, the reality was rather more complicated. Longstanding contests internal to each country over the *Amistad*'s historical relevance and inherent blind spots in AMISTAD America's cultural pluralist rhetoric forestalled productive alliances between the Sierra Leoneans and the Americans. And more significant, the underlying neoliberal ethos of AMISTAD America's NGO-status and of its tourism-oriented economic structure called into question the potential for the trans-Atlantic collaboration to secure effective structural transformation.

Productive dialogue among the participants in AMISTAD America's port visit was mitigated from the outset by the discrepant expectations about the value of slave trade monuments that often complicate interactions between Africans who live in communities with easily identifiable markers of the slave trade and their American, especially African American, visitors who are there to mourn the losses of history, place, family, and dignity inflicted by slavery. With their memories of the Sierra Leone and U.S. government's *Amistad* publications, Haffner and DeSouza-George's plays, and the 1993 public art movement, AMISTAD America's Sierra Leonean hosts carried aboard the recreated schooner a deeply entrenched and actively contested discourse that was situated largely outside the boundaries of AMISTAD America's declared domain.

For them, the 1839 uprising and its aftermath signified the globalized moral economy of canniballike excess consumption, the valences of transnational citizenship, postcolonial modernity's locus in the trans-Atlantic slave trade, and local and international governmental eagerness to coopt histories of resistance. In other words, since their government's publication of *Sierra Leonean Heroes* in 1987 the *Amistad* narrative had served as a central modality through which localized meanings of Sierra Leonean nationalism and claims to state power were contested. This is not to say that the *Amistad*-instigated debates did not acknowledge Sierra Leone's historical commonalities with the United States or the benefits of trans-Atlantic cultural and political organizing around the 1839 rebellion. Rather, it is to say that the port visit, much to AMISTAD America's credit, reignited twenty-year-old discussions with histories that were, however, too capillary and too rooted in local political demands to consistently or effectively incorporate the interests and agendas of the American visitors.

Take, for example, Wuru Bujay's January 7, 2008, commentary in *The Standard Times*, titled "Sierra Leone's National Heritage? Going . . . Going . . . Gone?" Bujay cites two incidents related to AMISTAD America's visit to critique the Ministry of Tourism and Monuments and Relics Commission for failing the nation's interests but shows no interest in developing a conversation with the American organization. First, Bujay points to the Americans' refusal to commence the official landing ceremony while the U.S. flag was touching the ground in order to castigate the ministry for neglecting the symbols with which the Sierra Leonean nation imagines itself as a coherent community. As if taking a page from Benedict Anderson's description of nationalist projects elsewhere, Bujay suggests that it would be "helpful to our national cohesion if as a people with a common focus" national symbols were standardized and respected ("Sierra Leone's National Heritage?"). Second, Bujay cites the example of a Sengbe Pieh monument rumored to have been donated from the United States for the occasion of the port visit as new proof of how the Ministry of Tourism fails persistently to capitalize on Sierra Leone's other international slave trade tourist draw, Bunce Island. He declares, "Bunce Island affords us the rare opportunity of actualizing our endless dreams of raking in millions from our tourist potentials, but certainly not in its present state and condition. Of course US Dollar Millionaires do want to see African historic sites but not at their peril" ("Sierra Leone's National Heritage?"). While this attention to preserving a historical monument of the slave trade no doubt resonated equally with the AMISTAD America representatives, the primarily pecuniary advantage Bujay foresees must have discomfited them no less equally. And even though Charlie Haffner, too, might bristle at Bujay's baldly money-grabbing proposition, Bujay's combined attention to symbols of the national imaginary and to the material benefits of commemorating the past speaks more to *Amistad Kata-Kata* and the 1993 public art movement than to the pluralist rhetoric of AMISTAD America. After all, it was the Mende priest in *Amistad Kata-Kata* who prescribed a more active approach to memorializing Sengbe Pieh and the other *Amistad* mutineers as a cure for Sierra Leone's economic ills.

AMISTAD America's representatives arrived with at least two distinctly American interpretive frameworks of their own, neither of which elicited easy recognition of or by their Sierra Leonean counterparts. The first is found in how Captain Emeritus Bill Pinkney approached Sierra Leone as many African American visitors to West Africa do to gain a "home in my soul" and allow him to identify with the "continent Africa as more than the birth place of those generations unknown to me" (Pinkney). In other words, he hoped to achieve psychic reparation for the enduring damage of slavery. As Saidiya Hartman points out in her evocative analysis of slave route tourism, the grief work and the necessary reverence for the object of loss required to repair the psychic breach of enslavement rests uneasily with the material reparations anticipated by their African counterparts. Part of the discrepancy stems from the fact that the African American "returnee" does not necessarily encounter "Africa in its contemporaneity" because "the present is eclipsed by an earlier moment—the event of captivity and the experience of enslavement in the Americas" (Hartman, "The Time of Slavery" 762–63). Furthermore, the monumentality of the Middle Passage means that the process of mourning—recognizing loss and replacing the lost object through identification—can recognize no more than the moment of rupture. Thus, mourning only attenuates loss and magnifies the alienation of guest from host (766–67). The *Amistad* replica's captain emeritus admits as much when, after proclaiming that he finally acquired the home in his soul, he simultaneously writes that in the Sierra Leoneans he sees "faces I had seen hundreds of times before, in Chicago, Jackson, Mississippi, Baltimore, everywhere I had seen black people in America" Pinkney). This example that Pinkney provides as evidence of his identification with the people of his newfound homeland suggests quite the opposite. When he looks at Sierra Leoneans he sees the African Americans with whom he shares his alienation. In effect,

Pinkney's declaration reaffirms his diasporic status, and, if it does not compound the rupture dividing him from someone like Wuru Bujay, it does little to bridge it.

AMISTAD America's cultural pluralist rhetoric represents the second of the Americans' fraught approaches. The language of intercultural dialogue and respect in AMISTAD America's mission statement reappeared repeatedly in the blog posts and other public documents produced by the organization during its visit. AMISTAD America Webmaster Wojtek Wocowski drew careful attention, for instance, to the interfaith welcome ceremony, noting in particular how a local Imam prayed in front of a U.S. flag for the Americans' safety (Wocowski). *Amistad* Captain Eliza Garfield, in turn, suggested that she and her hosts enjoyed a mutually respectful and level interchange when she tells of how the Sierra Leoneans' "smiles, their laughter and their direct questions (What are you doing for Sierra Leone?) keep all of us going throughout each long hot day" (Garfield). This kind of pluralism, however, celebrates difference without attending adequately to the enduring structural inequalities that produce those differences. The question Garfield cites, "What are you doing for Sierra Leone?" suggests that the Americans' rhetoric did not translate to many of the Sierra Leoneans, or if it did, it was resisted as if international recognition and respect were insufficient to improving their immediate material conditions. In fact, unofficial Sierra Leonean responses to the *Amistad* port visit underscore the degree to which Sierra Leoneans were unwilling to concede the erasure of the structural differences separating them from their American counterparts. While Freetown's *Awoko* newspaper supportively reprinted AMISTAD America's claim that the port visit would generate important "international recognition" for Sierra Leone for something other than "blood diamonds and the brutal civil war" ("U.S. Schooner Arrives Tomorrow"), in another article it divulged that "many assembled at the wharf grumbled that African American descendants of slaves are better off than Sierra Leoneans" ("Sierra Leonean Onboard Replica Slave Ship").[4] Even Sam S. Sesay's winning essay in the U.S. Embassy-sponsored contest highlighted global structural inequalities over the kind of pluralism promulgated by AMISTAD America. The Government Model Secondary School pupil explained that he admired the mutineers for asserting their liberty but also "for the simple fact that these Africans were stock illiterate, they however defended themselves in the white man's Court of Law . . . in a foreign land amongst strangers" and "for their aptitude in learning a foreign language—both spoken and written English—in so short a period whilst in detention in the United States" ("U.S. Embassy Awards Students"). Taken together, *Awoko*'s report, Sesay's essay, and Garfield's aside point to the chasm separating AMISTAD America's multicultural rhetoric from the Sierra Leoneans' insistence on highlighting the stark geopolitical asymmetries of economic privilege and sociopolitical security separating Sierra Leoneans from Americans of all races.[5]

To what extent guest and host heard each across the gulf of their discrepant expectations and interpretive frameworks remains unclear. Charlie Haffner complained that ultimately "the exercise was more an American thing—planned, implemented from America. The ship and crew came along with their agenda and we only fitted [sic] in between" (personal correspondence July 7, 2010). As a writer whose *Amistad* play targeted the intersection of U.S. and Sierra Leonean political hegemonies, Haffner is equally quick to spread the blame to his own government for welcoming the AMISTAD American crew as little more than a "courtesy" and for failing to recognize the cultural and economic investments that could be made by actively memorializing the slave trade past (personal correspondence July 7, 2010). Furthermore, Haffner laments that apart from the large crowds that gathered for the ship tours, the museum exhibit was "not well attended" and that in general the event was "not as big as it would have been if it happened in Ghana or Senegal who [sic] understand what an event of this nature . . . means politically and socio-economically" (personal correspondence July 7, 2010). This last point should be read skeptically, of course, but the first two critiques are enlightening for how they suggest that the American and Sierra Leonean *Amistad* performances during the port visit were staged in significant part for each other, not with each other. No doubt the thousands of visitors to the *Amistad* replica benefited greatly by learning more about the material culture of the slave trade and about local histories of resistance to it. But for as earnestly as Haffner and AMISTAD America might have envisioned a collaborative cross-border cultural encounter, productive engagement was mitigated by prerogatives rooted in separate national histories and material circumstances and in the discrepant ideological positions engendered by those prerogatives.

Yet, despite their different expectations of the port visit, AMISTAD America and Sierra Leoneans such as Charlie Haffner and Wuru Bujay expressed a shared faith in the redemptive power of slave-route tourism. From the moment that AMISTAD America announced its plans to build the $2 million, seventy-seven-foot vessel with nineteenth-century methods in dockyards open to fee-paying audiences visiting the living history museum of Mystic, Connecticut, it located itself securely in the matrices of global tourism. Haffner's praise for Ghana's and Senegal's slave-routes tourist infrastructure commitments and his chagrin over Sierra Leone's failure to pursue a similar development program align him more closely with AMISTAD America than his critiques would otherwise indicate. Likewise, Bujay's desire to see "US Dollar Millionaires" flood Sierra Leone's slave-trade monuments is not altogether different from AMISTAD America's reliance on the entry fees at its home port. Tourism does not, however, lead consistently to the cultural or economic practices capable of radically transforming current structural geopolitical inequalities. Tourism's structural requirements favor the neoliberal rhetoric of multiculturalism and commodify experience in such a way as to turn what could be a substantive, systematic critique of historical structural inequalities into a prepackaged, individualized experience of penitence, salvation, and reconciliation.[6] Thus, my second reason for focusing on AMISTAD America's port visit is because it highlights the dangers facing the *Amistad* rebellion's contemporary artist-activists as they develop a discourse of the future. Neoliberal capitalism's ability to appropriate the language of memorialization may, in fact, prove to be the most intractable impediment to the development of a transnational political practice, and potentially the most resistant to the summons entailed in the question, "What are you doing for Sierra Leone?"

The narrative and performative strategies employed by museums dedicated to slavery and the slave trade, as AMISTAD America's recreated schooner is, often represent the violence of enslavement in ways that minimize that violence and depoliticize the mourning they otherwise so effectively generate. Consider, for example, the dynamics that emerge at the popular slave barraccoons in Ghana, a country that Charlie Haffner holds in such high esteem for marrying tourism and memorialization. The sign at the entryway of Ghana's Elmina Castle reads, "In everlasting memory of the anguish of our ancestors. May those who died rest in peace. May those who return find their roots. May humanity never again perpetrate such injustice against humanity. We the living vow to uphold this" (qtd. in Hartman, "The Time of Slavery" 758).[7]

The invocation, and ones similar to it in Senegal and in AMISTAD America's rhetoric, implores the tourist to remember as an act of redress and simultaneously as insurance against future injustice. As Saidiya

Hartman notes, such mourning can function as a powerful "counternarrative to the exclusions of U.S. national history and a personal seizure and appropriation of the narrative resources made available by tourism" (769). But mourning, still so necessary for expressing the grief over wrongs that have not yet ended, also risks obliterating "the other through identification" and minimizing "the very terror it sets out to represent through . . . mundane reenactments," risks only exacerbated by the market requirements of a tourist economy in which "atrocity becomes a commodity for transnational consumption" (771, 773, 760). In other words, the individuated experience of mourning and consumption generated by tourism's structural demands runs counter to slave-route tourism's imperative to forge a collective politics in opposition to globalized structural inequalities.

For AMISTAD America, the problem of individuated and commodified mourning is exacerbated by its imbrication as a de facto nongovernmental organization with emergent regimes of neoliberal governmentality. Insofar as AMISTAD America assumes the responsibility for historical education from a state that increasingly wants to privatize schooling, it is, effectively, an NGO. Charles R. Hale contends that the "cultural project" of neoliberalism is "to harness and redirect the abundant political energy of cultural rights activism" through NGOs precisely like AMISTAD America (Hale 496). Like other nongovernmental organizations, AMISTAD America endeavors to channel activist impulses toward social change, but, like other NGOs, it also actively competes for finances and expertise from the private sector and otherwise operates more like private-sphere corporations than state enterprises or the activist communities that typically launch nongovernmental organizations in the first place (Abélès 249). This expansion of a market logic into NGO management practices has only been exceeded by the proliferation of NGOs themselves as neoliberal rationalities have assumed a dominant place in political culture globally (Park and Richards 1319). As states shed social services, NGOs—and private enterprises, where there is money to be made—take up the burden. Hale asserts that NGOs have become so essential for the operations of neoliberal governmentality, in fact, as to proclaim: "If, under classic liberalism, the quintessential agent of discipline is the Panoptic state penitentiary, under neoliberalism, it is the professionalized NGO" (Hale 496). To be fair, AMISTAD America is hardly alone in its reproduction of neoliberalism through its NGO operations; Charlie Haffner and Raymond DeSouza-George regularly accept commissions for educational plays from NGOs as a way to support their artistic projects and are thus complicit.

Entwined as slave-route tourism and NGO operations are in AMISTAD America's cultural practice and in Charlie Haffner's vision for tourist development projects, they magnify the hazard neoliberal rationalities pose to the political visions expressed in the majority of *Amistad* texts examined in this book. As the language of management, privatization, self-care, and choice, along with market rationalities generally, permeate further into everyday life, resistance to the idea that individuals are entirely responsible for their well-being becomes increasingly difficult. The refusal by neoliberals to view chronic impoverishment and insecurity historically elides the way that the slave trade enabled select populations in select countries to amass the capital with which they secured long-term economic dominance over the communities from whom they stole labor and other material recourses. Under neoliberalism, the commodification of individual human bodies cannot be taken as a fundamental component of the psychological process of enslavement—or, in DeSouza-George's case, as a root cause of Sierra Leone's civil war—because neoliberal rationalities reduce bodily commodification to yet another market opportunity to be exploited for personal, rather than collective, advantage. Nor can oppositional diasporic temporal and spatial formations easily challenge the particularisms of race and nation because neoliberal hegemony produces its own globalized forms of chrononormativity and networked spatiality. Taken together, neoliberalism's market logic and its insistence on the individual as the primary unit of political and economic identity further erode the unfinished promise of epistemological decolonization. Apart from obfuscating the historical and structural hermeneutics that have been so central to decolonizing projects, neoliberalism also renders collective organizing, action, and self-representation as quaint artifacts of a past, misguided age. Thus, consent to this neoliberal logic reproduces inequality, and *The Broken Handcuff* and Clifford Mason's Joe Cinquez novels risk giving way to Steven Spielberg's neoliberal parable of individual salvation.

My goal here is not to dismiss the efforts of organizations such as AMISTAD America or of cultural activists such as Charlie Haffner to make the *Amistad* history the foundation for new daily economic and political practices. Nor is it to reject tourism or NGO projects out of hand. It is not even to suggest that neoliberal capitalism is the only threat facing African and African American communities seeking to fulfill the promise of justice that motivated Sengbe Pieh and his fellow mutineers to take up cane knives and assert their freedom. Rather, by highlighting the limits of slave-route tourism and by emphasizing neoliberal capitalism's pernicious appropriation of the rhetoric of liberty and equality to exacerbate dependence and inequality, my desire is to highlight the principal shared risks that Sierra Leoneans and Americans face as they look unsteadily on the future. Moreover, it is to propose that these common risks are more insidious than the discrepant prerogatives that mitigated the collaborative possibilities of AMISTAD America's Freetown visit. Where a collective process that embraces alterity can minimize the negative impact of differential privilege and history, a logic that erases historical and structural difference in the name of individual liberty and equality nullifies altogether the claims that the past makes on the future. One need look no further than Steven Spielberg's *Amistad* for an example of how dangerously neoliberal rationalities empty historical slave rebellions of their power to articulate the will to collective freedom. Taken together, AMISTAD America's neoliberal organizational structure, Charlie Haffner's openness to tourism, and the ease with which Steven Spielberg coopts the *Amistad* story to celebrate neoliberal individualism underscore the dangers that the authors and readers of *Amistad* texts must confront if they are to produce a future-oriented politics that avoids getting caught, like Walter Benjamin's angel of history, with its back turned to the future. Future dangers demand rebellious futures, and rebellious futures demand a careful accounting of the past's claims on the present.

By attending to the shortcomings of tourism and NGO educational projects and to the looming threat of neoliberal rationalities, I ultimately want to refocus on the narratives themselves. While slave-route tourism offers the potential to translate memorial practice into tangible future-oriented action, by no means is it the only logical process by which to do so, and it is certainly not the most viable tactic for resisting neoliberal hegemony. Expressive culture narrative, however, gives writers and artists tools to deconstruct hegemonic rationalities, to enact new interpretive paradigms, and to imagine alternate realities to the lived world. The aesthetic temporal, spatial, and character liberties permitted to creative culture producers may not supplant the accounts produced by rigorous disciplinary historical practice, but they supplement them by generating configurations of possibility unavailable to standard historical narrative. In this respect, historical fictions such as the *Amistad* texts are adamantly future-oriented. As historical narratives, the majority of the *Amistad* texts discussed here ethically impel their audiences to reimagine the past and present of the social world around them in order to envision just futures. At root, they demand an accounting of how individuals and communities build new societies from the wreckage of the slave trade, colonialism, political independence, and civil war, which is to demand more broadly how communities worldwide construct new socialities in the wake of global capitalism's reorganization of nearly every aspect of daily life. By making these demands, the writers and visual artists compel us to ask how we can make a just society from the radical inequalities that shape our world. In the end, all of the plays, novels, paintings, and films explored in these pages implore us to imagine the rebellious futures that loom on the horizon.

Notes

Introduction

1. Described in Opala, "*Ecstatic Renovation!*"10.

2. Notably, the other monumental text to initiate the study of slave rebellions from the perspective of the enslaved, Herbert Aptheker's *American Negro Slave Revolts*, followed *The Black Jacobins* just five years later, in 1943.

3. Several book-length studies analyze the literary and cultural "afterlives" of armed uprisings against enslavement. Mary Kemp Davis's *Nat Turner before the Bar of Judgment* and Albert Stone's *The Return of Nat Turner: History, Literature, and Cultural Politics in Sixties America*, for example, conceptualize the place of a discrete slave rebellion in American cultural and racial politics. Taking a comparative approach to investigating the relationship between slave rebellions and modernity, Adéẹ̀kọ́'s *The Slave's Rebellion* enlists Paul Gilroy's revision of Hegel's master-slave dialectic to compare subject formation in Yoruba and African diaspora narratives about slave resistance. In *The Slumbering Volcano: American Slave Ship Revolts and the Production of Rebellious Masculinity*, Maggie Montesinos Sale examines the rhetoric of revolution and heroic masculinity in nineteenth-century narratives about the *Amistad* and *Creole* shipboard slave rebellions. Jack Shuler's *Calling Out Liberty: The Stono Slave Rebellion and the Universal Struggle for Human Rights* explores how the Slave Code, written in response to the 1739 uprising on the Stono Plantation, structured virtually all subsequent literary and cultural analyses of race and freedom in the United States. Though it is not about a slave rebellion per se, Jennifer Wenzel's *Bulletproof: Afterlives of Anticolonial Prophecy in South Africa and Beyond* traces the cultural afterlives of the millenarian Xhosa cattle killing movement in nineteenth-century South Africa. Wenzel offers especially valuable insights for how to read the complex maneuvers by which later writers translate the failure of an uprising into the as-yet unrealized promise of a dream deferred. The Haitian Revolution, of course, remains the perpetual subject of artistic production and scholarly inquiry.

4. For a detailed analysis of how Bontemps reads Gabriel Prosser's compromised leadership as a commentary on 1930s radical organizing, see Adéẹ̀kọ,

chapter 4. For more on how Bontemps's novel *Drums at Dusk* figures the Haitian Revolution as a commentary on the threat of fascism in the 1930s, see Thompson.

5. If William Styron's Pulitzer-Prizing-winning novel *The Confessions of Nat Turner* continues to draw more scorn than praise, it is because his civil rights/black power-era novel refuses to read its protagonist's rebellion as being motivated by a politicized will to freedom. By reading enslavement as an individuated experience of sexual neurosis and psychological insecurity, as Styron does, Nat Turner cannot produce a structural critique of chattel slavery or imagine a utopian transformation of human relations. For more on the Styron controversy and on the cultural afterlives of the Nat Turner rebellion, see Davis and Stone.

6. The following list includes only those works not addressed directly elsewhere in this book. From 1968 to 1973, John Quincy Adams' and Roger Baldwin's 1840 Supreme Court arguments were republished, as were John Barber's 1840 chronicle, Emma Sterne's 1953 narrative, and William Owens' 1956 history of the revolt; at least two children's books on the revolt were rushed to bookstores (Kromer, *Amistad;* Hunt, *The Amistad Mutiny*) as were two new popular and scholarly monographs (Martin, *The Amistad Affair*; Cable, *Black Odyssey*); a Manhattan art gallery featuring African American artists opened as the Cinque Gallery; John A. Williams and Charles F. Harris published two collections of writings on black history and culture under the names *Amistad 1* and *Amistad 2*; and countless African Americans added "Cinque" to their given or adopted African names. The 1980s and 1990s saw the publication of another batch of histories (Chambers and Lee, Jurmain, Steady, Zeinert), an illustrated history (Golden Legacy), plays (Thorpe, Peters, Maddy), visual art (Bah, Hamilton), and novels (Pate, Pesci). The only other period with a comparable interest in the rebellion was the mid-1930s through World War II, with works published or staged by Muriel Rukeyser, Owen Dodson, Robert Hayden, Bucklin Moon, and Blair Niles.

7. For a survey of the literature on the technology and organization of the slave ship, see Rediker. My account here of the *Amistad* incident necessarily simplifies what was a highly complex contest of claims, counterclaims, behind-the-scenes machinations, and media interventions. For detailed histories, see Jones, *Mutiny on the Amistad,* and Osagie, *The Amistad Revolt.*

8. Given that the *Amistad* legal case focused primarily on questions about international commerce and separation of powers, it provided little by way of precedent for subsequent legal considerations of slavery. In this way, the *Amistad* case was significantly different from the 1739 Stono rebellion in South Carolina, which led the South Carolina government to craft the Negro Act, a comprehensive legal code that institutionalized the practice of chattel slavery and "would become a model for slave codes in the American colonies and in the United States for years to come, providing another pillar of support for the plantation regime" (Shuler 4).

9. Such forms of display had begun at the very moment of the Africans' landing in New London, Connecticut, when the prison warden designed a scheme to charge visitors a penny and a half to gawk at the captives. While still in prison, a wax model maker nearly suffocated one of the Africans in his attempt to cast a mold of the man's head for a traveling display (Dinsmore 53).

10. For more on the relationship between missionary activity and colonialism, see Mudimbe.

11. For more on how historians have grappled with Sengbe Pieh's rumored participation in the slave trade, see Jones, "Cinque of the *Amistad* a Slave Trader?"

12. For useful historical analyses of Atlantic capitalism, slavery, and modernity, see Piot, Baucom, and Shaw. For histories of Africa's involvement in the Atlantic slave trade, see Thornton, *Africa and Africans in the Making of the Atlantic World, 1400–1800,* and Miller, *Way of Death.* See also Smallwood, Lovejoy, and Inikori and Engerman.

13. It is worth noting on this point that Josee Lahai received nearly all of the supplies for his paintings of Sengbe Pieh and other figures from Christian missionaries based on a medical mission ship docked nearby (Lahai, 2000).

14. For a brief sampling of the scholarship on the Haitian Revolution and the Enlightenment, see Garraway, Nesbitt, Fischer, and Buck-Morss.

15. See Mamdani. The most influential writings on patrimonial politics in Sierra Leone include the essays collected in Ibrahim Abdullah et al., *Between Democracy and Terror.* See also Reno and Richards.

16. I am thinking here of arguments made by Gikandi, Ferguson, and George.

17. Sale also explores the cultural responses to the *Amistad* slave rebellion, but she focuses almost exclusively on cultural production in the immediate aftermath of the rebellion and the U.S. legal battle.

18. My attention to the reading and viewing publics of popular literatures has been reinforced and nuanced in large part by Stephanie Newell's introduction to her edited volume, *Readings in African Popular Fiction.*

Chapter 1

1. Foster enjoyed widespread support from the Bay Area's black community, including the Black Panthers, but was targeted by the SLA for allegedly authorizing an identity card system for Oakland school students. To the SLA the scheme smacked of fascism and appeared to be designed to inure black youth to repressive surveillance technologies (Avery and McLellan 133–35). The Foster assassination drew widespread condemnation and scorn from the Left, which tended to view the action as adventurist, elitist, and wholly irresponsible. Speaking on behalf of the National Alliance against Racism and Oppression, Angela Davis

declared, "[W]e dissociate ourselves entirely from this sort of thing," and Black Panther Huey Newton "denounced the SLA as 'enemies of the people'" (qtd. in "The Hostage: A Game of Terror" 20). Despite a few accolades for the Hearst kidnapping, the SLA never shed the taint it acquired after the Foster killing.

2. I borrow "guerrilla theater" from Vin McLellan and Paul Avery's SLA history, *The Voices of Guns* (17). The phrase, however, was bandied about regularly to characterize the SLA, appearing in articles from the left-wing newspaper *The San Francisco Phoenix* (Hinckle 12) to the mainstream serial *Newsweek* ("The Hostages: A Game of Terror" 18). See also Bryan and "20 Questions We'd Ask Symbionese."

3. The rumor that Cinque worked as a slave trader upon his return to West Africa has plagued *Amistad* scholars for decades. The first documented citation that Cinque entered the slave trade was in William A. Owens' 1953 novel *Slave Mutiny: The Revolt on the Schooner* Amistad, although rumors had circulated prior to the novel's publication and gained widespread currency in 1969 when C. Vann Woodward repeated it in his presidential address to the annual meeting of the Organization of American Historians (Jones, "Cinqué of the Amistad a Slave Trader?" 3, no. 7; McFeely 6). In pursuing the debate, *Amistad* historian Howard Jones scrutinized extant missionary records and Owens' meticulous notes and found no conclusive evidence—nary any evidence at all—to prove the assertion one way or the other (6). For more on the debate, see Jones, "Cinqué of the Amistad a Slave Trader?" and Osagie, *The Amistad Revolt*.

4. Henegan's assertion that Cinque entered the slave trade generated so many letters to the editor in protest, that *Dawn* ran a follow-up story by Henegan five months later that pursued the issue further, concluding still that Cinque did likely work as a slave trader upon his return (Henegan, "Did Cinque Enter the Slave Trade?" 2).

5. Hinckle points out that Hearst's namesake "by all accounts of Che scholarship left to right, was a KGB agent with a crush on Che who nonetheless dutifully spied on him for her bureaucratic Russian bosses" (1).

6. See Shank.

7. Magee and Davis were charged and, initially, tried jointly. Magee's legal strategy differed radically from Davis'. Magee forced the dismissal of successive judges, often without the prior knowledge and against the wishes of Davis and her legal team. Where Davis wanted to speed along the pretrial phase so that she could get bail, Magee, who was facing the death penalty, sought to stretch the case out as long as possible. Also, Davis felt that she could get a more favorable verdict in the state courts, and Magee hoped to get his case into the federal system where he believed he would have a better chance to argue that his 1963 conviction should be overturned and that he could not be convicted for the Marin case because he never should have been in the courtroom in the first place. Eventually, their cases were severed. For more on their judicial strategies, see *New York Times* coverage by Stern and Caldwell.

8. Magee flatly denies the accusation of attempted rape (Thiel, chapter 2). Given how frequently whites falsely accused black men of rape as a mechanism of social control, it is likely that Magee was falsely imprisoned for speaking out against established white authority. And he does not deny his tendency to speak out loudly and aggressively against racial injustice: "When I was about twelve years old down in Louisiana I used to see cases where a white man kick a nigger in the ass just for fun. For some reason or another, I couldn't tell you why . . . I don't go for that . . . If I see it I try to stop it—don't care if they got fifty guns—I don't allow no dogs to drive over me, I still don't" ("Interview with Dave Stevens, August 18, 1971").

9. Even though the armed courtroom takeover was preceded by numerous gun battles between the police and the Black Panthers and bombings by the Weathermen, for the Left it represented a bold "new stage of combat" and "one of the heaviest military actions" enacted in its ambitious revolutionary struggle ("Ruchell vs. Reagan" 12). Coming shortly after the Pentagon Papers revealed a government program to conceal the extent of the U.S. military campaign in Southeast Asia and just three months after the killings by National Guardsmen and police of a dozen unarmed protestors at Kent State University, Jackson State College, and in Augusta, Georgia, the courtroom takeover and hostage taking appeared to be a first step in turning "the prerevolutionary situation" that was believed to characterize global political relations at that moment into full-fledged revolution (Katsiaficas viii). Perhaps the radical Left newspaper *The Berkeley Tribe* captured the extravagant rhetoric best when it declared, "These were the first prisoners-of-war to attempt liberating themselves and others with guns in hand, consciously deciding that death-in-struggle is better than life-in-solitary. That they fell minutes later, killed by maniacs who would rather unleash a slaughter than allow their system to be defied, makes little difference" ("We Are the Revolution" 2). See also "Eulogy to Three Murdered Revolutionaries."

10. Special thanks go to Claude Marks who first introduced me to Ruchell Magee's use of the *Amistad* history and for giving me access to the collection of audio and print materials on both Magee and the Symbionese Liberation Army that he has collected for the Freedom Archives, an audio archive chronicling the American radical Left located in San Francisco, California.

11. See the introduction to this work, note 6, for details.

12. According to Avery and McLellan, in the early 1970s, the California Department of Corrections boasted the title of being the third largest "unified prison system in the world—save only the national systems of China and the Soviet Union" (47), and under Governor Reagan's and his successors' direction, its population would only balloon over the next three decades.

13. On account of the perceived failure of the courts to provide fair and impartial trials to black defendants, point number eight of the Black Panthers' ten-point platform demanded the release of all African American prisoners from U.S. penitentiaries and jails (The Black Panthers, 163). See also R. Chrisman.

14. John Cluchette, one of the Soledad Three accused with George Jackson of murdering a white prison guard, declared: "Under the existing social order men and women are sent to prison for labor (free labor) and further economical gain (money) by the state. Where else can you get a full day's work for two to sixteen cents an hour, and these hours become an indeterminate number of years? This is slave labor in the 20th century America" (qtd. in Cummins 194). It should be noted that one of the major rallying points for the Left was the indeterminate sentencing law. Under indeterminate sentencing, individuals convicted of crimes were sentenced for an indeterminate period of time wherein release would be determined by prison staff at such time as the prisoner demonstrated his or her rehabilitation. The policy gave prison authorities tremendous Orwellian power to extort "good behavior" and unduly punish individuals who voiced criticisms of any kind. The abolition of indeterminate sentencing was one of the central demands made by prison activists and was discontinued in California in 1977 (Cummins 253). See also, "Prisoners in Rebellion: The Folsom Prisoners Manifesto of Demands and Anti-Oppression Platform" (65–74). For more on the relationship between incarceration and slavery, see Political Prisoners of Parish Prison (1) and Seale (2).

15. Magee and Larry West (also known as Maharibi Muntu) jointly authored at least two essays, "Ruchell Magee Speaks Out" for *The Black Panther* and "The Right to Kill," which appeared in *The Berkeley Tribe*. Magee's supporters dismissed the contention made by the mainstream media that West was the brains behind Magee's political thinking and legal work (Ruchell Magee Committee for Black Prisoners 41). The committee takes pains to cast Magee as a maligned revolutionary and dismisses the charge, quoting West himself as no less an authority. In my opinion, there is little to gain by deciphering Magee's thinking from West's. Clearly, West influenced Magee. Magee found West to have useful opinions and a valuable voice, otherwise he would not likely have worked with him on the essays. Very few intellectual projects are undertaken in isolation from others, and Magee was developing his ideas about incarceration and enslavement in San Quentin at a moment when, according to one inmate, prison yard status was based on one's theoretical knowledge about revolution (Cummins 138). Magee produced his texts in a milieu of secret study groups and contraband copies of Mao, Fanon, and Marx and likely formed his critical frameworks within a larger circle of readers than just West.

16. For additional information about Magee's ideological position, see his "Statement to the Court," "Letters to Angela," "His Own Story," "Pigs Cut Down Judge Haley," and "Wake Up Oppressed People (Open Address to the President.)" See also B. Barber; Kaufman, "Ruchell and Angela," "Prisoners of War," and "Free Ruchell Magee."

17. A growing body of scholarship on postcolonial and ethnic minority crime fiction points to the routine rejection of narrative closure and

legal justice in the works of these writers. See Siddiqi, Christine Matzke and Susanne Mülheisen, Christian, Gosselin, Fischer-Hornung and Meuller, and Soitos. For a more general analysis of the idelogical work of the detective novel, see Porter.

18. Historian Konrad Tuchscherer contends that the name 'Sengbe Pieh' is itself a historical anachronism no less alienating than the name 'Cinque.' While he believes that 'Sengbe' is likely the revolt leader's birth name, he notes that 'Pieh' only shows up in the historical record in the second half of the twentieth century and that it was unlikely that individuals like Sengbe would have had surnames as they are used in contemporary Sierra Leone (pers. correspondance).

19. For the most complete and nuanced analysis of the RUF/SL's intellectual genealogy and self-serving rhetoric, see Abdullah et al., *Between Democracy and Terror*.

20. In the campaign, dozens of young male artists worked alongside volunteer clean-up crews to claim long stretches of public space, often found along the perimeter walls of schools, government buildings, and even the national prison, and filled it with portraits of political and cultural leaders of Sierra Leone's and Africa's past.

21. For more detailed analysis of youth as a social category in West Africa, see Cruise O'Brien. For a detailed historical and ethnographic account of Sierra Leone's urban youth associations, see Nunley. See also Opala, "*Ecstatic Renovation!*" (5–6).

22. The artist Alusine Bangura chose to place his portraits of nationalist heroes and political martyrs on the outer walls of the Public Works Department, a decision that is profound in both its irony and its idealism. Not so fondly nicknamed the Public Waste Department by Freetown residents, the PWD was an inefficient and corrupt institution whose failure during the APC era to keep cities clean and streets serviceable signified for many one of the most blatant symbols of the country's problems. Indicative of the level of corruption in the agency, Will Reno notes that one government official diverted bulldozers from the PWD to the Kono district for personal use on his diamond mining plot (108). Bangura's selection of this site for his paintings signifies deliberate irony for its juxtapositions of anticolonial, antislavery, and nationalist figures with an institution that had long enabled greed and abuse of power. The choice also indicates a great deal about how Bangura and his fellow Portuguese Town Youth Organization members hoped Sierra Leone could remake its institutions with the end of the APC domination of the government. Bangura's heroes, all lionized for their selflessness and dedication to the greater good of society, mark the civic institution with the none-too-subtle reminder about its purpose to serve not the individuals selected to run it, but the community at large. (I thank Abu Bakarr Kalokoh for reminding me of the PWD nickname.)

23. In this respect, the public art movement paralleled a similar effort, named "Set/Setal" that had taken place in Senegal a few years prior. There, youth covered public walls with elaborate murals drawing from similar sets of local and global imagery. For more on Set/Setal, see Diouf and Bugincourt and Diallo.

24. See McElroy for a history of Jocelyn's portrait.

25. Originally, Jocelyn's portrait contributed to the narrative strategies developed by the abolitionist-supported Amistad Defense Committee to cast the mutineers as noble patriots fighting for the preservation and sanctity of individual liberty (Sale chapter 2; McElroy et al. 35). African American businessperson, philanthropist, and abolitionist James Forten funded Jocelyn's work and contributed the painting to the Amistad Defense Committee.

26. ECOMOG was the peace-keeping force of the Economic Community of West African States (ECOWAS), developed initially to stabilize neighboring Liberia after Charles Taylor and other militia leaders launched military campaigns to topple the Doe regime. Taylor provided material support to Foday Sankoh's RUF/SL, in part, to punish the Sierra Leonean government for allowing ECOMOG to base its operations in Sierra Leone.

27. For the finalized Bangura image with text, see Opala, " 'Ecstatic Renovation!' Street Art Celebrating Sierra Leone's 1992 Revolution," 203.

28. Opala, "*Ecstatic Renovation!*" 4.

Chapter 2

1. Having little factual basis on which to explain their bondage, enslaved Africans often believed their white slavers to be cannibals, and the *Amistad* revolt was just one of many motivated by the fear of being eaten by whites. Alan Rice documents that fears of cannibalism sparked the revolt aboard the *Prince of Orange* off the coast of San Domingo in 1737 when more than one hundred slaves jumped overboard, of whom thirty-three drowned (Rice 112). Likewise, the 1729 revolt on board the *Annibal* occurred after the slaves heard rumors that they were to be eaten (112). Guest details some of the broader metaphoric links between cannibalism and identity, as does Nunes.

2. *Sierra Leonean Heroes* was published in an expanded version with fifty biographies a year later. My citations refer to the longer 1988 edition.

3. Prior to this publication the only attention given to the revolt in terms of its relevance to Sierra Leonean history appeared in an article by historian Arthur Abraham, "Sengbe Pieh: A Neglected Hero?" published in *The Journal of the Historical Society of Sierra Leone* in 1978. Given the very limited readership of the journal, the article did not have the kind of impact that *Sierra Leonean Heroes* would.

4. The full text of the biography reads:

Sengbe Pieh was a Mende farmer whose extraordinary courage in resisting slavery earned him a lasting place in the histories of Sierra Leone and the United States.

Sengbe was captured in his rice farm in January, 1839 and ultimately sold to a Spanish slave trader near modern Sulima. He was then transported across the Atlantic to Havana, Cuba and sold at an auction, along with forty-eight other Sierra Leoneans, to a Spanish sugar planter named Jose Ruiz. The Spaniard placed his slaves aboard a ship called the Amistad for a short trip to his plantation, but on the third day at sea, Sengbe pulled a loose spike from the deck and broke his chains and those of his fellow slaves. He discovered cane knives in the cargo hold, armed his men, mostly Mende, and led them onto the deck. They killed the captain and drove the crew overboard, and then Sengbe ordered their would-be master to sail the Amistad back to Sierra Leone. The Spaniard tried to trick the Africans by turning the ship toward Cuba at night, but a storm drove the Amistad northeast along the coast of the United States. Sengbe and his men were captured by the United States Navy off Long island [sic], New York, and charged with murder and piracy, but a dedicated group of American abolitionists came immediately to their defence.

The Americans formed the "Amistad Committee" which recruited prominent lawyers to argue for the captured Mendes who were finally freed when former President John Quincy Adams argued their case before the United States Supreme Court. Sengbe Pieh, also known as James [sic] Cinque in the United States, became a celebrity in the free Northern States, and thousands of people bought his portrait and paid to see him speak on the evils of slavery. Sengbe returned with his men to Sierra Leone in January, 1842 together with the first of many American missionaries to come to these shores. In the United States the Amistad Committee, originally set up for the defence of Sengbe and his fellow Mendes, continued to fight for an end to slavery and, after emancipation, set up hundreds of schools and colleges for the newly freed slaves.

Today, Sengbe's picture hangs in some public buildings and black colleges in the United States, and no history book on the American slavery era is complete without an account of his courageous deeds. Although still largely unknown in his own country, Sengbe Pieh deserves to be recognized as one of the most famous and influential Sierra Leoneans who ever lived. (30)

5. Though most copies of the book ended up in the hands of government ministers who distributed them as political favors—many of which in turn were sold for a profit—they were originally intended for free distribution to schools and school-aged children (Opala, "Ecstatic Renovation!" 8–9).

6. Let me emphasize that numerous individuals participated in the making of this text and fought to shape the book's message in ways that challenged Momoh's politicization of the project. For the purposes of this study, however, I am interested primarily in the way *Sierra Leonean Heroes* voices official governing power.

7. In his inauguration speech, Momoh declared a "New Order" for Sierra Leone, laying out the conditions for a project of constructive nationalism that called on all Sierra Leoneans at every level of society to prioritize their national identities over their ethnic, religious, and class affiliations, but moreover to not let personal greed hinder the nation-state's development (Momoh 11).

8. Stevens' shadow state accumulation left health, education, public works, and civil service infrastructures decimated around the country. By 1987, after two years of Momoh's presidency, Sierra Leone's life expectancy rate was the lowest in the world, and its levels of relative spending power and literacy were little better (United Nations Development Programme 128).

9. At the time of publication, *The Amistad Revolt* was available in its entirety at http://www.sierra-leone.org/heroes.html.

10. By telenovela, I am referring to the soap opera televisual form popular throughout Latin America. Like U.S. soaps, Latin American telenovelas and the Sierra Leonean plays of the 1980s dramatize romantic intrigue and familial conflict and depict a fantasy world of wealth, luxury, and upward class mobility. Unlike the open narrative of the U.S. form, the telenovela and these Sierra Leonean plays "roll to definite climatic endings" (Sturken and Cartwright 320).

11. Haffner walked a fine line with any depiction of political conflict. The previous president, Siaka Stevens, jailed a group of actors who staged a play on the nineteenth-century anticolonial leader Bai Bureh on the grounds of "inciting rebellion" (Opala, "Bai Bureh: The Making of a National Symbol" 2). Also during Stevens' reign, two other playwrights, (Pat) Yulisa Amadu Maddy with *Big Berrin* and John Kolosa Kargbo with *Poyotong Wahala*, overtly depicted government corruption and only thinly veiled their critiques of specific politicians and scandals. Maddy was imprisoned (Karefa-Smart 879, Etherton 334, Rowe 58), and more significantly, the government established a script approval office, thus bringing to a quick halt any theater critical of the government. When Momoh came to power in 1985, he relaxed government control over the theater community, which resulted in the number of theater groups swelling from just over a half dozen at the end of the Stevens' regime to nearly forty by 1988 (Kargbo 1892). However, in 1988, the Freetown municipal government shut down the city's premier theater, a two-thousand-seat hall, ostensibly because of the damage done to it

by its audiences (Karefa-Smart 880), although it was widely speculated that the move came about out of fear that drama posed too big of a threat to Momoh's weakly held hegemony. For a broader contextualization of this period in Sierra Leone, see Hollist and Cumale and Warritay. For a broader contextualization of political theater, see Kerr.

12. For more on this aspect of the play, see Osagie, *The Amistad Revolt.*

13. I am substituting page numbers for the traditional act/scene citations used for dramatic texts because the typescript copy of *Amistad Kata-Kata* that Haffner gave me marks act and scene changes with spacing rather than numbers, making it nearly impossible to determine actual acts and scenes.

14. The spelling of his name varies from account to account, though usually appearing as Grabo or Grabeau.

15. In my typescript copy, Sengbe does not insist on his birth name at the slave auction house, but he does in a recorded stage performance from 1990.

16. As a note about the staging, racial difference was marked primarily by clothing. The Spaniards were costumed in Western pants and jackets, and the *Amistad* Africans, in loin cloths. Additionally, whiteness was marked linguistically. The actors playing the Spaniards, curiously, inflected their English with what was commonly understood to be an American accent, rather than a Spanish-accented English.

17. These three lines comprise the chorus of a much longer narrative song about the *Amistad* revolt that Haffner's theater troupe wrote and performed regularly beginning as early as 1985 or 1986. This self-reference encodes yet another layer of intertextuality.

18. The importance of the symbol to the public identity of the party can be gauged by the fact the A.P.C.'s self-published history printed only a few years earlier was titled *The Rising Sun: A History of the All People's Congress Party of Sierra Leone.*

Chapter 3

1. For a historical overview of neoliberalism, see Harvey and Brown.

2. Laurie Oullette elucidates especially clearly, and with a welcome recognition of the comedy of her chosen text, how neoliberal technologies endeavor to produce self-disciplining citizens for the market-oriented state. The body of scholarship on neoliberal citizenship and the technologies of subject formation is too rich and extensive to catalog here.

3. For more on neoliberalism's cooptation of progressive multiculturalism, see Duggan.

4. Charles R. Hale argues that neoliberals also discovered they could harness the energies of racial and ethnic affinity groups by calling on them

to act as corporate entities with a stake in the neoliberal state rather than as counterhegemonic forces seeking to transform it (487).

5. For an extended development of this argument, see Goldberg, *The Threat of Race* and *Multiculturalism*.

6. See also Lim and Ngai.

7. To what degree these discourses actually operated in black communities or whether they have been magnified and overstated by a predominantly white media with its own anxieties about racial inequality and African American claims of persistent racism is not entirely clear. Certainly, it is easy to identify a hostile undercurrent (and a gleeful neoconservative voice) suggesting that hard-working, economically successful immigrants prove once and for all that African Americans overstate the negative impact of race. Moreover, to suggest that continental Africans are somehow historically immune from racism is to willfully disregard not just colonialism but a long history of pernicious representation in scholarly studies, political writing, creative literature, the popular media, and development discourse. For an expression of the generalized fascination with the new African immigration, see Roberts.

8. For a compelling analysis of liberal individualism in *Schindler's List*, see Loshitsky. For a contextualization of masculinity in Spielberg's earlier films, see Sexton.

9. In a *New York Times* Sunday Magazine feature, Spielberg said of his motives, " 'Well, we were already talking to Theo about slavery and where he came from and who his great-great grandparents might have been . . . So when I heard the story, I immediately thought that this was something I would be pretty proud to make, simply to say to my son, 'Look, this is about you' " (Dubner 231).

10. See also Mercer.

11. My brief discussion here simplifies the complex dynamics of race, masculinity, and citizenship at work. My thinking is additionally informed by, among others, Carby, Blount and Cunningham, Golden, Wallace, Gray, Harper, and Jeffords.

12. Styron's novel came under almost immediate attack, especially by African American writers, for pathologizing Nat Turner and all but dismissing the structural critiques of slavery that might have motivated the rebellion. For more on African American responses in the 1960s, see Clark and Friedman and Malin. For more recent scholarly assessments of the controversy and of Styron's troubling gendered characterization, see Davis, Stone, and Adéẹ̀kọ́.

13. In her work on the neoliberal undercurrents of reality television programming, Anna McCarthy makes a compelling argument about how the visual representation of trauma and suffering on such shows is structured to produce a privatized philanthropy rather than structural, societal change. Future scholarship might develop a similar argument about *Amistad*'s depiction of the mutineers' traumatized bodies.

14. A phenomenon of 1980s Reagan-era Hollywood cinema, the cross-racial buddy narrative has much older antecedents in the literature of James Fennimore Cooper, Mark Twain, and Herman Melville. By making the manly homosocial relationship unencumbered by domestic responsibility the privileged site for pursing the "higher ideals" of "Truth, Nature, and Innocence," the genre has long explored the utopian ideals of American identity (Wiegman 48–49). In Hollywood releases of the 1980s and '90s, such as *48 Hours*, *Beverly Hills Cop*, *Lethal Weapon*, and *Cry Freedom*, white and black male protagonists get thrown into "situations that they would have rather avoided, and in which they are interdependent and ultimately . . . come to understand each other to solve the poisonous problem of racial conflict" (Guerrero 242). Typically, narrative resolution in the buddy film results from the psychological maturation of the white male character, which comes from his interactions with his black buddy. In light of the close friendship that forms between the two, the men prove that multiracial societies with a history of racial conflict can, in fact, achieve racial equality. Simultaneously, however, the genre typically subordinates an idealized black masculinity to the subjective needs of the white male protagonists, thereby reinscribing patriarchal racial hierarchy. The black men in these works are customarily uncomplicated and perfectly self-assured in their identities; in short, they require nothing and gain nothing from their buddy adventures. The equality shared at film's end, thus, masks a deeper persistent racial inequality. *Amistad*'s narrative departs only marginally.

15. The children he refers to are not his own, but the three girls and one boy who were also aboard the *Amistad* at the time of the revolt.

16. The rebel leaders infantilization and move back toward authority through acts of self-discovery also call to mind Valerie Smith's arguments about African American narrative.

17. Perhaps the most famous example of this rhetorical demand for manhood as a civil rights tactic came during the 1968 Memphis Sanitation Workers Strike where picketing employees wore clapboards and carried signs reading, "I AM A MAN." For an analysis of the gendered implications of the striking workers' discursive tactics, see Estes.

18. I would argue that the abolitionist's primary narrative function in both works is to situate what is otherwise a story about global trade and Africanness in a firmly American milieu. The media and academic commentary accompanying the film attests to how successfully Spielberg fashioned the narrative as a uniquely American story. As Spielberg's first directorial effort following his landmark World War Two holocaust drama *Schindler's List*, *Amistad* generated a wealth of commentary in excess of its break-even box office returns. Apart from the coverage of Chase-Riboud's lawsuit and the usual film reviews that accompany a major Hollywood release, discussion of the film focused almost exclusively on the conjoined questions of historical accuracy and its contribution

to understanding African American historical experience. In op-ed pieces, letters to the editor, and radio talk shows, historians, creative writers, cultural critics, and the like debated such topics as the relevance of the rebellion to African American history and debates on race (Adjaye; Fontenot Jr.; Forman Shockley II; Dargis et. al.; and Thornton, "*Amistad* and African Slavery") and problems of historical representation, including the gross mischaracterization of attorney Roger Baldwin and the Christian abolitionists who spearheaded the *Amistad* defense campaign, and the historical liberties taken in depicting John Quincy Adams' meeting with Cinqué (Dalzell, Lemisch, Briley, Goldstein, Bresnick, Nagel, Vidal).

19. It is difficult to discern to what degree the filmmakers were conscious of how radical the claim to consummate American citizenship would have been for an African American in 1839. As a composite figure, Joadson's character is underdeveloped in any way that would reveal the political implications of his socio-economic subject position. Likewise, pinpointing his actual political commitments as a black American in 1839 and as an abolitionist—for there is a tremendous difference of political agenda between James Forten, Henry Highland Garnet, and David Walker, the figures Franzoni identifies as models for Joadson (Spielberg et. al. 44)—is made all the more difficult by how infrequently his character articulates any expression of political opinion. In the words of one critic, it is Joadson, "and not Cinque who remains the black cipher in the film. If Cinque is the irrepressibly verbal Black Other who, with translation, reveals himself as not just human, but eminently assimilable with his modesty, his irritation in the face of bureaucracy, and, over time, even his garb, the ex-slave-turned-abolitionist that Freeman plays is an inscrutable mystery" (Yarborough 39). For more on the cultures of protest in northern black communities during the period, see Horton.

20. See also Foner, "Hollywood Invades the Classroom," and Will.

21. For more detailed discussion on neoliberlism's blindness to the shortcomings of its own claims to color blindness, see the special issue of *PMLA* on comparative racialization (2008) and, in particular, the essays by Shih, Mills, Dirlik, and Eng.

22. Kodat makes a similar argument by tracing out how the film resolves the mutual crises of natural law and capital during the nineteenth century.

23. For a discussion of Chase-Riboud's sculptural practice, see the special issue of *Callaloo* (Summer 2009) on her sculpture, poetry, and fiction.

24. Osagie notes that Vivian provokes in Sengbe a parallel formulation of death. Toward the end of the novel, Vivian sings a song comparing the *Amistad* rebellion to Gabriel Prosser's 1800 insurrection. The song "paints a picture of heroism that allows Sengbe Pieh to see the historic proportions of his actions and his imminent place in history: 'At that moment,' Sengbe Pieh recalls, 'I can think of nothing more wonderful than to die' " ("Spirit of the Amistad" 839, quoting *Echo of Lions* 273). The parallel is not exact in that Covey's death and

rebirth in Vivian's company are more akin to Sengbe's earlier transformation under Henry Braithwaite's tutelage, whereas Sengbe's response to Vivian's song signals his sense of historical fulfillment. But it remains an important parallel insofar as it signals the political victories to come.

25. See Appadurai's global flows model, described in *Modernity at Large*.

26. Ashraf H. A. Rushdy notes that Cinque's planned obfuscation parallels President Adams' decision to hide an assassination threat from his wife. Adams withholds the information because he fears that Louisa's emotional constitution is too fragile to handle the news. Rushdy argues that because the novel takes great pains to demonstrate Louisa Adams' emotional durability, it implicitly critiques John Quincy Adams' sexist attitude about his wife. By tracing out significant narrative parallels between the ex-president and Cinque—neither of whom holds any evidence of his wife's fragility—Rushdy convincingly reads Cinque's decision to obscure "the worst" from Bayeh Bia in similar terms (270).

Chapter 4

1. In chapter 2 of his book, Richards lays out a complex argument about the modernity of patrimonial politics and the post-cold war crisis of patrimonialism, which incurred a crisis of modernity. In the other major book on the war, *Between Democracy and Terror*, Abdullah and colleagues subject Richards' arguments to careful—and warranted—critique but make parallel claims about the failure of the nation-state to deliver its promised political subjectivity. See Bangura in particular.

2. See Abdullah et al., *Between Democracy and Terror*.

3. Explanations for Sierra Leone's civil war frequently cite the state's colonial history. Political scientist Will Reno, for example, argues that the legacy of colonial economic practices and colonial-era chieftancy policies facilitated the formation of a corrupt shadow state in which "bigmen" exploited vulnerable laborers and illegally smuggled diamonds, which in turn fueled the armed conflict (chapter 2). In studies of the intellectual foundations of the rebel militia that initiated the civil war, Ibrahim Abdullah and Ismail Rashid note that early rebel leaders—radicalized students and lumpen youth inspired by Qaddafi's Green Book and the antiapartheid struggle in South Africa—were motivated by an anti-imperialist rhetoric and located postcolonial political failures within a longer colonial history (Abdullah 47–49; Rashid 79). See also Smillie, Gberie, and Hazelton, and Keen. For a broader critical overview of Africanist work on modernity and colonialism, see George, Gikanki, Korang, Cooper, Desai, Mudimbe, and Comaroff and Comoroff, *Modernity and Its Malcontents*.

4. For a historical analysis of Atlantic capitalism, slavery, and modernity, see Piot, Baucom, Thornton, Lovejoy, Miller, and Inikori and Engerman.

5. Julius Spencer details the history and politics of Sierra Leonean drama.

6. DeSouza-George's deployment of language in the play is fascinatingly complex and deserves a study of its own, but let it suffice here to say that the African foot-soldiers of the slave trade speak Mende, just as most of the rebel soldiers fighting in the guerilla forces did at that point in the civil war; a chorus depicting the greed and corruption of everyday life speak Krio, the lingua franca shared by nearly everyone in the country; and the heroes speak English.

7. Sierra Leone did not become a crown colony proper until 1807, but DeSouza-George's earlier date is more symbolically significant. Clarkson is remembered to this day in Sierra Leone for a prayer that he wrote upon his retirement to England for the future success of Freetown's repatriated African settlers. Nearly one hundred years before Kipling, Clarkson expressed virtually the same sentiments about the white man's burden that would organize Kipling's famous poem on the subject. Because of that, the prayer has served as a powerful symbol of colonialism and the knowledge/power nexus of colonial governmentality. As the lights come up on the stage, the audience hears the first lines of the poem and sees Clarkson himself reciting them.

8. Peterson provides an excellent historical analysis of Sierra Leone's formation as an Enlightenment project and of eighteenth-century British imperialism. For more on eighteenth-century imperialism and Enlightenment thought, see Wilson, Nussbaum, and Kazanjian.

9. Adelaide Smith Casely-Hayford's short story "Mister Courifer" explores the complicated dynamics of mimicry and colonial culture in Freetown's elite Krio community, as does Syl Cheney Coker in his poetry and fiction. For more on the historical formation of Krio identity see Wyse and Kanneh.

10. Murphy's and Osinubi's rereadings of the West African literary canon for traces of the trans-Atlantic slave trade offer a compelling and necessary rethinking of the relationship between slavery and colonialism in the critical discourse. We might situate Manthia Diawara in this camp as well. Diawara's critical autobiography *In Search of Africa* is less explicitly informed by Hegelian theories of slavery and subjectivity than Mbembe's and Adéẹ̀kọ́'s, but it argues that the reliance of African intellectuals on African American writing and art to theorize their own identities produced a set of discourses on colonial modernity, freedom, and subjectivity that were substantially informed by the experience of slavery. For similar arguments about the South African context see Masilela, Baderoon, and Chrisman.

11. Similar arguments can be found in Piot, Geschiere, and Shaka.

12. Ngugi himself wrote in response to Chinua Achebe's earlier defense of writing in English, in which Achebe identifies English as a forced inheritance that African writers have every right to Africanize (62). Moreover, he suggests, the continent's richly polyglot heritage demands a few lingua francas for the sake of convenience (58). Ngugi and Achebe's arguments remain the primary

poles around which the language debate continues, energetically, to fuel debate among African writers. See, for instance, the proceedings of the Asmara Conference (Cantalupo).

13. Similarly, Shaw argues that the predatory nature of Atlantic slave-trade modernity "resonates all too strongly with the violence of Sierra Leone's rebel war" (17).

14. See also Prestholdt's insightful scholarship on precolonial consumer culture in Africa, especially his analysis of how African consumer desires dictated trade and production globally.

15. In this respect, Gikandi echos James Ferguson, who makes a similar claim about modern space. Like Gikandi, Ferguson finds few of the Africans he studies have abandoned the developmentalist notions of modernity so important to the discourses of decolonization. What has changed, Ferguson argues, is that the temporal emphasis of popular understandings of modernity has given way to a spatial focus, which is to say that people no longer believe themselves to be catching up to modern societies but rather that they are stuck below them. Development does not, then, hinge on transformation over time, but on movement upward (174–75).

16. For more on colonial capitalism and temporality, see Atkins. Hanchard offers one of the rare discussions of slavery and temporality in the African context.

17. This focus on temporality and the commodified body also complicates Ian Baucom's argument in *Spectres of the Atlantic* that the twentieth century repeats or discontinuously extends the eighteenth century. For Baucom, the eighteenth and twentieth centuries represent a discontinuous *longue duree* because of the way that each is defined by speculative finance capital rather than commodity capital. The shared historicization of the slave trade and late-twentieth-century capitalism in DeSouza-George's and Lahai's work, however, turns not on finance capital but on the commodity and the commodification of human bodies. The difference is due largely to Baucom's reliance on the records and archives of slave trade financiers rather than on the experience of the African bodies in which they traded. While this focus on commodity capital does not necessarily challenge Baucom's chronology of a long twentieth century, it does demand the reassessment of the implications of his argument.

Conclusion: Rebellious Futures

1. Charlie Haffner and the Freetong Players performed *Amistad Kata-Kata* for American audiences at the 1992 National Black Arts Festival in Atlanta, Georgia, and at the unveiling of Ed Hamilton's *Amistad* memorial sculpture in New Haven, Connecticut. Raymond DeSouza-George staged *The Broken Handcuff* at the 1994 Canadian Fringe Theatre Festival. Steven Spielberg hired Arthur

Abraham, the Sierra Leonean author of the U.S.I.S. pamphlet on the *Amistad* rebellion, as a historical and cultural consultant. And, Barbara Chase-Riboud and Charlie Haffner exchanged perspectives on memorializing slave rebellion at the 2006 "Slavery and Public History Symposium" sponsored by Yale University's Gilder Lehrman Center for the Study of Slavery, Resistance, and Abolition.

2. *The Christian Science Monitor* reproduced much of this rhetoric in an article on the ship and Spielberg's film as human rights activist projects. See Grant.

3. Freetown's *Awoko* and *Exclusive* newspapers reported on the results of the contest. For the full text of Government Model Senior Secondary School student Sam S. Sesay's winning entry, see "U.S. Embassy Awards Students."

4. Another Freetown newspaper, *The Standard Times*, also reprinted the portion of AMISTAD America's press release about international recognition.

5. Saidiya Hartman's investigation of the memory and meaning of the slave trade in Ghana points to how commonly the conflict between the Sierra Leoneans and AMISTAD America is replayed between West Africans and American tourists, especially African Americans seeking to either reconnect with the "motherland" or, in Hartman's case, ambivalently wanting their hosts to admit culpability for the historical horrors endured by those sent off to the Americas. As Hartman notes repeatedly in *Lose Your Mother*, for those living in countries at the bottom of the United Nations Human Development Index in no small part due to U.S. economic and foreign policy, any discussion of past horrors must simultaneously acknowledge present-day structural inequalities.

6. For a detailed analysis of this point, see Magelssen.

7. There is a growing body of research on slave-route tourism, much of which examines the problematics of memorializing practices and the competing agendas of African diaspora tourists and local African communities. See Hasty, Bruner, Ebron, Tillet, and Hartman, *Lose Your Mother*. See also Phillips, *The Atlantic Sound*.

Works Cited

Abdullah, Ibrahim. "Bushpath to Destruction: The Origin and Character of the Revolutionary United Front (RUF/SL)." *Between Democracy and Terror: The Sierra Leone Civil War*. Ed. Ibrahim Abdullah. Dakar: CODESRIA, 2004. 41–65.

Abdullah, Ibrahim, et al. "Lumpen Youth Culture and Political Violence: Sierra Leoneans Debate the RUF and the Civil War." *Africa Development* 22.3–4 (1997): 171–214.

Abdullah, Ibrahim, et al. *Between Democracy and Terror: The Sierra Leone Civil War*. Ed. Ibrahim Abdullah. Dakar: CODESRIA, 2004.

Abélès, Marc. "Rethinking NGOs: The Economy of Survival and Global Governance." *Indiana Journal of Global Legal Studies* 15.1 (Winter 2008): 241–258.

Abraham, Arthur. *The Amistad Revolt: An Historical Legacy of Sierra Leone and the United States*. Freetown, Sierra Leone: United States Information Service, 1987.

———. "Sengbe Pieh: A Neglected Hero?" *The Journal of the Historical Society of Sierra Leone* 2.2 (1978): 22–30.

Achebe, Chinua. *Things Fall Apart*. New York: Anchor, 1994.

Adams, John Quincy. *The Amistad Case: The Most Celebrated Slave Mutiny of the Nineteenth Century. Two Volumes in One: Africans Taken in the Amistad. The Argument of John Quincy Adams before the Supreme Court of the United States*. New York: Johnson Reprint Corp., 1968.

Adéẹkọ, Adélékè. *The Slave's Rebellion: Fiction, History, Orature*. Bloomington: Indiana University Press, 2005.

Adjaye, Jospeh K. "*Amistad* and the Lessons of History." *Journal of Black Studies* 29.3 (1999): 455–459.

Akosah-Sarapong, Kofi. "Freetown's Traveling Theater." *West Africa* 28 December–8 January 1989.

Alexander, Elizabeth. "Can You Be BLACK and Look at This? Reading the Rodney King Video(s)." *Black Male: Represenations of Masculinity in Contemporary American Art*. Ed. Thelma Golden. New York: Whitney Museum of American Art, 1994.

Allen, Robert L. *Black Awakening in Capitalist America*. New York: Doubleday, 1969.

All Peoples Congress Secretariat. *The Rising Sun: A History of the All People's Congress Party of Sierra Leone*. Freetown: A.P.C., 1982.

AMISTAD America, Inc. "Mission Statement." amistadamerica.org. n.d. Web. 2 May 2009.

———. "Amistad Arrives in Freetown." amistadamerica.org. 7 December 2007. Web. 7 July 2010.

Anderson, Benedict. *Imagined Communities: Reflections on the Origin and Spread of Nationalism*. New York: Verso, 1991.

Appadurai, Arjun. *Modernity at Large: Cultural Dimensions of Globalization*. Minneapolis: University of Minnesota Press, 1996.

Apter, Emily. "Introduction: World Borders, Political Borders." *PMLA* 117.1 (2002): 68–71.

Aptheker, Bettina. "Social Functions of Prisons in the United States." *If They Come in the Morning*. Ed. Angela Davis. New York: Signet, 1971.

Aptheker, Herbert. *American Negro Slave Revolts*. New York: Columbia University Press, 1943.

Atkins, Keletso. *The Moon Is Dead! Give Us Our Money! The Cultural Origins of an African Work Ethic, Natal, South Africa, 1843–1900*. Portsmouth: Heinemann, 1993.

Aubry, Erin. "Culture Clash: African Americans and African Immigrants Seek Path to Common Ground." *Los Angeles Times* 14 July, 1994, sec. J12. Web. 25 June 2009.

Avery, Paul, and Vin McLellan. *The Voices of Guns*. New York: G. P. Putnam's Sons, 1977.

Baderoon, Gabeba. "The African Oceans: Tracing the Sea as Memory of Slavery in South African Literature and Culture." *Research in African Literatures* 40.4 (Winter 2009): 89–107.

Bah, Chernoh. "Martin Luther King, Jr. and Sengbe Pieh." c. 1992. Acrylic on canvas. The King Center, Atlanta, Georgia.

Bai, Matt. "Is Obama the End of Black Politics?" *New York Times* 10 August, 2008, sec. Magazine. Web. 6 October 2008.

Bangura, Amadu. "Sengbe Pieh, or Joseph Cinque." 1993. Mural. Freetown, Sierra Leone.

Bangura, Yusuf. "Understanding the Political and Cultural Dynamics of the Sierra Leone War: A Critique of Paul Richards' *Fighting for the Rainforest*." *Africa Development* 22.3–4 (1997): 117–148.

Barber, Bob. "'Not Guilty!' Magee's Own Testimony." *Muhammad Speaks* 13 April 1973: 4–5.

Barber, John Warner. *A History of the Amistad Captives*. New York: Arno, 1969.

Baucom, Ian. *Specters of the Atlantic: Finance Capital, Slavery, and the Philosophy of History*. Durham: Duke University Press, 2005.

Bayart, Jean-Francois. *The State in Africa: The Politics of the Belly*. Trans., Mary Harper, Christopher Harrison, Elizabeth Harrison. New York: Longman, 1993.

Bederman, Gail. *Manliness and Civilization: A Cultural History of Gender and Race in the United States, 1880–1917*. Chicago: University of Chicago Press, 1995.

Benjamin, Walter. "Theses on the Philosophy of History." *Illuminations*. Trans. Harry Zohn. New York: Schoken Books, 1968.

Berkman, Ronald. *Opening the Gates: The Rise of the Prisoners' Movement*. Lexington, MA: Lexington Books, 1979.

Black Panthers, The. "The Black Panther Party: Platform and Program." *The Sixties Papers: Documents of a Rebellious Decade*. Ed. Judith Clavir Albert and Stewart Edward Albert. New York: Praeger, 1984. 159–164.

Blount, Marcellus, and George P. Cunningham, eds. *Representing Black Masculinities*. New York: Routledge, 1996.

Bresnick, Adam. "Telling Everyone's Story." *TLS* 20 February 1998: 18.

Briley, Ron. "The Study Guide *Amistad*: A Lasting Legacy." *The History Teacher* 31.3 (May 1998): 390–4. Web. 2 June 2001.

Brooks, Daphne Ann. *Bodies in Dissent: Spectacular Performances of Race and Freedom, 1850–1910*. Durham: Duke University Press, 2006.

Brown, Wendy. "American Nightmare: Neoliberalism, Neoconservativism, and De-Democratization." *Political Theory* 34.6 (December 2006): 690–714.

Bruner, Edward M. "Tourism in Ghana: The Representation of Slavery and the Return of the Black Diaspora." *American Anthropologist* 98.2 (1996): 290–305.

Bryan, John. "Mix Berkeley Racial Consciousness: Black Prison Revolt—You've Got S.L.A." *The San Francisco Phoenix* 15 March 1974: 7, 10.

Buck-Morss, Susan. "Hegel and Haiti." *Critical Inquiry* 26.4 (Summer 2000): 821–865.

Bugincourt, Jacques, and Amadou Diallo. *Set Setal: Des Murs Qui Parlent*. Dakar: ENDA, 1991.

Bujay, Wuru. "Sierra Leone's National Heritage? Going . . . Going . . . Going . . . Gone?" *The Standard Times*. Freetown, Sierra Leone. 7 January 2008. Web. 15 July 2010.

Cable, Mary. *Black Odyssey: The Case of the Slave Ship Amistad*. New York: Penguin Books, 1971.

Caldwell, Earl. "Davis Co-Defendant Takes Spotlight." *The New York Times* 21 March 1971: 58.

Cantalupo, Charles. *Against All Odds: African Languages and Literatures in the 21st Century*. Eritrea: Hdri, 2007.

Carby, Hazel. *Race Men*. Cambridge, MA: Harvard University Press, 1998.

Casely-Hayford, Adelaide Smith. "Mister Courifer." *Unwinding Threads: Writing by Women in Africa*. Ed. Charlotte H. Bruner. Portsmouth, NH: Heinemann, 1983.

Césaire, Aimé. *The Collected Poetry*. Trans. Clayton Eshleman and Annette J. Smith. Berkeley and Los Angeles: University of California Press, 1984.

Chambers, Veronica, and Paul C. Lee. *Amistad Rising: A Story of Freedom*. San Diego: Harcourt Brace, 1998.

Chase-Riboud, Barbara. "Slavery as a Problem in Public History: Or Sally Hemmings and the 'One Drop Rule' of Public History." *Callaloo* 32.3 (Summer 2009): 826–831.

———. "Barbara Chase-Riboud v. DreamWorks et. al." O'Donnell and Shaeffer. United States District Court, 1997.

———. *Echo of Lions*. New York: Morrow, 1989.

Chatterjee, Partha. *The Nation and Its Fragments: Colonial and Postcolonial Histories*. Princeton, NJ: Princeton University Press, 1993.

Cheevers, John. "SLA-Vacaville Link." *The Daily Cal* 4 March 1974: 1, 5.

Chrisman, Laura. *Postcolonial Contraventions: Cultural Readings of Race, Imperialism, and Transnationalism*. New York: Manchester University Press, 2003.

Chrisman, Robert. "Black Prisoners, White Law." *Contemporary Black Thought: The Best from the Black Scholar*. Ed. Robert Chrisman and Nathan Hare. New York: The Bobbs-Merrill, 1973.

Christian, Ed, ed. *The Postcolonial Detective*. New York: Palgrave Macmillan, 2001.

Clark, John Henrik, ed. *William Styron's Nat Turner: Ten Black Writers Respond*. Boston: Beacon, 1968.

Comaroff, Jean and John. "Criminal Obsessions, after Foucault: Postcoloniality, Policing, and the Metaphysics of Disorder." *Law and Disorder in the Postcolony*. Ed. Jean Comaroff and John Comaroff. Chicago: University of Chicago Press, 2006: 273–298.

———. "Occult Economies and the Violence of Abstraction: Notes from the South African Postcolony." *American Ethnologist* 26.2 (1999). Web. 6 May 2003.

———. "Millenial Capitalism: First Thoughts on a Second Coming." *Public Culture* 12.2 (Spring 2000): 291–343.

———, eds. *Modernity and Its Malcontents: Ritual and Power in Postcolonial Africa*. Chicago: University of Chicago Press, 1993.

Conteh-Morgan, Earl, and Mac Dixon-Fyle. *Sierra Leone at the End of the Twentieth Century: History, Politics, and Society*. New York: Lang, 1999.

Cooper, Frederick. *Colonialism in Question: Theory, Knowledge, History*. Berkeley and Los Angeles: University of California Press, 2005.

Cruise O'Brien, Donal B. "A Lost Generation? Youth Identity and State Decay in West Africa." *Postcolonial Identities in Africa*. Ed. Richard Werbner and Terrence Ranger. London: Zed Books, 1996.

Cumale, Kwame, and Batilloi Warritay. "Theatre for the People." *West Africa* 16 December 1985: 2641–2642.

Cummins, Eric. *The Rise and Fall of California's Radical Prison Movement*. Palo Alto: Stanford University Press, 1994.

Dalzell, Frederick. "Dreamworking 'Amistad': Representing Slavery, Revolt, and Freedom in America, 1839 and 1997." *New England Quarterly* 71.1 (1998): 127.

Dargis, Manhola, et al. "Arguing *Amistad*." *LA Weekly* 19–25 December, 1997: 36–40.

Davis, Angela Yvonne, and Angela Davis Defence Committee. *If They Come in the Morning: Voices of Resistance*. New York: Signet, 1971.

Davis, Mary Kemp. *Nat Turner before the Bar of Judgment*. Baton Rouge: Louisiana State University Press, 1999.

Desai, Gaurav. *Subject to Colonialism: African Self-Fashioning and the Colonial Library*. Durham: Duke University Press, 2001.

Desouza George, Raymond E. Personal interview. 22 June 2006.

———. *The Broken Hancuff (Give Me Free)*. Freetown, Sierra Leone: unpublished.

Diawara, Manthia. *In Search of Africa*. Cambridge: Harvard University Press, 1998.

Dinsmore, Charles Allen. "Interesting Sketches of the Amistad Captives." *The Yale University Library Gazette* 9.3 (1935): 51–55.

Diouf, Mamadou. "Urban Youth and Senegalese Politics: Dakar 1988–1994." *Public Culture* 8 (1996): 225–249.

Dirlik, Arif. "Race Talk, Race, and Contemporary Racism." *PMLA* 123.5 (October 2008): 1363–1379.

Dodson, Owen. "Amistad." Unpublished, 1939.

Dubner, Stephen J. "Steven the Good." *Steven Spielberg: Interviews*. Ed. Lester D. Friedman and Brent Notbohm. Jackson: University Press of Mississippi, 1999.

DuBois, W. E. B. *The Suppression of the Atlantic Slave-Trade to the United States of America 1638–1870*. New York: Harvard Historical Studies, 1896.

Duggan, Lisa. *The Twilight of Equality: Neoliberalism, Cultural Politics, and the Attack on Democracy*. Boston: Beacon, 2004.

Ebron, Paulla. "Tourists as Pilgrims: Commercial Fashioning of Transatlantic Politics." *American Ethnologist* 26.4 (1999): 910–932.

Edwards, Brent Hayes. *The Practice of Diaspora: Literature, Translation, and the Rise of Black Internationalism*. Cambridge, MA: Harvard University Press, 2003.

Eller, Claudia. "Novelist Urges Court to Block Spielberg Film." *Los Angeles Times* 18 November, 1997, sec. D: 1+.

———. "Spielberg Lawsuit Pits Author vs. *Auteur*." *Los Angeles Times* 24 October 1997, sec. D, 5+.

Eng, David L. "The End(s) of Race." *PMLA* 123.5 (October 2008): 1479–1493.

Estes, Steve. " 'I *AM* a Man!' Race, Masculinity, and the 1968 Memphis Sanitation Strike." *Labor History* 41.2 (2000): 153–170.

Etherton, Michael. *The Development of African Drama*. New York: Africana, 1982.

"Eulogy to Three Murdered Revolutionaries." *The Black Panther* 29 August 1970: 7.

Fanon, Frantz. *The Wretched of the Earth*. New York: Grove, 1963.
Ferguson, James. "Decomposing Modernity: History and Hierarchy after Development." *Postcolonial Studies and Beyond*. Ed. Ania Loomba, Suvir Kaul, Matti Bunzl, Antoinette Burton, and Jed Esty. Durham: Duke University Press, 2005.
Ferme, Mariane C. *The Underneath of Things: Violence, History, and the Everyday in Sierra Leone*. Berkeley and Los Angeles: University of California Press, 2001.
Fischer, Sibylle. *Modernity Disavowed: Haiti and the Cultures of Slavery in the Age of Revolution*. Durham: Duke University Press, 2004.
Fischer-Hornung, Dorothea, and Monika Mueller, eds. *Sleuthing Ethnicity: The Detective in Multiethnic Crime Fiction*. Madison and Teaneck: Fairleigh Dickenson University Press, 2003
Foner, Eric. "Hollywood Invades the Classroom." Editorial. *New York Times* 20 December, 1997, sec. A: 13.
Forman, Seth. "*Amistad, Schindler*: Black and Jewish Identity." *Midstream* September/October 1998: 37–38.
Fotentot Jr., Chester J. "Black Misery, White Guilt and Amistad." *MELUS* 24.1 (1999): 235–243.
"Free Ruchell Magee." *The Black Panther* 6 February 1971: 10–11.
Friedman, Melvin J., and Irving Malin, eds. *William Styron's* The Confessions of Nat Turner: *A Critical Casebook*. Belmont, CA: Wadsworth, 1970.
Garfield, Eliza. "Voyage Logbook." amistadamerica.org. Amistad America, Inc. 14 December 2007. Web. 7 July 2010.
Garraway, Doris L., ed. *Tree of Liberty: Cultural Legacies of the Haitian Revolution in the Atlantic World*. Charlottesville: University of Virginia Press, 2008.
George, Olakunle. *Relocating Agency: Modernity and African Letters*. Albany: State University of New York Press, 2003.
Geschiere, Peter. *The Modernity of Witchcraft*. Charlottesville: University of Virginia Press, 1997.
Gikandi, Simon. "Globalization and the Claims of Postcoloniality." *South Atlantic Quarterly* 100.3 (Summer 2001): 627–658.
Gilmore, Ruth Wilson. *Golden Gulag: Surplus, Crisis, and Opposition in Globalizing California*. Berkeley and Los Angeles: University of California Press, 2007.
———. "Globalisation and US Prison Growth: From Military Keynesianism to Post-Keynesian Militarism." *Race and Class* 40.2/3 (October 1998): 171–188.
Gilroy, Paul. *The Black Atlantic: Modernity and Double Consciousness*. Cambridge, MA: Harvard University Press, 1993.
Goldberg, David Theo. *The Threat of Race: Reflections on Racial Neoliberalism*. Malden, MA: Wiley-Blackwell, 2009.
———. "Racisms without Racism." *PMLA* 123.5 (October 2008): 1712–1716.
———, ed. *Multiculturalism: A Critical Reader*. Oxford: Oxford University Press, 1994.

Golden Legacy. *Joseph Cinque and the Amistad Mutiny*. Golden Legacy Illustrated History Magazine. Vol. 10. Seattle, WA: Baylor Publishing & Community Enterprise, 1983.

Golden, Thelma, ed. *Black Male: Representations of Masculinity in Contemporary American Art*. New York: Whitney Museum of American Art, 1994.

Goldstein, Warren. "Why Bad History Is Bad for Culture." *Chronicle of Higher Education* 44.31 (10 April, 1998): A64.

Government of Sierra Leone. *Sierra Leonean Heroes: Fifty Great Men and Women Who Helped to Build Our Nation*. 2nd ed. Freetown: Government of Sierra Leone, 1988.

Grant, Bill. "Filmmaker and Boat Builders Hew Lessons of Human Rights." *Christian Science Monitor* 19 December 1997, sec. Features: 10. Web. 5 February 2009.

Gray, Herman. "Black Masculinity and Visual Culture." *Black Male: Representations of Masculinity in Contemporary American Art*. Ed. Thelma Golden. New York: Whitney Museum of American Art, 1994.

Guerrero, Ed. "The Black Image in Protective Custody: Hollywood's Biracial Buddy Films of the Eighties." *Black American Cinema*. Ed. Manthia Diawara. New York: Routledge, 1993.

Guest, Kristen, ed. *Eating Their Words: Cannibalism and the Boundaries of Identity*. Albany: State University of New York Press, 2001.

Haffner, Charlie. "Re: Amistad Kata-Kata Script." Message to the author. 25 July 2010. Email.

———. "Re: Amistad Kata-Kata Script." Message to the author. 7 July 2010. Email.

———. Personal interview. 19 September 1998.

———. *Amistad Kata-Kata*. Unpublished manuscript. Freetown, Sierra Leone.

Hale, Charles R. "Cultural Politics of Identity in Latin America." *Annual Review of Anthropology* 26.1 (1997): 567–591.

Hall, Stuart. "Cultural Identity and Diaspora." *Diaspora and Visual Culture: Representing Africans and Jews*. Ed. Nicholas Mirzoeff. New York: Routledge, 2000.

———. "Old and New Identities, Old and New Ethnicities." *Culture, Globalization, and the World System*. Ed. Anthony D. King. Minneapolis: University of Minnesota Press, 1997.

Hamilton, Ed. "Amistad Memorial." 1992. Scuplture. New Haven, Connecticut.

Hanchard, Michael. "Afro-Modernity: Temporality, Politics, and the African Diaspora." *Public Culture* 11.1 (1999): 245–268.

Harper, Phillip Brian. *Are We Not Men? Masculine Anxiety and the Problem of African-American Identity*. New York: Oxford University Press, 1996.

Hartman, Saidiya V. *Lose Your Mother: A Journey along the Atlantic Slave Route*. New York: Farrar, Strauss, and Giroux, 2007.

———. "The Time of Slavery." *South Atlantic Quarterly* 101.4 (Fall 2002): 757–778.

———. *Scenes of Subjection: Terror, Slavery, and Self-Making in Nineteenth-Century America*. New York: Oxford University Press, 1997.

Harvey, David. *A Brief History of Neoliberalism*. Oxford: Oxford University Press, 2005.

Hasty, Jennifer. "Rites of Passage, Routes of Redemption: Emancipation Tourism and the Wealth of Culture." *Africa Today* 49.3 (Fall 2002): 47–76.

Hayden, Robert. "Middle Passage." *Cross Section 1945: A Collection of New American Writing*. Ed. Edwin Seaver. New York: Book Find Club, 1945.

Henegan, Lucius H. "Did Cinque Enter the Slave Trade?" *Dawn Magazine* 8 February 1975: 2.

———. "There Was Another Cinque But He Found His Freedom." *Dawn Magazine* 31 August 1974: 15.

Hinckle, Warren. "Debray Enters SLA Handicap." *The San Francisco Phoenix* 12.16 1974: 1, 12.

Hollist, Onipede A. "An Analytic Survey of the Post Colonial Fiction in English of Sierra Leone." Ph.D. Dissertation. University of South Florida, 1991.

Horton, James and Lois. *In Hope of Liberty: Culture, Community, and Protest among Northern Free Blacks, 1700–1860*. New York: Oxford University Press, 1997.

"Hostage: A Game of Terror, The." *Newsweek* Februrary 25 1974: 18–21.

Hunt, Bernice Kohn. *The Amistad Mutiny*. New York: McCall, 1971.

Hurley, E. Anthony. "'Is He, Am I, a Hero?' Self-Referentiality and the Colonial Legacy in Aime Cesaire's *Toussaint Louverture*." In *Tree of Liberty: Cultural Legacies of the Haitian Revolution in the Atlantic World*. Ed. Doris L. Garraway. Charlottesville: University of Virginia Press, 2008.

Inikori, Joseph, and Stanley Engerman, eds. *The Atlantic Slave Trade: Effects on Economies, Societies, and Peoples in Africa, the Americas and Europe*. Durham: Duke University Press, 1992.

James, C. L. R. *The Black Jacobins: Toussaint L'Ouverture and the San Domingo Revolution*. New York: Vintage Books, 1963, 1989.

Jeffords, Susan. *The Remasculinization of America: Gender and the Vietnam War*. Bloomington: Indiana University Press, 1989.

Jocelyn, Nathaniel. "Joseph Cinque." 1839. Oil on canvas. New Haven Museum, New Haven, Connecticut.

Johnson Gosselin, Adrienne, ed. *Multicultural Detective Fiction: Murder from the "Other" Side*. New York: Garland, 1999.

Jones, Howard. Letter. *New York Times* 1 January 1998, sec. A: 21. Web. 29 January 2009.

———. "Cinqué of the Amistad a Slave Trader? Pepetuating a Myth." *Journal of American History* 87.3 (2000). Web. 6 February 2001.

———. *Mutiny on the Amistad: The Saga of a Slave Revolt and Its Impact on American Abolition, Law, and Diplomacy*. New York: Oxford University Press, 1987.

Jurmain, Suzanne. *Freedom's Sons: The True Story of the Amistad Mutiny*. New York: Lothrop Lee and Shepard Books, 1998.

Kanneh, Kadiatu. *African Identities: Race, Nation, and Culture in Ethnography, Pan-Africanism, and Black Literatures*. New York: Routledge, 1998.

Karefa-Smart, Peter. "Theatre and Social Change." *West Africa* 10–16 May 1988: 879–880.

Kargbo, Kolosa. "In Search of a Venue." *West Africa* 10–16 October 1988: 1892.

Kasirika, Kaidi, and Maharibi Muntu. "Prison or Slavery?" *Contemporary Black Thought: The Best from the Black Scholar*. Ed. Robert Chrisman and Nathan Hare. New York: Bobbs-Merrill, 1973.

Katsiaficas, George. "Introduction." *Liberation, Imagination, and the Black Panther Party: A New Look at the Panthers and Their Legacy*. Ed. Kathleen Cleaver and George Katsiaficas. New York: Routledge, 2001.

Kaufman, Robert. "Ruchell Magee." *If They Come in the Morning*. Ed. Angela Y. Davis. New York: Signet, 1971.

Kazanjian, David. *The Colonizing Trick: National Culture and Imperial Citizenship in Early America*. Minneapolis: Minnesota University Press, 2003.

Keen, David. *Conflict and Collusion in Sierra Leone*. Oxford: Curry, 2005.

Kerr, David. *African Popular Theater*. Portsmouth, NH: Heinemann, 1995.

Kodat, Catherine Gunther. "Saving Private Property: Steven Spielberg's American DreamWorks." *Representations* 71.Summer (2000): 77–105.

Korang, Kwaku Larbi. *Writing Ghana, Imagining Africa: Nation and African Modernity*. Rochester: Rochester University Press, 2004.

Kromer, Helen. *Amistad: The Slave Uprising Aboard the Spanish Schooner*. Cleveland, OH: Pilgrim, 1973, 1997.

Lahai, Josee. Personal interview. 11 December 2000.

———. "Sengbe Pieh." 1993. Mural. Freetown, Sierra Leone.

Lemisch, Jesse. "Black Agency in the *Amistad* Uprising: Or, You've Taken Our Cinque and Gone." *Souls: A Critical Journal of Black Politics, Culture, and Society* 1.1 Winter (1999): 57–70.

Lim, Shirley Jennifer. *A Feeling of Belonging: Asian American Women's Public Culture, 1930–1960*. New York: New York University Press, 2006.

Loomba, Ania, et. al. *Postcolonial Studies and Beyond*. Durham: Duke University Press, 2005.

Loshitzky, Yosefa, ed. *Spielberg's Holocaust: Critical Perspectives of Schindler's List*. Bloomington and Indianapolis: Indiana University Press, 1997.

Lovejoy, Paul. *Transformations in Slavery: A History of Slavery in Africa*. 2nd ed. Cambridge: Cambridge University Press, 2000.

Lowe, Lisa. *Immigrant Acts: On Asian American Cultural Politics*. Durham, NC: Duke University Press, 1996.

Magee, Ruchell "Cinque." "Personal correspondence." 9 March 2002.

———. "Wake Up Oppressed People (Open Address to the President)." Transcript. Tamal, California, 1972.

———. "Miscarriage of Justice: A Revolutionary Play." *Berkeley Tribe* 19–26 November 1971: 8–9.

———. "Statement to the Court." *If They Come in the Morning*. Ed. Angela Y. Davis. New York: Signet, 1971.

———. "Letters to Angela." *If They Come in the Morning*. Ed. Angela Y. Davis. New York: Signet, 1971.

———. "Pigs Cut Judge Haley Down." *Berkeley Barb* 30 July–5 August 1971: 3, 8.

———. "Interview with Dave Stevens, August 18." KPFK, 1971.

———. "His Own Story." *Black Politician* April 1971: 13–15.

———. "Interview, Unmarked Audio Recording." Freedom Archives, San Francisco.

Magee, Ruchell, and Larry "Muntu" West. "The Right to Kill." *Berkeley Tribe* 4–11 June 1971: 12–13.

———. "Ruchell Magee Speaks Out." *The Black Panther* 13 February 1971: 8.

———. "Ruchell Magee Speaks Out (continued)." *The Black Panther* 20 February 1971: 8.

Magelssen, Scott. "Making History in the Second Person: Post-touristic Consideration for Living Historical Interpretation." *Theatre Journal* 58.2 (May 2006): 291–312.

Mamdani, Mahmood. *Citizen and Subject: Decentralized Despotism and the Legacy of Late Colonialism*. New York: Oxford University Press, 1997.

Martin, Christopher. *The Amistad Affair*. New York: Abelard-Schuman, 1970.

Martin, B. Edmon. *All We Want Is Make Us Free: La Amistad and the Reform Abolitionists*. Lanham, MD: University Press of America, 1986.

Masilela, Ntongela. " 'The Black Atlantic' and African Modernity in South Africa." *Research in African Literatures* 27.4 (1996): 88–96.

Mason, Clifford. *Jamaica Run: A Joe Cinquez Mystery*. New York: St. Martin's, 1987.

———. *The Case of the Ashanti Gold: A Joe Cinquez Mystery*. New York: St. Martin's, 1985.

Matzke, Christine, and Susanne Mühleisen. *Postcolonial Postmortems: Crime Fiction from a Transcultural Perspective*. Amsterdam: Rodopi, 2006.

Mbembe, Achille. *On the Postcolony*. Berkeley and Los Angeles: University of California Press, 2001.

McCarthy, Anna. "Reality Television: A Neoliberal Theater of Suffering." *Social Text* 25.4 (Winter 2007): 17–41.

McElroy, Guy C., et al. *Facing History: The Black Image in American Art, 1710–1940*. San Francisco, Washington, DC: Bedford Arts, Corcoran Gallery of Art, 1990.

McFeely, William S. "Cinque, Tall and Strong." *The Journal of American History* 87.3 (2000): 949–950.

Melancon, Trimiko. "Politics of Belonging: Race, Freedom, and Subjectivity in Barbara Chase-Riboud's *Echo of Lions*." *Callaloo* 32.3 (Summer 2009): 845–854.

Mercer, Kobena. *Welcome to the Jungle: New Positions in Black Cultural Studies.* New York: Routledge, 1994.

Miller, Joseph. *Way of Death: Merchant Capitalism and the Angolan Slave Trade, 1730–1830.* Madison: University of Wisconsin Press, 1996.

Mills, Charles. "Racial Liberalism." *PMLA* 123.5 (October 2008): 1380–1397.

Momoh, Joseph Saidu. "Address by His Excellency the President Major-General Dr. Joseph Saidu Momoh Delivered on The Occasion of His Inauguration." Freetown, Sierra Leone: Sierra Leone Government, 1986.

Moon, Bucklin. *Primer for White Folks.* Garden City, NY: Doubleday Doran, 1945.

Mudimbe, V. Y. *The Invention of Africa: Gnosis, Philosophy, and the Order of Knowledge.* Bloomington and Indianapolis: Indiana University Press, 1988.

Murphy, Laura. " 'Obstacles in the Way of Love': The Enslavement of Intimacy in Crowther and Aidoo." *Research in African Literatures* 40.4 (Winter 2009) 47–64.

———. "Into the Bush of Ghosts: Specters of the Slave Trade in West African Fiction." *Research in African Literatures* 38.4 (Winter 2007): 141–152.

Nagel, Paul. "The Real John Quincy Adams." Editorial. *New York Times* 20 December, 1997, sec. A: 13.

Nesbitt, Nick. *Universal Emancipation: The Haitian Revolution and the Radical Enlightenment.* Charlottesville: University of Virginia Press, 2008.

Newell, Stephanie. *Readings in African Popular Fiction.* Bloomington and Indianapolis: Indiana University Press, 2002.

Newman, Richard. "Not the Only Story in 'Amistad': The Fictional Joadson and the Real James Forten." *Pennsylvania History* 67.2 (2000): 218–239.

Ngai, Mae. M. *Impossible Subjects: Illegal Aliens and the Making of Modern America.* Princeton: Princeton University Press, 2005.

Ngugi, wa Thiong'o. *Decolonising the Mind: The Politics of Language in African Literature.* Portsmouth, NH: Curry, Heineman, 1986.

Niles, Blair. *East by Day.* New York: Toronto: Farrar and Rinehart, 1941.

Nunes, Zita. *Cannibal Democracy: Race and Representation in the Literature of the Americas.* Minneapolis: University of Minnesota Press, 2008.

Nunley, John W. *Moving with the Face of the Devil: Art and Politics in Urban West Africa.* Urbana and Chicago: University of Illinois Press, 1987.

Nussbaum, Felicity. *The Global Eighteenth Century.* Baltimore: Johns Hopkins University Press, 2005.

Nyang'oro, Julius E. "Hemmed In? The State in Africa and Global Liberalization." *States and Sovereignty in the Global Economy.* Ed. David A. Smith, Dorothy J. Solinger, and Steven C. Topik. New York: Routledge, 1999.

Ong, Aihwa. *Flexible Citizenship: The Cultural Logics of Transnationality.* Durham: Duke University Press, 1999.

Opala, Joseph A. Personal interview. 17 May 2000.

———. *"Ecstatic Renovation!" Street Art Celebrating Sierra Leone's 1992 Revolution.* Freetown: Sierra Leone Adult Education Association, 1994.

———. " 'Ecstatic Renovation!' Street Art Celebrating Sierra Leone's 1992 Revolution." *African Affairs* 93 (1994): 195–218.

———. "Bai Bureh: The Making of a National Symbol." Upublished manuscript.

Osagie, Iyunolu Folayan. "Spirit of the Amistad: Figurations of Women in *Echo of Lions*." *Callaloo* 32.3 (Summer 2009): 832–844.

———. *The Amistad Revolt: Memory, Slavery, and the Politics of Identity in the United States and Sierra Leone.* Athens and London: University of Georgia Press, 2000.

Osinubi, Taiwo Adetunji. "Chinua Achebe and the Uptakes of African Slaveries." *Research in African Literatures* 40.4 (Winter 2009): 25–46.

Oullette, Laurie. " 'Take Responsibility for Yourself': *Judge Judy* and the Neoliberal Citizen." *Reality TV: Remaking Television Culture.* Ed. Susan Murray and Laurie Oullette. New York: NYU Press, 2004.

Owens, William A. *Black Mutiny: The Revolt on the Schooner Amistad.* Baltimore, MD: Black Classic, 1953, 1968, 1997.

Palmer, Eustace. "Personal correspondence." Accra: African Literature Association Conference, 2006.

Park, Yun-Joo, and Patricia Richards. "Negotiating Neoliberal Multiculturalism: Mapuche Workers in the Chilean State." *Social Forces* 85.3 (March 2007): 1319–1339.

Pate, Alexs. *Amistad.* New York: DreamWorks, 1997.

Patterson, Orlando. *Slavery and Social Death: A Comparative Study.* Cambridge, MA: Harvard University Press, 1982.

Pearsall, Robert Brainard, and Symbionese Liberation Army. *The Symbionese Liberation Army. Documents and Communications.* Amsterdam: Rodopi, 1974.

Pesci, David. *Amistad: A Novel.* New York: Marlowe, 1997.

Peters, Jonathan. "The Gentleman." Unpublished manuscript. Freetown, Sierra Leone.

Peterson, John. *Province of Freedom: A History of Sierra Leone, 1787–1870.* London: Faber and Faber, 1969.

Phillips, Caryl. *The Atlantic Sound.* New York: Vintage Books, 2000.

Pinkney, William. "Voyage Logbook." amistadamerica.org. Amistad America, Inc. 22 December 2007. Web. 7 July 2010.

Piot, Charles. *Remotely Global: Village Modernity in West Africa.* Chicago: University of Chicago Press, 1999.

Political Prisoners of Parish Prison. "Angola-Slave Labor Camp of Louisiana." *The Black Panther* 13 March 1971: 7.

Porter, Dennis. *The Pursuit of Crime: Art and Ideology in Detective Fiction.* New Haven: Yale University Press, 1981.

Prestholdt, Jeremy. *Domesticating the World: African Consumerism and Genealogies of Globalization*. Berkeley and Los Angeles: University of California Press, 2008.

"Prisoners in Rebellion: The Folsom Prisoners Manifesto." *If They Come in the Morning*. Ed. Angela Davis. New York: Signet, 1971.

"Prisoners of War." *Berkeley Tribe* 8–15 1971: 12–13.

Radhakrishnan, R. *Diasporic Meditations: Between Home and Location*. Minneapolis: University of Minnesota Press, 1996.

Rashid, Ismail. "Student Radicals, Lumpen Youth, and the Origins of the Revolutionary Groups in Sierra Leone, 1977–1996." *Between Democracy and Terror: The Sierra Leone Civil War*. Ed. Ibrahim Abdullah. Dakar: CODESRIA, 2004. 66–89.

Rediker, Marcus. *The Slave Ship: A Human History*. New York: Penguin, 2007.

Reno, William. *Corruption and State Politics in Sierra Leone*. Cambridge, UK: Cambridge University Press, 1995.

Rice, Alan. " 'Who's Eating Whom': The Discourse of Cannibalism in the Literature of the Black Atlantic from Equiano's *Travels* to Toni Morrison's *Beloved*." *Research in African Literature* 28.4 (1998): 107–121.

Richards, Paul. *Fighting for the Rain Forest: War, Youth & Resources in Sierra Leone*. Portsmouth, NH: Heinemann, 1996.

Rimer, Sara, and Karen W. Arenson. "Top Colleges Take More Blacks, but Which Ones?" *New York Times* 24 June, 2004. Web. 29 January 2009.

Roberts, Sam. "More Africans Enter U.S. Than in Days of Slavery." *New York Times* 21 February 2005. Web. 21 February 2005.

Rodriguez, Dylan. *Forced Passages: Imprisoned Radical Intellectuals and the U.S. Prison Regime*. Minneapolis: University of Minnesota Press, 2006.

Rosen, Gary. " 'Amistad' and the Abuse of History." *Commentary* February 1998: 46–51.

Rowe, Sylvester Edundayo. "Sierra Leone's Newly-Born Theater." *African Arts* 9.1 (1975): 56–59.

"Ruchell and Angela." *Berkeley Tribe* 2–8 July 1971: 12–13.

Ruchell Magee Committee for Black Prisoners. "Ruchell Magee: Slave Rebel." *Black Scholar* (October 1972): 41–43.

Ruchell Magee Defense Committee. "State Courts in Violation of Own Law: Press Release." San Francisco, California, 1971.

"Ruchell Magee's Struggle to Fight for the Rights of All Black People." *The Black Panther* Saturday, 12 June 1971: 13–14.

"Ruchell vs. Reagan (an interview)." *Berkeley Tribe* 14–20 August 1971: 8–9, 12–13.

Rukeyser, Muriel. "The 'Amistad' Mutiny." *Primer for White Folks*. Ed. Bucklin Moon. New York: Doubleday, 1945.

Rushdy, Ashraf H. A. "Representing the Constitution: Embodiments of America in Barbara Chase-Riboud's 'Echo of Lions.'" *CRITIQUE: Studies in Contemporary Fiction* 36.4 (1995): 258.

Sale, Maggie Montesinos. *The Slumbering Vocano: American Slave Ship Revolts and the Production of Rebellious Masculinity*. Durham: Duke University Press, 1997.

Scott, James C. *Domination and the Arts of Resistance*. New Haven: Yale University Press, 1990.

Seale, Bobby. "The Police State and Reagan's Slave Labor Schemes." *The Black Panther* 20 March 1971: 2.

Sexton, Roy. "'Steven Doesn't Understand No': Masculinity and Escapism in the Films of Steven Spielberg." *Henry Street* 5.1 (1995): 59–74.

Shaka, Femi Okirimuete. *Modernity and the African Cinema*. Trenton: Africa World, 2005.

Shank, Gregory. "Looking Back: Radical Criminology and Social Movement." *Social Justice* 26.2 (1999): 114.

Shaw, Rosalind. *Memories of the Slave Trade: Ritual and the Historical Imagination in Sierra Leone*. Chicago: University of Chicago Press, 2002.

Shih, Shu-mei. "Comparative Racialization: An Introduction." *PMLA* 123.5 (October 2008): 1347–1362.

Shockley II, Madison T. "So Why Do I Still Feel Like a Slave?" *Los Angeles Times* 19 January 1998: B5.

Shuler, Jack. *Calling Out Liberty: The Stono Slave Rebellion and the Universal Struggle for Human Rights*. Jackson: University of Mississippi Press, 2009.

Siddiqi, Yumna. *Anxieties of Empire and the Fiction of Intrigue*. New York: Columbia University Press, 2008.

"Sierra Leonean on Board Replica Slave Ship," *Awoko Newspaper*. Freetown, Sierra Leone. 11 December 2009. Web. 10 July 2010.

Smallwood, Stephanie. *Saltwater Slavery: A Middle Passage from Africa to American Diaspora*. Cambridge: Harvard University Press, 2008.

Smillie, Ian, Lansana Gberie, and Ralph Hazleton. "The Heart of the Matter: Sierra Leone, Diamonds, and Human Security." Ottawa: Partnership Africa Canada, 2000.

Smith, Valerie. *Self-Discovery and Authority in Afro-American Narrative*. Cambridge, MA: Harvard University Press, 1987.

Soitos, Stephen F. *The Blues Detective: A Study of African American Detective Fiction*. Amherst: University of Massachusetts Press, 1996.

Spencer, Julius. "A Historical Background to the Contemporary Theatre in Sierra Leone." *International Journal of Sierra Leone Studies* 1 (1988): 26–35.

Spencer, Suzette. "On Her Own Terms: An Interview with Barbara Chase-Riboud." *Callaloo* 32.3 (Summer 2009): 736–757.

Spillers, Hortense J. "Mama's Baby, Papa's Maybe: An American Grammar Book." *Diacritics* 17.2 (Summer 1987): 65–81.

Spielberg, Steven, dir. *Amistad.* Dreamworks, 2007.

Spielberg, Steven, Debbie Allen, and Maya Angelou. *Amistad: "Give Us Free."* New York: DreamWorks, 1997.

Spivak, Gayatri. *Death of a Discipline.* New York: Columbia University Press, 2005.

Steady, Filomina Chioma. *Women and the Amistad Connection: Sierra Leone Krio Society.* Rochester, VT: Schenkman Books, 2001.

Stern, Sol. "The Campaign to Free Angela Davis and Ruchell Magee." *New York Times* 27 June 1971. Web 18 May 2001.

Sterne, Emma Gelders. *The Long Black Schooner: The Voyage of the Amistad.* New York: Alladdin Books, 1953.

Stone, Albert E. *The Return of Nat Turner: History, Literature, and Cultural Politics in Sixties America.* Athens: University of Georgia Press, 1992.

Sturken, Marita, and Lisa Cartwright. *Practices of Looking: An Introduction to Visual Culture.* New York: Oxford University Press, 2001.

Styron, William. *The Confessions of Nat Turner.* New York: Vintage International, 1968 (1993).

Symbionese Liberation Army. "Communique to the San Francisco Phoenix." *The San Francisco Phoenix* 4 April 1974.

Tarawalie, Amadu, and Mustapha Lawal Turay. "Sengbe Pieh and ECOMOG." 1993. Mural. Freetown, Sierra Leone.

Thiel, Mark A. *How Many More Years.* Unpublished manuscript, 1997.

Thompson, Mark Christian. "Voodoo Fascism: Fascist Ideology in Arna Bontemps's Drums at Dusk." *MELUS* 30.3 (Fall 2005): 155–177.

Thornton, John. "*Amistad* and African Slavery." *The History Teacher* 31.3 (1998): 384–385.

———. *Africa and Africans in the Making of the Atlantic World, 1400–1800.* 2nd ed. Cambridge: Cambridge University Press, 1998.

Thorpe, John. *Chap Am So: The Amistad Victory.* Unpublished manuscript.

Tillet, Salamishah. "In the Shadow of the Castle: (Trans)Nationalism, African American Tourism and Goree Island." *Research in African Literatures* 40.4 (Winter 2009): 122–141.

Triulzi, Allessandro. "African Cities, Historical Memory and Street Buzz." *The Post-Colonial Question: Common Skies, Divided Horizons.* Ed. Iain Chambers and Lidia Curti. New York: Routledge, 1996.

Tuchscherer, Konrad. "Re: Sengbe Slave Trader Controversy." Message to the author. 22 November 2010. Email.

"20 Questions We'd Ask Symbionese." *The San Francisco Phoenix* 4 April 1974.

United Nations Development Programme. *Human Development Report 1990.* New York: Oxford University Press, 1990.

United States. Department of State. *United States Information Agency*. Web. 23 August 2000.

"U.S. Embassy Awards Sierra Leonean Students for Writing about Amistad." *Awoko Newspaper*. Freetown, Sierra Leone. 20 December 2007. Web. 8 July 2010.

"U.S. Schooner Arrives in Freetown December 9th." *Standard Times*. Freetown Sierra Leone. 5 December 2007. Web. 3 January 2011.

"U.S. Schooner Arrives Tomorrow." *Awoko Newspaper*. Freetown, Sierra Leone. 7 December 2007. Web. 8 July 2010.

Vidal, Gore. "Reel History: Why John Quincy Adams Was the Hero of the Amistad Affair." *New Yorker* 10 November 1997: 112.

Wallace, Michelle. *Black Macho and the Myth of the Superwoman*. New York: Verso, 1994 (1978).

"We Are the Revolution." *Berkeley Tribe* 1–21 August 1970: 2–3.

Weinraub, Bernard. "Spielberg Film Faces Charge of Plagiarism." *New York Times* 13 November, 1997, sec. B: 1+.

Wenzel, Jennifer. *Bulletproof: Afterlives of Anticolonial Prophesy in South Africa and Beyond*. Chicago: University of Chicago Press, 2009.

Wiegman, Robyn. "Fiedler and Sons." *Race and the Subject of Masculinities*. Ed. Harry Stecopoulos and Michael Uebel. Durham: Duke University Press, 1997.

Will, George. F. "'Amistad' Redeems Hollywood." *Deseret News* 18 December, 1997. Web. 22 January 2009.

Williams, John A., and Charles F. Harris. *Amistad 2*. New York: Random House, 1971.

———. *Amistad 1*. New York: Random House, 1970.

Wilson, Kathleen, ed. *A New Imperial History*. Cambridge: Cambridge University Press, 2006.

Wocowski, Wojtek. "Voyage Logbook." amistadamerica.org. Amistad America, Inc. 22 December 2007. Web. July 7, 2010.

Wyse, Akintola. *The Krio of Sierra Leone: An Interpretive History*. London: Hurst, 1989.

Yarborough, Richard. "Arguing Amistad." *LA Weekly* 19–25 December 1997: 39–40.

Zeinert, Karen. *The Amistad Slave Revolt and American Abolition*. North Haven, CT: Linnet Books, 1997.

Index